Bonds of Community

THE LIVES OF FARM WOMEN IN
NINETEENTH-CENTURY NEW YORK

Nancy Grey Osterud

CORNELL UNIVERSITY PRESS

ITHACA AND LONDON

First published 1991 by Cornell University Press.
First printing, Cornell Paperbacks, 1991.
Third printing 1996.

International Standard Book Number (cloth) 0-8014-2510-7
International Standard Book Number (paper) 0-8014-9798-1
Library of Congress Catalog Card Number 90-41814
Printed in the United States of America
Librarians: Library of Congress cataloging information
appears on the last page of the book.

⊗ The paper in this book meets the minimum requirements
of the American National Standard for Information Sciences—
Permanence of Paper for Printed Library Materials, ANSI Z39.48-1984.

Bonds of Community

Contents

Acknowledgments

This book is dedicated to the women of the Nanticoke Valley who have generously shared their lives with me and helped me to understand the lives of their mothers and grandmothers. Janet Bowers Bothwell realized there was a story to tell and offered me the opportunity to undertake this project; she and Larry Bothwell have been a constant source of guidance and support over the years. I am especially grateful to those who allowed me to read their ancestors' diaries and papers: Dorothy Lawton Ames and Leigh Ames; Alleyne Davey Bostwick; Janet Bowers Bothwell; Myra Dudley Carman; Anita Jackson Dunbar; Louise Gates Gunsalus, Paul Gunsalus, and Sue Gunsalus Bakken; Evelyn Bailey LaDue, Jane Daniels Youngs, and Deborah Youngs; Doris DuBois Lee; Richard J. Rozelle; Olive Gould Smith, Claude Smith, and Marion Swan Smith; Jennie L. Whittaker; Barbara DuBois Yarrington; Ralph Young and Margaret Young Coles. Others who facilitated the local research include Don Baker, Richard Barons, Gloria Comstock, Mary Crockett, Eleanor Swan, and Shirley L. Woodward. Stefan Bielinski, Lawrence Bothwell, Marjorie Hinman, and Ross McGuire made the resources of the New York State Museum and Archives, the Broome County Historian's Office, and the Broome County Historical Society available to me. The Maine Town Historian, Nanticoke Valley Historical Society, Broome County Historian, and the Broome County Historical Society graciously granted permission to quote from the documents cited in the bibliography.

Friends and colleagues inside and outside academic institutions and historical museums have listened patiently to my reflections and shared insights of their own. Particular thanks go to Susan Amussen, Patricia Foster Haines, Kathy Kerns, Walter Meade, Virginia Scheer, Judith Wellman, and the members of the Upstate New York Women's History Conference; to students and faculty in History and Gender Studies at Lewis and Clark College and the research group on American women in Portland, Oregon, especially Jane Atkinson, Dorothy Berkson, Gina Bonner, Virginia Darney, Nancy Porter, Mary Kay Tetreault, and Jean Ward; and to the far-flung but closely connected network of people concerned with rural women's history, especially Sarah Deutsch, Sarah Elbert, Elizabeth Hampsten, Joan Jensen, Lu Ann Jones, Seena Kohl, and Mary Neth. I have benefited from the comments of Hal Barron, Tom Dublin, John Mack Faragher, James Henretta, John Knodel, Allan Kulikoff, Jack Larkin, and other colleagues at meetings of the Berkshire Conference on Women's History, the Social Science History Association, and the Association of Living Historical Farms and Agricultural Museums. At Brown University, Mari Jo Buhle, Howard Chudacoff, and Frances Kobrin Goldscheider provided helpful advice as I completed the first draft of this book.

For financial support during research and writing, I am grateful to the American Council of Learned Societies, for a Fellowship for Recent Recipients of the Ph.D. supported in part by the National Endowment for the Humanities; to San Jose State University and Lewis and Clark College, which both granted leaves of absence, research time, and travel funds; to the Historian-in-Residence Program of the New York State Historical Resources Center at Cornell University, funded by the New York Council for the Humanities and the New York State Council on the Arts; and to the Nanticoke Valley Historical Society. Cornell University Press editors Peter Agree and Patty Peltekos, and manuscript editor Marilyn Sale, along with indexer Jill Harris and proofreader André Lambelet, have helped this book make the transition from manuscript to print.

Portions of this book previously appeared as " 'She Helped Me Hay It as Good as a Man': Relations among Women and Men in an Agricultural Community," in *"To Toil the Livelong Day": American Women at Work, 1780–1980,* edited by Carol Groneman and Mary Beth Norton, copyright © 1987 by Cornell University, and used by permission of the publisher, Cornell University Press. Portions of Chapter 10 were published as "The Valuation of Women's Work: Gender and the Market in a Dairy Farming Community during the Late Nineteenth Century," in *Frontiers* 10, no. 2 (1988); I thank the Frontiers Collective for permission to reuse this material.

Finally, I thank my family and friends in New York, Ohio, Oregon,

Utah, and California for living with me as I lived imaginatively in the Nanticoke Valley.

NANCY GREY OSTERUD

Santa Cruz, California

Bonds of Community

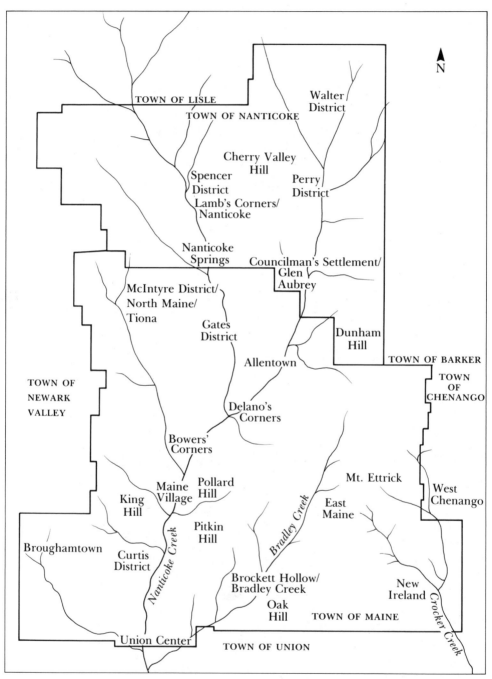

Nanticoke Valley neighborhoods in the late nineteenth century

No Separate Spheres

When Sarah M. Grimké signed her 1838 *Letter on the Equality of the Sexes and the Condition of Women* "Thine in the bonds of womanhood," she gave the term "bonds" a new dimension; women were not only oppressed, they were also united by their common condition. Nancy F. Cott has persuasively argued that Grimké "must have composed her phrase with care, endowing it intentionally with the double meaning that womanhood bound women together even as it bound them down."[1] As middle-class women found their lives becoming more tightly circumscribed by the prescriptions and proscriptions of gender, they developed a consciousness of their common condition and a sense of sisterhood which enabled them to question and even challenge the limits of their "sphere." The feminist movement that emerged in the mid-nineteenth century, Cott concludes, was based on these contradictory meanings of the bonds of womanhood.

The bonds of kinship and labor had an equally contradictory significance in the lives of rural women during the nineteenth century. In contrast to urban women, whose position was increasingly defined by their difference from men, rural women were defined through their relationships with men. The kinship system identified them as wives and mothers, daughters and sisters. They gained access to land, the most important resource in an agricultural society, only through husbands and sons, fathers and brothers. Their labor remained integral to farm family economies as agriculture commercialized. Unlike ur-

1. Nancy F. Cott, *The Bonds of Womanhood: "Woman's Sphere" in New England, 1780–1835* (New Haven: Yale University Press, 1977), 1.

1

ban middle-class women, whose work was devalued as families became more involved in the capitalist marketplace, farm women
contributed to commodity production in concrete and visible ways.
Indeed, in some regions of rural Pennsylvania and New York it was
women's traditional tasks—butter and cheese making and poultry
raising—that became the major source of cash income for farm
families.[2] At the same time, it was almost impossible for rural women
to support themselves outside male-headed farm households. The
bonds of kinship and labor which linked women to men were powerful and nearly all-encompassing.

Although rural women were legally and materially subordinated to
men within farm families, they were also central to the kinship system
and mode of production on which rural society was founded. Women
responded to their situation by emphasizing those aspects of rural life
in which they had a legitimate place and focusing their energies on
activities they shared with men. On farms, women voluntarily participated in the most labor-intensive and highly valued work and nurtured an ethic of mutuality in work and decision making between
husbands and wives. They drew on their kindred for support in their
marriages, creating cross-gender cooperation within and between
households. Women extended the norms of reciprocity which governed relationships among kin to their neighborhoods and the entire
community. They upheld the principle of kinship as the basis for social organization and opposed the formation of exclusive and impersonal interest groups. The social activities women organized for their
families, neighborhoods, and churches all involved men and children
as well as women themselves. The strategies rural women adopted,
like the problems they confronted, were the inverse of those followed
by urban middle-class women. Defined in relation to men rather than
as distinct from them, rural women tried to transform the bonds of
kinship and labor into sources of sharing and strength, renegotiating
the terms of gender relations and modifying them in a more symmetrical and egalitarian direction.

This book examines the meaning of gender in the lives of women
in a rural agricultural community in New York during the second
half of the nineteenth century. Based on diaries, letters, and recollections as well as on census data, church records, and maps from the
Nanticoke Valley in Broome County, it reconstructs women's life histories and analyzes how gender structured women's interactions with

2. Joan M. Jensen, *Loosening the Bonds: Mid-Atlantic Farm Women, 1750–1850* (New
Haven: Yale University Press, 1986), 79–141.

their families and neighbors, their place in the farm family economy, and their participation in community organizations.

I conceptualize the gender system as it was defined in Gayle Rubin's classic article "The Traffic in Women": the gender system is the entire set of social arrangements by which a society transforms biological males and females into masculine men and feminine women and brings them together in heterosexual marriage.[3] This definition implies a feminist critique of the dominant ideology of sexual difference, for it points out the disjunction between biological sex and the *disjunction between biological sex and characteristics* gendered characteristics ascribed to individuals. More positively, it asserts that gender is socially constructed and culturally interpreted, not natural and universal. It also suggests that gender systems are not historically invariant but constituted and reconstituted over time. Rubin argues that gender divisions are created and maintained through social arrangements that, more or less successfully, impose gendered identities on women and men and structure their relations with one another.

Gender is a relational system. Symbolically, what is "feminine" is defined in terms of its difference from what is "masculine"; neither term makes sense without the other. While cultural discourse may emphasize the distinction between masculinity and femininity, gender also defines how men and women are supposed to interact in social practice. Gender is always reciprocal. At the same time, it is rarely symmetrical. In modern Western European thought, "man" was regarded as absolute and "woman" as relative; gendered men set a standard for humanity that women could never quite meet. Civil society was regarded as composed of male heads of households who exercised authority over women and children. Property ownership and political representation provided a material and legal basis for masculine power; inequalities in access to resources and to the public domain enforced women's subordination to men within the family. Masculine power, however, was neither absolute nor arbitrary. Like all forms of social power, it was carefully bounded and regulated by other forms of hierarchy and other centers of authority. Furthermore, because gender pertains to the most intimate forms of human interaction, sexuality and reproduction, the relational aspect of the system is of paramount importance. Women and men may be brought together as "opposite sexes," but brought together they must be. As Rubin suggests, kinship and heterosexual marriage are central

3. Gayle Rubin, "The Traffic in Women: Notes on the 'Political Economy' of Sex," in *Toward an Anthropology of Women*, ed. Rayna R. Reiter (New York: Monthly Review Press, 1975), 157–210.

features of the gender system. The norms of conjugal relationships are gender-specific, but both husbands and wives are supposed to behave in ways that maintain an orderly household. Each must know what to expect of the other as well as what the other expects. Since gender is a fundamental principle of social order, both women and men must understand and conform to its dictates.

At the same time that gender imposes identities on individuals and shapes their interactions with one another, the system is riddled with contradictions. Fundamental, of course, is the fact that women and men vary more as individuals than they do as sexes. Strong women and gentle men are always appearing to derange the neat dichotomies, and the constant need to discipline deviants makes the artificial character of the system apparent. Furthermore, although women and men do not make history under conditions of their own choosing, they do make history. Every generation of young people renegotiates the terms of manhood and womanhood. While gender must be reconstituted in each generation, historical changes in other dimensions of social organization cause shifts in gender relations or create opportunities for redefinition. As the disadvantaged parties in the modern Western European gender system, women have individually and collectively taken advantage of whatever flexibility existed in their situation, sought to increase their resources and enlarge their freedom of action, and maintained their own alternative visions of how human relationships might be conducted. Women do not always directly challenge the dominant gender system and advance alternatives; the emergence of feminist movements requires a complex conjunction of social-historical circumstances. But women have always struggled to mitigate the inequalities of their situation and to improve the quality of their lives.

The dominant paradigm of gender relations in nineteenth-century American women's history is epitomized by the phrase "separate spheres," a phrase used during the early nineteenth century to define the proper realms of women and men. Prescriptive literature stressed the difference between women's and men's work, place, and character; relations between the sexes were seen in terms of complementarity rather than commonality. Earlier notions of gender relations had emphasized their hierarchical character, the subordination of women to men in all aspects of life in which both were intimately involved. The ideology of separate spheres, on the other hand, emphasized the disjunction between women and men while concealing the inequalities between them. Rooted in the social experiences of urban middle-class families, this ideology embodied the separation between workplace and household and between income-producing and non-income-producing labor which accompanied commercialization and industrialization. Middle-class women became solely responsible for the home while men assumed the primary responsibility for earning money. This distinction between women's and men's activities was interpreted as a fundamental difference between the feminine and masculine characters. Women, who nurtured children and mediated family relationships, were described as naturally selfless, sensitive, virtuous, and pious; men, who competed in the rough-and-tumble world of the capitalist marketplace and popular politics, were seen as strong willed and decisive, rational and practical. Ideally, women's supposed passivity and men's activity balanced each other; women were to be protected by men, while men would be softened and elevated by female influence. The ideology of separate spheres rationalized women's exclusion from the emerging public world and assigned to the private life of the family responsibility for maintaining civic virtue and social stability in a time of moral uncertainty and rapid change. The very words "separate spheres" implied that women's field of action, although distinct from that of men, was neither incomplete nor secondary. The notion that women had a domain of their own within which they enjoyed considerable autonomy and power obscured the fact that they were being excluded from crucial areas of social life and were still subordinated to their fathers and husbands. The ideology of separate spheres mystified the connections between men and women, public and private, capitalism and the family, at the same time that it was based on them.[4]

Studies of the lives of women in nineteenth-century America have been subtly shaped by the ideology of separate spheres at the same time that they have subjected it to a feminist critique.[5] In an attempt

4. On the ideology of separate spheres, see Cott, *The Bonds of Womanhood*; Ann Douglas, *The Feminization of American Culture* (New York: Knopf, 1977); Mary P. Ryan, *Womanhood in America from Colonial Times to the Present* (New York: Franklin Watts, 1983), 113–65, and *The Empire of Mothers: American Writings on Women and the Family, 1830–1860* (New York: Haworth Press, 1982). Mary P. Ryan, *Cradle of the Middle Class: The Family in Oneida County, New York, 1790–1865* (Cambridge: Cambridge University Press, 1981), and Leonore Davidoff and Catherine Hall, *Family Fortunes: Men and Women of the English Middle Class: 1780–1850* (Chicago: University of Chicago Press, 1987), offer brilliant analyses of the centrality of domestic ideology to the formation of the middle class in the United States and England.

5. Linda K. Kerber arrived at a similar conclusion in her analysis of the conceptual frameworks adopted by historians of American women since the 1960s. Kerber criticizes the confusions that historians' use of the rhetoric of separate spheres has involved and clarifies the various meanings of these terms. She distinguishes "separate spheres," an ideology imposed on women that reinforced and concealed their subordination,

to see women as historical actors rather than as the passive victims of male domination, historians of women have emphasized how women created a separate culture within their societally prescribed sphere. Rooted in such shared experiences as childbirth and enacted primarily in friendship, this "female world of love and ritual" was a source of intimacy and support for individual women and provided the basis for a distinctly feminine sensibility and form of cultural expression. In the classic formulation of this perspective, Carroll Smith-Rosenberg contrasted relations between women with those between women and men, arguing that while women were emotionally intimate and expressive with their female friends, women and men were more distant and their interaction remained stiffly formal even after they were married. The problem with Smith-Rosenberg's analysis is that, while she read women's correspondence with women to ascertain the quality of female friendships, she relied on prescriptive literature rather than first-person sources for her characterization of relations between women and men. Following the tenets of nineteenth-century ideology, Smith-Rosenberg assumed that middle-class women and men were members of "alien groups" who were unable to communicate with each other beyond the gender-segregated conventions of Victorian marriage.[6]

This notion of women's culture tends to encapsulate women within their separate sphere. Historians have focused on women's reproductive experiences and domestic activities in isolation from the men in their families and households, and they have explored the places where women gathered together but not those in which they interacted with men. When Marilyn Ferris Motz sought to elucidate the

"women's culture," a set of work practices and social relations created by women, and "woman's place," the constraints and possibilities that were "socially constructed both *for* and *by* women." My book fits into what Kerber calls the third stage of feminist historiography, which takes "an interactive view of social process" and explores "how women's allegedly 'separate sphere' was affected by what men did, and how activities defined by women in their own sphere influenced and even set constraints and limitations on what men might choose to do." Although I have moved further from the rhetoric of separate spheres than Kerber did in this passage, I share her conclusion that historians of women must deconstruct the dichotomies between public and private, masculine and feminine, and construct a relational and dynamic analysis of women's place. Linda K. Kerber, "Separate Spheres, Female Worlds, Woman's Place: The Rhetoric of Women's History," *Journal of American History* 75 (1988): 9–39.

6. Carroll Smith-Rosenberg, "The Female World of Love and Ritual: Relations between Women in Nineteenth-Century America," *Signs* 1 (1975): 1–25. Smith-Rosenberg reprinted this essay in *Disorderly Conduct: Visions of Gender in Victorian America* (New York: Knopf, 1985), 53–76, and discussed it in the introductory essay, "Hearing Women's Words: A Feminist Reconstruction of History," 25–39.

meaning of kinship in women's lives, for example, she studied women's correspondence with one another. Not surprisingly, Motz concluded that women relied on their female kin for support in the transitions and crises of their adult lives. Motz drew her characterization of relations between women and men, not from the prescriptive literature as Smith-Rosenberg did, but from juridical definitions of the status of women; rather than emphasizing the psychological distance between women and men, Motz stressed women's legal and economic subordination. Still, like Smith-Rosenberg, Motz did not read personal correspondence between women and men. Cross-gender interaction is missing from her account of kinship, and women's relations with one another seem entirely distinct from their relations with men.[7]

Women's relationships with men have rarely been examined in the same depth and with the same concern for women's experiences and perspectives. But, as John Mack Faragher reminds us, the vast majority of women lived in families, and "the cultural expectation was that husbands and wives, despite their differences, would reach some ordered harmony within the bonds of marriage."[8] Marriage was a process of adjustment, involving both conflict and accommodation, in which men as well as women participated. The bonds of womanhood and the bonds of marriage were closely intertwined, for the gender system ultimately defined women in terms of their relationships with men, however much it emphasized the divergence between the sexes. To attain a comprehensive perspective on women's experience, historians must examine women's relationships with their fathers and brothers, husbands and sons, as well as their ties to other women.

Women remain the primary subjects in this analysis of gender relations. Adopting gender as a theoretical framework does not mean abandoning a women-centered approach and subsuming women under such concepts as "the family" or "the household."[9] Rather, this

[margin annotation: Marriage = adjustment]

7. Marilyn Ferris Motz, *True Sisterhood: Michigan Women and Their Kin, 1820–1920* (Albany: SUNY Press, 1983).

8. John Mack Faragher, *Women and Men on the Overland Trail* (New Haven: Yale University Press, 1979), 2; see also Faragher, "History from the Inside Out: Writing the History of Women in Rural America," *American Quarterly* 33 (1981): 537–57.

9. Jane Atkinson maintains that a relational analysis of gender should augment, but not supersede, a "women-centered" approach. I share Atkinson's concern that analytical categories not be substituted for social actors in feminist social theory. Jane Monnig Atkinson, "Gender Studies, Women's Studies, and Political Feminism: A View from Anthropology," unpublished paper, Center for Advanced Study in the Behavioral Sciences and Lewis and Clark College, December 1984.

perspective incorporates the feminist insight that families and households involve sets of relationships which are more or less unequal and conflictual.[10] Modes of analysis which treat the family or household as a unit fail to scrutinize its internal divisions and misconstrue its external relations; they uncritically reproduce male dominance and present cultural constructions as natural facts. The approach adopted here, by contrast, regards families and households as characterized by gender and generational relations and constituted by kinship; it analytically dissolves families into the relations that compose them and examines the kin relationships that operate within and between households.

The heuristic value of this approach is that it allows women's relationships with men and with other women to be examined within a single analytical framework. Too often, historians assume that cross-gender and same-gender relations were mutually exclusive, based on opposing principles and incompatible in practice. Smith-Rosenberg regards homosocial relationships as freely chosen and characterized by sisterly identification and sympathy; she counterposes them to heterosexual relations, which she presumes were compulsory and characterized by difference and distance. She fails to examine how the bonds of womanhood, especially between older and younger generations, might have entailed conflict and enforced the prescriptions and proscriptions of femininity.[11] Equally important, she fails to investigate how women and men might seek to communicate with and understand one another. Ellen Kate Rothman's study of courtship correspondence illuminates the extraordinary efforts courting couples made to form an "intimate acquaintance" beyond the conventions of cross-gender interaction, founding their mutual trust on candor and commonality rather than following the stereotyped rituals of

10. For feminist critiques of the concept of the family in the social sciences, see *Rethinking the Family: Some Feminist Questions*, ed. Barrie Thorne with Marilyn Yalom (New York: Longman, 1982), especially Barrie Thorne, "Feminist Rethinking of the Family: An Overview," 1–24, and Jane Collier, Michelle Z. Rosaldo, and Sylvia Yanagisako, "Is There a Family? New Anthropological Views," 25–39. Rayna Rapp, Ellen Ross, and Renate Bridenthal, "Examining Family History," *Feminist Studies* 5 (1979): 174–200, critique the assumptions underlying recent work in the history of the family. Some feminist anthropologists, sociologists, economists, and historians regard the household as a more useful analytical concept, but others question the assumptions underlying that concept as well. For both sides of the debate, see *Households and the World-Economy*, ed. Joan Smith, Immanuel Wallerstein, and Hans-Dieter Evers (Beverly Hills, Calif.: Sage, 1984), especially Diana Wong, "The Limits of Using the Household as a Unit of Analysis," 56–63.

11. Christine Stansell, "Revisiting the Angel in the House: Revisions of Victorian Womanhood," *New England Quarterly* 60 (1987): 471.

sentimental conversation.[12] Finally, historians of "women's culture" presume that women turned to one another as an alternative to their relationships with men and that the qualities characterizing their relationships with one another were confined to their separate sphere. But women also responded to the gender system by trying to create greater mutuality in their relationships with men, breaking down the barriers between cross-gender and same-gender relationships and drawing on their female networks to nurture respect and understanding between women and men.

This book investigates the balance and interaction between elements of conjunction and disjunction in relationships among women and men. In what aspects of family, work, and social life did women participate jointly with their husbands and kinsmen? How many of their activities were gender-marked, linking them primarily with other women in their families, neighborhoods, and community? How did these two dimensions of women's lives intersect? Whether or not women inhabited a separate sphere, a gender-defined realm of experiences and activities they did not share with men, not only depended on the given conditions of women's lives but also involved women's responses to those conditions. The creation of a distinctive "women's culture" takes gender divisions as its basis and builds on the elements of separation between women and men; it emphasizes those experiences which women shared with one another rather than those which tied them to men. The attempt to create a common culture between women and men may begin with the same conditions but moves in the opposite direction; it stresses the things that united women and men across the boundaries of gender and builds on those aspects of life in which women and men interacted on the basis of mutual interests rather than on the basis of their differences. Both of these responses were open to American women during the nineteenth century. This book demonstrates that some women sought mutuality in cross-gender relationships rather than retreating into a separate women's culture and analyzes the social-structural conditions that made their efforts effective.

Exploring such large questions within the confines of a single community offers several significant advantages. First, focusing narrowly makes it possible to examine the problem in depth: to trace the

12. Ellen Kate Rothman, *Hands and Hearts: A History of Courtship in America* (New York: Basic Books, 1984). Karen Lystra, *Searching the Heart: Women, Men, and Romantic Love in Nineteenth-Century America* (New York: Oxford University Press, 1989), concurs with this conclusion.

course of individual lives and ascertain common patterns and to illuminate the processes of adjustment through which women and men worked out their relationships within the framework of cultural definitions of gender. Second, this approach makes it possible to attain a comprehensive view: to analyze the interactions among the familial, economic, and social dimensions of women's lives and to investigate the dynamics that shaped the meaning of the gender system as a whole. Third, it enables the problem to be situated in a long-term historical context: to trace life histories and intergenerational transitions and to examine the social-historical conditions within which the gender system took shape and was reshaped.

Choosing the small Nanticoke Valley community as the setting for this study allows the integration of actor-oriented perspectives with social-structural ones. This is important because all social formations are, in the final analysis, composed of social relationships, no matter how mystified, reified, and alienated they may have become. The capitalist marketplace, no less than the family farm, places people in certain positions and constrains their interaction; similarly, the gender system constructs women and men as gendered subjects and brings them together in patterned ways. People's sense of self and interpretation of the world are based on their social experience, and social meaning resides in the ways various perspectives are integrated or counterposed in the culture. People are active participants in rather than passive objects of this process. Too often, social scientists treat subjectivity separately from causality, as if people's lives were determined by external forces beyond their comprehension or control and the meanings they make of their experience have nothing to do with the factors that shape their situation. While this approach may reflect the alienation and sense of powerlessness that pervades modern social life, it replicates rather than penetrates the mystification and reification of social relations. Just as there is a dialectical relationship between social experience and social structure, so there is a dialectical relationship between meaning and causation. The analysis moves back and forth between women's experiences and their position, exploring the perspective women developed on their situation and their active efforts to transform it. Women's attempts to create alternatives to male dominance were not utopian but were firmly rooted in the resources their social world offered them and in the experiences of relative equality they had enjoyed. It was only through women's consciousness and collective activity, however, that these resources were mobilized and rural gender relations reshaped in the direction of mutuality.

"The Rural Community" describes the web of spatial and social relations within which women conducted their lives, tracing the emergence of community through the process of settlement and the maintenance of social stability in spite of demographic decline and economic contraction during the late nineteenth century. Women had a central place in the kinship system. Although they were formally subordinated to men and gained access to land only through their fathers and brothers, husbands and sons, women were not isolated in male-dominated households. People sustained vital links with their kin in the open-country neighborhoods formed around clusters of related families. Friendship among neighbors followed the model of kinship as well. While the vertical lines in local networks usually followed the inheritance of property by men, the horizontal ties that flowed from intermarriage among neighbors were forged by women. This network of family and neighbors was a crucial resource for women, who played a vital role in the provision of mutual aid. Indeed, women shaped the kinship system to their own purposes, strengthening their position within their households by crossing the boundaries between one household and the next.

"Rural Women's Lives" focuses on courtship and marriage, childbearing, and widowhood. These crucial transitions simultaneously defined women in terms of their relationships with men and constituted a distinctively feminine life experience. Nanticoke Valley women emphasized the familial dimension of these transitions. Couples courted within an informal, gender-mixed milieu and enjoyed relative freedom from parental supervision; they interacted in flexible and intimate, rather than stiff and stereotyped, ways. Women controlled childbirth and they often chose to have their husbands as well as kinswomen present when they gave birth. The anomalous positions of single women and deserted wives illuminate the centrality of cross-gender relationships, for women without husbands still did not conduct their lives separately from men. Instead of elaborating a distinct women's culture, rural women nurtured respect and reciprocity between women and men in their families and kin groups.

"Women's Work on Family Farms" analyzes how work structured women's interactions both with their husbands and with other women. The division of labor in farm households assigned distinct tasks to women and men. Yet the distribution of tasks was flexible, varying within and between households. Men and women shared responsibility for the dairy operation, the most important source of cash income, allocating labor in various ways and often exchanging tasks. The gender division of labor in dairying was more variable and

flexible than in any other farm operation, providing a basis for cooperation across gender lines.

Women's domestic labor was devalued according to the terms of
the capitalist marketplace. Throughout the nineteenth century, however, farm people did not entirely accept the standards of the market.
Men and women produced useful things as well as marketable commodities. Both valued the "living" their land and labor yielded, priz-
ing their relative independence from the vagaries of prices and the
power of merchants. Their resistance to incorporation in the capitalist
market involved a conscious, collective avowal of alternative ways of
thinking about value as well as a defense of local autonomy. At the
same time, there was a clear gender difference in the extent to which
women and men accepted the standards of the marketplace. While
men conceived of their work relationships with men outside of their
immediate household—including their male kin—as relations of exchange, involving the buying and selling of goods and services among
independent producers, women did not apply this market metaphor
to the work they shared with other women. Rather, they extended the
norms of kinship to their female friends and neighbors, sharing work
within the context of reciprocal but long-term and diffuse bonds of
mutual aid. Just as men's relations with their male kin were mediated
by property, so men's cooperative work with other men was mediated
by market models; just as women's kinship bonds depended on direct
personal assistance, so women's cooperative work with other women
depended on ties forged through multifarious forms of help given
and received over time. Women, to a greater degree than men, espoused standards of value and notions of social relations which were
opposed to the pecuniary and impersonal standards of the capitalist
marketplace. Yet rural women did not regard their practices and values as distinctly feminine. Instead, they sought to sustain mutuality in
relations between women and men within their families, households,
and neighborhoods and to encompass the entire community in networks of reciprocity.

Men's and women's lives also differed in their temporal rhythms
and spatial dimensions. Men's tasks were sequential, while women's
were simultaneous; men's work varied seasonally, while women's
work was more repetitive. Women complained of monotony in part
because their chores confined them to the household and farmyard.
Men frequently met others in the ordinary course of their labor,
while women had to create occasions for social contact. These differences in the spatial and temporal qualities of men's and women's
lives, coupled with the formal exclusion of women from the public

domain, could have led to sharp gender differences in social life. Men might have dominated community-wide organizations while women were restricted to more informal and less frequent contacts with relatives and neighbors, and husbands and wives might have had different social networks.

"Patterns of Sociability" shows that in the Nanticoke Valley, formal and informal social activities tended to counteract and overcome, rather than extend and reinforce, the separation between women and men which arose from their patterns of labor. Husbands and wives had joint social networks in part as a result of women's active efforts to create a common social life. Couples visited back and forth with their kin and neighbors. The Grange simultaneously advocated equal rights for women and defended the common commitment of women and men, and parents and children to family farming. There were some single-sex organizations in the community; but while men's groups conducted their business alone, women's groups regularly included men in their activities. Men attended quilting parties, sewing circles, and ladies' aid society socials. Women formed auxiliary organizations in response to their exclusion from the decision-making bodies in such gender-mixed organizations as the churches, but they did not use these auxiliaries to create female enclaves; rather, women drew men into the activities they sponsored and used these organizations to expand their role within the larger institutions. In all these ways, mutuality was a strategy of empowerment for rural women.

My sources include both first-person documents and public records. The diaries, letters, and reminiscences of local residents are most important. These not only provide information about the common activities and crucial events in people's lives but also illuminate their thoughts and feelings. The dimension of subjectivity is crucial; only first-person sources directly express people's own interpretations of their experience. I chose to study the Nanticoke Valley largely because an extraordinary number and range of first-person sources have survived there and were generously made available to me by local residents. I have analyzed more than three dozen manuscript collections that date from the period between the Civil War and the turn of the twentieth century. Most are collections of diaries, although some collections contain correspondence, autobiographies, and family histories as well. While a few diaries cover only a single year, many continue through multiple volumes from youth to old age. Some especially rich manuscript collections include the diaries of several family members. When the diaries kept by different individuals are sequential, they highlight the continuities and changes in particular families over time; when they are simultaneous, they illuminate similarities and differences in individuals' perspectives on and responses to events which are sometimes related to their gender or generational position. While I focused on women's diaries, I also found men's diaries to be valuable, for they reveal the degree to which men's activities and consciousness intersected with those of their mothers, sisters, wives, and daughters. A few diaries were kept jointly by women and men; as husbands and wives shared the recording of their activities, they developed a common perspective on their family experiences. As a whole, the manuscript collections represent farm and nonfarm women at all stages of life and in a variety of family situations. They also represent nearly the entire range of the socioeconomic scale. With the exception of the Irish Catholics (whose omission I explain), they represent all of the community's cultural and religious groups as well.

I have placed the first-person accounts in relation to the reconstructed life histories of everyone who lived in the Nanticoke Valley during the late nineteenth century.[13] My primary sources for the reconstruction of the local population are the manuscript schedules of the federal and New York State censuses of population, the membership records of local churches, and a series of maps showing the location of family farms and households. (Vital records were not kept in New York State until the early twentieth century.) I traced families' economic histories through the manuscript schedules of the federal and New York State censuses of agriculture and industry, town tax records, wills, deeds, and account books. Comparison of the diarists to those whose life histories have been reconstructed from public records shows that they were not unusual in their life histories, ways of making a living, forms of social participation, or even degree of literacy. Indeed, they are distinguished not by the fact that they kept diaries, for the population as a whole was highly literate and accustomed to record keeping, but by the accident that their writings have survived to the present, usually because their descendants remained in the community during the twentieth century.[14]

13. This was not a reconstitution of persistent families but a complete enumeration of everyone who resided in the community, however briefly, during this period. Many records are incomplete, but the whole population is included in aggregate analyses.

14. The families that remained were neither richer nor poorer than those which moved away. The children of both the poorest and the wealthiest families in the community tended to depart during the late nineteenth century. By World War I, however,

While the first-person sources illuminate the meanings people found in life-historical events and social-historical developments, the public records elucidate the dynamics of continuity and change in the community. I traced the development of the economy through the manuscript censuses of agriculture and industry, business directories, and newspaper advertisements, as well as business papers and account books. The history of local institutions is documented by the records of town government, religious organizations, and various social and political groups. The town histories included in the 1885 and 1900 Broome County histories incorporated primary materials, as did historical articles published in local newspapers during the early twentieth century. I have used all these sources to reconstruct as comprehensive a picture as possible of the context within which women conducted their relationships with others.

Finally, my investigation has been profoundly influenced by the presence of the past in the landscape of the Nanticoke Valley and in the memories of its contemporary residents. In the nine years since I began research for an exhibition on women's lives at the local historical society, I have explored the hills and valleys, fields and woods of the Nanticoke Valley, retracing as best I could the pathways of the nineteenth-century diarists as they fetched the cows, visited the neighbors, and went to market. Together with their descendants or the current occupants of their houses, I have searched the attics and cellars of their dwellings as well as enjoyed innumerable cups of tea in their parlors and kitchens. I have sat in their chairs, hefted their tools, and tried on their clothing. Above all, I have contemplated their photographs. Exploring their spaces, handling their artifacts, and seeing their faces have helped me to answer some questions but have raised others; three-dimensional evidence is powerfully concrete but mute and mysterious. Still, whatever sense these pages convey of the vivid reality of these people in the past comes from the contact I have had with the places, things, and images they have passed down to the present. This book is as much their legacy as it is the product of my labor; I have reassembled the fragments they left behind and tried to discern a pattern that speaks to our present as well as for their past.

---

valley residents could commute to jobs in nearby cities. Families unable to make a living from farming could remain in their ancestral farmhouses while working in industrial jobs. Wealthier people, too, could hold professional positions without having to relocate.

PART I

THE RURAL
COMMUNITY

CHAPTER ONE

The Nanticoke Valley

By industry and intelligent farming they have done much to improve the locality.

—Hamilton Child, compiler, *Gazetteer,* 1872

In the Nanticoke Valley, the landscape reveals the presence of the past. The indigenous inhabitants left scarcely a trace; Native Americans lived so lightly on the land that after their removal only the names of streams recall them. The imprint of the first European Americans is still evident in the rectilinear grid of property lines which surveyors imposed on the irregular topography two centuries ago. This order remained more notional than actual for another half-century, for the land was owned long before it was settled, but the surveyors' grid provided the framework within which farms were laid out. The pattern of farmsteads and fields, open-country neighborhoods and villages was established by the mid-nineteenth century. The roads along which a modern traveler passes follow their original routes, paralleling the creeks and running along the ridges more often than connecting the valley with the hills. In the uplands, the irregular clustering of residences reflects the relatively close proximity of nineteenth-century farmsteads. In some isolated neighborhoods houses have fallen into cellarholes and fields grown up to brush, but along farm-to-market roads people who commute to work in the city have renovated old houses. The landscape is still open, the result of generations of winters spent clearing the forest. In the valleys settlement is denser; houses line the roads and pastures stretch back to the wooded hills or down to the tree-lined creek. The village that serves as the center of the community seems more continuous with than

distinct from the surrounding countryside. There is enough space behind most houses for a big garden and a barn, or even to pasture a
cow. The vernacular Greek and Gothic Revival architecture indicates
the limits of the village's growth in the nineteenth century. In the
twentieth century, artisan shops and mercantile stores have been converted into residences; the interchangeability of public and domestic
spaces in village buildings suggests the small scale on which local life
was conducted during the nineteenth century.

Geographically as well as architecturally, the community was small
in scale. The Nanticoke Creek, which defines the topography, flows
south through the towns of Nanticoke and Maine into the Susquehanna River at Union, a little west of Binghamton. From its mouth to
its source is a distance of fifteen miles; its major branches extend for
about five miles on each side. The central valley is narrow. For most
of its length, the valley is just a quarter-mile across and bounded by
fairly steep slopes on both sides. It broadens whenever two or three
branches of the creek come together, but above these confluences the
branch valleys are narrower and the ridges higher. The uplands follow a similar progression. The hills in the southern section are gentle, although they are frequently broken by rocky ledges; to the
north, the land is rougher, the slopes steeper, and the hills higher.
The Nanticoke Valley forms a distinct geographical region.

The earliest published description of the Nanticoke Valley, in
Child's *Gazetteer and Business Directory of Broome and Tioga Counties,
N.Y. for 1872–3*, interpreted the landscape in terms of its human uses.
After describing the rich resources of the forest and tracing the
streams that powered numerous sawmills, Child remarked the dubious quality of the land: the soil in Maine was "a gravelly loam largely
intermixed with the underlying slate" and that in Nanticoke "a slaty
loam underlaid by hardpan." Child emphasized the achievements of
the inhabitants, who "are chiefly engaged in lumbering and dairying." The volume listed artisans, merchants, and manufacturers and
described the crossroads hamlets and villages in which their shops
were located. Finally, Child compiled the annals of the community,
giving the names of those who claimed to have been the first settlers,
recounting anecdotes that dramatized the settlers' encounter with the
wilderness, and dating the foundation of churches and schools.
Child's description of the Nanticoke Valley stressed the transformation of the natural topography in the process of settlement, signifying
that this was an orderly rural landscape.[1]

1. Hamilton Child, comp., *Gazetteer and Business Directory of Broome and Tioga Counties, N.Y. for 1872–3* (Syracuse, N.Y.: published by Child and printed at the Journal
office, 1872), 120–24.

The 1876 *Combination Atlas Map of Broome County, New York, Compiled, Drawn and Published from Personal Examinations and Surveys by Everts, Ensign and Everts of Philadelphia* contains a powerful graphic representation of the pattern of settlement in the Nanticoke Valley. Incorporating detailed local information into a standard format, the maps of Maine and Nanticoke show the location, ownership, and acreage of farms as well as the courses of streams and roads; mills, shops, stores, postoffices, schoolhouses, churches, and cemeteries are all indicated by small symbols. The land was densely settled. Only the steepest ridges remained uninhabited; there were farms on the broad slopes of the highest uplands and sawmills on the narrowest of streams. The 1876 map projects an image of the community as a finely wrought patchwork quilt of family farms.[2]

In the minds of local residents, however, the Nanticoke Valley was not simply a composite of individual farms; people were not scattered randomly across the land. Rather, they belonged to open-country neighborhoods, groups of adjacent farm families who exchanged work and socialized with one another. Each neighborhood was identified by name to residents and outsiders, although only those which centered on a hamlet had their names recorded on the 1876 map. Some were known by the name of the earliest settlers, and others by the name of their school district. Each neighborhood had a distinct social identity. Children who attended the local schools grew up with a sense of belonging together; many intermarried and continued to live nearby. Proximity was based on and reinforced by kinship and shared experience. The vernacular geography of Nanticoke Valley residents, which spoke of "Allentown" and "Mt. Ettrick," "Delano's Corners" and "New Ireland," was not recorded on any map. But the relationships it expressed bound the inhabitants of one farm to the next, crossing property lines with ties of friendship. These shaped the lives of women and men as surely as the creek shaped the land and the settlers reshaped the landscape. The local community was a social and historical rather than simply a geographical formation.

Settlement, 1787–1855

This region of south-central New York was opened for European American settlement after the Revolutionary War. The destruction of Native American villages and the defeat of the Iroquois Confedera-

2. *Combination Atlas Map of Broome County, New York, Compiled, Drawn, and Published from Personal Examinations and Surveys by Everts, Ensign and Everts* (Philadelphia: 1876).

tion were followed by the removal of the indigenous inhabitants; by the 1780s, Native Americans no longer constituted an obstacle to European American expansion. The Nanticoke Valley was included in a vast tract of land purchased by a group of Massachusetts investors in 1787. Many of the sixty original proprietors, who lived in Berkshire County, Massachusetts, never saw this territory; for them western land was a speculative commodity, an investment from which they hoped to profit by selling their holdings at ever-increasing prices to actual settlers. The developers had the tract surveyed and divided into plots of approximately 300 acres, which they offered for sale.[3]

The earliest settlers arrived in the Nanticoke Valley around 1793. Some were relatives of the Massachusetts proprietors and took up portions of their families' landholdings, but most had to purchase land from the proprietors or their agents. Generally they bought land on short-term contracts, for they lacked the capital to purchase land outright. Settlers struggled to meet their payments by selling timber and potash, hiring themselves out to others on a seasonal basis, and borrowing from better-off relatives. Those who had only their labor to invest squatted on forested land, spent several years clearing it, and then sold their improvements to later arrivals. For the settlers, migration to the Nanticoke Valley represented an opportunity to develop farms primarily through their own labor.[4]

[handwritten margin note: bought land as investment]

[handwritten margin note: borrowed from relatives / struggle to pay]

3. The standard published histories of Broome County are: J. B. Wilkinson, *The Annals of Binghamton, and of the County connected with it, from the earliest settlement* (Binghamton, N.Y.: n.p., 1840); H. P. Smith, ed., *A History of Broome County* (Syracuse, N.Y.: D. Mason & Co., 1885); William S. Lawyer, ed., *Binghamton: Its Settlement, Growth, and Development and the Factors in Its History Together with a History of the Villages and Towns of the County* (n.p.: Century Memorial Publishing Company, 1900); William Foote Seward, ed., *Binghamton and Broome County, New York: A History* (New York and Chicago: Lewis Historical Publishing Co., 1924); and Lawrence Bothwell, *Broome County Heritage: An Illustrated History* (Woodland Hills, Calif.: Windsor Publications, 1983).

4. The first histories of the towns of Maine and Nanticoke were printed in Child, *Gazetteer*, 120–24. Information on local history is contained in turn-of-the-century newspaper articles, especially Helen Knapp Garrett, comp. and ed., "Early Scotch Settlers of West Chenango," *Whitney Point Reporter*, 1901–2, and the anonymous "Historical Sketches of Maine" and "Historical Sketches of Union Center," *Whitney Point Reporter*, 1914. Modern local histories include Robert J. Spencer and Clement G. Bowers, "Notes on the History of the Town of Maine" (manuscript, c. 1941–57); Earl H. Ingalls, "History of Maine: Town of Maine, Broome County, New York" (manuscript, c. 1943); Robert J. Spencer, "Glen Aubrey: A Brief History of the Village of Glen Aubrey, Town of Nanticoke, County of Broome, on the 125th Anniversary of the First Town Meeting, 1832–1957," *Bulletin of the Broome County Historical Society* 6 (1958): 3–13, and the manuscript version, c. 1957; Shirley L. Woodward, comp., *A Short History of Maine, New York* (Maine, N.Y.: Town of Maine, 1973); and Eleanor Brown Swan, *Story of the Valleys: Town of Nanticoke* (Nanticoke, N.Y.: Town of Nanticoke, 1981).

The people who came from New England and eastern New York left communities in which the settlement process had reached its culmination.[5] Farms had been divided so many times that they could no longer support more than one family, and cheap land was no longer available nearby. People were forced to turn to nonagricultural occupations or to migrate to less-developed areas.[6] By the second quarter of the nineteenth century, the rural areas of New England and eastern New York were also being affected by the economic changes that came with the expansion of capitalism.[7] The construction of turnpike roads and canals promoted internal trade,

5. New Englanders and New Yorkers were represented in equal numbers among the initial settlers. Natives of Massachusetts and Connecticut predominated among the earliest arrivals; a substantial number came from New Hampshire and Vermont in the 1820s. People from eastern New York, especially Otsego, Mohawk, and Albany counties, migrated to the valley fairly continuously between 1795 and 1855.

6. The classic statements of the demographic dimensions of the settlement process are Kenneth A. Lockridge, "Land, Population, and the Evolution of New England Society, 1630–1790," *Past and Present* 39 (1968): 62–80, and James A. Henretta, "The Morphology of New England Society in the Colonial Period," *Journal of Interdisciplinary History* 2 (1971): 379–98. This model has been criticized for its neglect of migration in Darrett B. Rutman, "People in Process: The New Hampshire Towns of the Eighteenth Century," *Journal of Urban History* 1 (1975): 268–92. Daniel Scott Smith, "A Malthusian-Frontier Interpretation of United States Demographic History before c. 1815," in *Urbanization in the Americas: The Background in Comparative Perspective*, ed. Woodrow Borah, Jorge Hardoy, and Gilbert A. Stetler (Ottawa: National Museum of Man, 1980), 15–23, integrates "land/population pressure" with migration.

7. For a general interpretation of social change in New England and eastern New York during the late eighteenth and early nineteenth centuries, see James A. Henretta and Gregory H. Nobles, *Evolution and Revolution: American Society, 1600–1820* (Lexington, Mass.: D.C. Heath, 1987). For the history of agriculture, see Jeremy Atack and Fred Bateman, *To Till Their Own Soil: Agriculture in the Antebellum North* (Ames: Iowa State University Press, 1987); Clarence H. Danhof, "The Farm Enterprise: The Northern United States, 1820–1860s," *Research in Economic History* 4 (1979): 127–91, and Clarence H. Danhof, *Change in Agriculture: The Northern United States, 1820–1870* (Cambridge: Harvard University Press, 1969); Paul W. Gates, *The Farmer's Age: Agriculture, 1815–1860* (New York: Holt, Rinehart and Winston, 1960). The classic analysis is that of Percy Wells Bidwell: Percy Wells Bidwell and John I. Falconer, *History of Agriculture in the Northern United States, 1620–1860* (Washington, D.C.: The Carnegie Institution, 1925); Percy W. Bidwell, "Rural Economy in New England at the Beginning of the Nineteenth Century," *Transactions of the Connecticut Academy of the Arts and Sciences* 20 (1916): 241–399; and Percy W. Bidwell, "The Agricultural Revolution in New England," *American Historical Review* 26 (1921): 683–702. George Rogers Taylor, *The Transportation Revolution, 1815–1860* (New York: Harper & Row, 1951), discusses commercialization as well as the impact of changes in transportation on the rural economy. Studies of the relationship between economic change and emigration from New England include Lois K. Matthews, *The Expansion of New England* (Boston, 1909); Richard J. Purcell, *Connecticut in Transition, 1775–1818* (Washington, D.C., 1913); Lewis D. Stilwell, *Migration from Vermont, 1776–1860* (Montpelier: Proceedings of the Vermont Historical Society, n.s. 5, 1937): 65–245; and Harold Fisher Wilson, *The Hill Country of Northern New England: Its Social and Economic History, 1790–1830* (New York: Columbia University Press, 1936).

and the agricultural economy became more commercially oriented. The expansion of market relations intensified the changes brought by the culmination of the settlement process. The capital costs of farming increased and inequalities in the distribution of wealth became more marked. Families migrated to the Nanticoke Valley not only in order to assure the future of their children or to maintain the position their parents had occupied but also to avoid sinking into the growing ranks of landless laborers.

The overwhelming majority of settlers came to the Nanticoke Valley as members of family groups. Relatively few were displaced youths who had been unable to get established in their home communities. Most were parents who had owned some property elsewhere but knew that their children would find it impossible to get started in farming if they remained where they were. Older couples joined their married children in the move west. Selling their relatively small but much-improved farms, these families acquired large tracts of forested land and began the process of farm making, just as many of their parents and grandparents had done a generation or two before.[8]

People from Scotland and Ireland who migrated to America in the 1830s also settled on Nanticoke Valley farms. The wholesale transformation of peasant farming by capitalist agriculture in their homelands led to economic and demographic crises that stimulated mass emigration. In Scotland, the shift to large-scale grazing disrupted crofters' traditional way of life and displaced many families. As Robert Hogg, who migrated from Scotland to Maine, N.Y., in the 1830s, described it at the turn of the century:

> It is long since emigration from the Highlands commenced. When the clans were broken up as far as the government could do it, they were obliged to emigrate or starve. And the brave and intelligent rushed from their native country with all the symptoms of reckless despair. The whole of our most valuable peasantry and operative manufacturers were leaving. All who have made enough money to

8. This analysis of the age and family status of Nanticoke Valley settlers is based on the manuscript schedules of the 1855 New York State census. In 1855, one-third of the population had been born in the community; two-thirds had come from somewhere else. Of the migrants, 37 percent had accompanied their parents to the valley when they were under the age of fifteen; another 7 percent had accompanied their parents when they were older than fifteen years of age. Fully 36 percent came as married couples; most already had children. No more than 20 percent of all migrants, then, came to the valley alone. Just 14 percent were single youths over fifteen; the family status of the rest cannot be ascertained because they were over the age of forty-five when they arrived. Similar patterns of family-based migration have been found in other rural communities during the nineteenth century; Robert E. Bieder, "Kinship as a Factor in Migration," *Journal of Marriage and the Family* 35 (1973): 429–39.

freight them over the Atlantic to procure a settlement in America, VanDiemen's Land or New South Wales are hurrying away as if inflicted by a plague.

The foundations of all this was the density of the population and the impossibility of procuring sufficient food and clothing to keep in existence in such a miserable state, with no prospects ahead but still darker times. . . . So it will be easy to see the necessity of emigration. . . . the best of them who could get away did so.

In Ireland, the exploitation of the peasantry was even more intense and the crisis was more dramatic. As Hogg saw it:

The very same transpired in Ireland only more so, as it was more densely inhabited; rents were higher, every acre reclaimed from bog or barren, only added to the amount of rent to be paid at the next term, and the owner receiving and spending all that hard-earned money in London. No wonder the Irishman fled to where there were brighter prospects ahead, and we have in the town of Maine many who immigrated about 1830 and 40, took up land and made homes for themselves and families who have grown up and are as good citizens as can be found in all the country.[9]

Irish peasants had adapted to the extortionate demands of their English landlords by subdividing their farms and cultivating potatoes, but this was a fragile and temporary solution. The Irish began to emigrate in search of better conditions even before the potato blight led to widespread famine. The first immigrants quickly became established in farming, while those who arrived later lacked the capital necessary to purchase land and spent years working as wage laborers before they became independent farmers.[10] The Scots and the Irish, like the Yankees and Yorkers, settled in the Nanticoke Valley with their kin; members of sibling groups arrived simultaneously or sequentially and helped one another get started.

[margin handwriting: Irish- wage laborers then farmers]

However diverse their places of origin, the people who settled the Nanticoke Valley during the early nineteenth century came in response to broadly similar conditions and with similar goals—to perpetuate their accustomed way of life, which had become impossible in their native communities. They took the risks that migration involved in order to find a new place where they could continue living in the old way.

9. Robert Hogg, "More Recollections of Scotland by Gulch," in "Early Scotch Settlers of West Chenango," ed. Garrett, *Whitney Point Reporter,* May 1901.

10. Kerby A. Miller, *Emigrants and Exiles: Ireland and the Irish Exodus to North America* (New York: Oxford University Press, 1985).

farming family undertaking

The traditional orientation of the people who migrated to the Nanticoke Valley shaped the way they settled the land. To them, farming was a family undertaking that involved more than a single generation. Nanticoke Valley settlers aspired not so much to accumulate a large property for themselves as to establish their children on farms of their own in the vicinity of the parental farmstead.[11] Not all of the settlers succeeded, but most devoted their labor and whatever capital they could accumulate to achieving this goal. Those young people whose parents had been unable to help them get started in farming in their native communities did not relinquish the ideal of intergenerational continuity; their experience underlined the value of parental assistance, rather than impressing them with the virtues of self-reliance. Those who had crossed the Atlantic did not surrender their allegiance to family ties either; as they left their parents and their native land behind, they turned their aspirations toward their children's future.

The families who settled in the Nanticoke Valley between 1790 and 1820 purchased land at widely scattered places throughout the valley.[12] Soon neighborhoods formed around them. Some multigen-

11. John J. Waters has illuminated the multigenerational orientation of New England families toward their farms: "The Traditional World of the New England Peasants: A View from Seventeenth-Century Barnstable," *New England Historical and Genealogical Register* 130 (1976): 3–22, and "Patrimony, Succession, and Social Stability: Guilford, Connecticut, in the Eighteenth Century," *Perspectives in American History* 10 (1976): 131–60. However, Waters believes that this orientation involved the identification of the family name with a particular piece of land. For the insight that this orientation could also be served by migration and replicated on new land, I am indebted to Mary P. Ryan, *Cradle of the Middle Class: The Family in Oneida County, New York, 1790–1865* (Cambridge: Cambridge University Press, 1981), 18–19, and James Henretta, "Families and Farms: *Mentalité* in Pre-Industrial America," *William and Mary Quarterly* 35 (1978): 3–32. A. Gordon Darroch, "Migrants in the Nineteenth Century: Fugitives or Families in Motion?" *Journal of Family History* 6 (1981): 257–77, argues that migration was a family strategy. Darroch analyzes the relationship between inheritance processes and migration, suggesting that the traditional goal of establishing sons on nearby farms might motivate men to uproot their growing families to move to new areas and that the decision to establish a single heir would lead to the chain migration of other children. Darroch's model fits the Nanticoke Valley; both entire kin groups and chains of relatives migrated to the community during the period of settlement. The migration of mature families to secure land for the next generation is extensively documented for Quebec: Gérard Bouchard, "Family Structures and Geographic Mobility at Laterrière, 1851–1935," *Journal of Family History* 2 (1979): 350–69; Gérard Bouchard, "Les systèmes de transmission des avoirs familiaux et le cycle de la société rurale au Quebec, du XVIIe au XXe siècle," *Histoire Sociale/Social History* 31 (1983): 35–60; and Gérard Bouchard and Isabelle de Pourbaix, "Individual and Family Life Courses in the Saguenay Region, Quebec, 1842–1911," *Journal of Family History* 12 (1987): 225–42.

12. This analysis of the settlement process is based on the reconstructed histories of more than two dozen families who settled in the Nanticoke Valley between 1790 and 1820 and remained in the community until 1855.

erational extended-family settlements were established in the process of migration, as parents and their married children or families of adult siblings moved to the valley simultaneously or in rapid succession. Other neighborhoods emerged over time as the numerous children who accompanied their parents to the valley or were born there grew up and founded farms of their own. Fathers with large tracts of forested land had their maturing sons clear new fields and divided the land among them when they married. Those who did not have enough capital to start with such large holdings helped their older sons buy land nearby, loaning them money, livestock, and tools in exchange for their continued help with the harvest; the youngest son usually inherited the parental farmstead. Soon adjacent farms were owned by fathers and sons, uncles and nephews, brothers and cousins. Kin-based neighborhoods were formed throughout the Nanticoke Valley as this process was repeated in family after family and from one generation to another.

Parents who arrived after 1820 followed the same pattern as those who had come thirty years before, establishing their sons on farms adjacent to their own.[13] The pace of settlement quickened during the third and fourth decades of the nineteenth century. As the valley became more populous, more newcomers purchased land near established neighborhoods. At the same time that kin groups proliferated, localities became more mixed in their composition. Some new migrants were relatives of long-established residents and settled near them, but others were quite different from their neighbors in their places of origin.

Intermarriage bound these people together, as children who grew up in the same neighborhood often married. Proximity and marriage were so closely connected that marriages among cousins and between groups of siblings were relatively common. At the same time, children of long-established residents married the children of newcomers; within particular neighborhoods, marriages even occurred across economic and ethnic lines. If kin were often neighbors, over time neighbors became kin. By the middle of the nineteenth century, the names by which many neighborhoods were known connoted not so much a single descent group as a social network of farm families. So many neighbors were kin that even among those who were not, rela-

13. This analysis of the settlement process after 1820, as well as the description of the pattern of settlement at mid-century, is based on a complete linkage between the manuscript schedules of the 1855 New York State census and the *Map of Broome County from Actual Surveys by Franklin Gifford and Emile Wenig* (Philadelphia: A. O. Gallup & Co., 1855), which was the first to show the places of residence of Nanticoke Valley families.

tionships were modeled on kinship; the expectation of continuing reciprocity shaped neighbors' interaction. Residents of open-country neighborhoods developed a sense of common identity.

Over time, these distinct neighborhoods coalesced into a community. In the early years, when settlement was sparse, people interacted primarily with their relatives and neighbors on the one hand and with merchants and creditors in Binghamton, Union, and Whitney's Point on the other. People who lived in Brockett Hollow might have been utter strangers to those in Broughamtown, although the two neighborhoods were just four miles apart. By mid-century, however, family farms were no longer islands of clearing in a sea of forest, neighborhoods no longer isolated settlements. As population density increased, contacts among local residents became more frequent, intense, and multifarious. The development of villages exemplifies this process. Growing up around artisan shops and mercantile stores, villages became centers for social interaction as well as business dealings. Union Center formed the southern gateway into the Nanticoke Valley. Farmers from Broughamtown and Brockett Hollow encountered one another as they traded in its mills, shops, and stores. By mid-century, Congregational and Methodist churches had been established there. Maine village, located midway up the creek, was the recognized center of the community. Its streets were lined with professional offices and specialty shops as well as the usual array of local businesses. The hotel provided refreshment for farmers from outlying areas and space for community gatherings. The Baptist, Congregational, and Methodist denominations all had churches in Maine village; some had branches in the smaller hamlets, but their ministers resided in Maine. Other villages were more limited in scope. Lamb's Corners, later called Nanticoke, served residents of the northwestern section of the valley, while Councilman's Settlement, renamed Glen Aubrey, was frequented by people who lived along the northeastern branch of the creek.

Religious institutions, like central places, fostered the development of social relationships among Nanticoke Valley residents. The churches brought people from different neighborhoods together along denominational lines for religious services, Sunday-school classes, prayer meetings, missionary and charitable societies. Interdenominational cooperation was also common. Some large camp meetings, cosponsored by all the evangelical churches, featured visiting preachers and drew people from throughout the valley. Other revivals took place in particular hamlets. For example, according to the history of the Wyoming Conference a revival that began in the

Maine village, looking east from King Hill toward Pollard Hill. Nanticoke Valley Historical Society.

nondenominational Sunday school in Lamb's Corners in the early 1850s "resulted in nearly one hundred conversions. This was virtually the establishing of the Methodist and Baptist churches in this place."[14] Church-sponsored social activities were even more inclusive. "Donations," which raised money for the church building or the minister's salary, were the most common community-wide gatherings at mid-century. People who did not belong to the congregation commonly attended donations, not simply to amuse themselves but also because such a demonstration of community spirit was expected. For the most part, denominational differences and geographical distinctions did not reinforce one another; congregations worked together

establishment of churches (handwritten marginal note)

14. This observation was made by the historian of the Wyoming Conference, the regional body to which the local Methodist churches belonged. Sections from A. J. Chafee's *History of the Wyoming Conference* have been incorporated into Mildred Garrett's 1973 manuscript, "A History of the Maine Methodist Church."

across denominational lines in particular localities, while denominational affiliations linked those from different neighborhoods.

The formation of town governments was perhaps the least important part of the process of community organization. The Town of Nanticoke was formed in 1831, when the area contained only 296 inhabitants, as a by-product of divisions among the more populous towns to the north. Local residents had difficulty agreeing to set up a government, and the first town meeting ended in a brawl when one faction attempted to burn the ballot box.[15] The creation of the Town of Maine, on the other hand, followed the community's maturation. Maine was set off from Union in 1848, when it already had approximately 1,800 residents. The men of Maine had been acting together to maintain public highways and operate school districts for more than thirty years; autonomy enabled them to assess and collect property taxes and elect their own representative to the Broome County Board of Supervisors.[16]

Stability, 1855–1880

The towns of Maine and Nanticoke contained 2,419 people in 1850 and 2,798 in 1855. The population grew much more slowly after the Civil War, when little land was available for new arrivals or for local sons who lacked capital; inmigration declined and outmigration increased. The Nanticoke Valley population reached 3,093 in 1870 and peaked at 3,128 in 1880. Between 1855 and 1880, then, the community stabilized.

This pattern of growth and stabilization resulted from the process of economic development.[17] By mid-century, the construction of turnpike roads, canals, and the Erie Railroad had connected the re-

15. Smith, *History of Broome County*, 394, 406–7, 420; Child, *Gazetteer*, 125. Nanticoke's first town meeting was held in 1832, a year of hotly contested state and national elections.
16. The formation of school and highway districts in the area of Union that became the town of Maine is described in Smith, *History of Broome County*, 616, 632; and in Belle North Johnson's undated manuscript, "Recollections of Brockett Hollow."
17. The major primary sources of information on the economic history of the Nanticoke Valley are the manuscript censuses of industry conducted in conjunction with the federal and New York State censuses of 1855 through 1880. Business directories are also useful: Andrew Boyd, comp., *Boyd's Binghamton City and Susquehanna Railroad Directory* (Binghamton, N.Y.: H. E. Pratt, Bookseller, 1871); Child, *Gazetteer*; and J. E. Williams, comp., *Williams' Binghamton City and Broome County Directory for 1881* (Binghamton, N.Y.: J. E. Williams, 1881). Additional information appears in newspapers and in county and town histories. This interpretation of Broome County's economic history was developed in collaboration with Ross McGuire and Lawrence Bothwell.

gion to national markets. Extractive industries that processed the resources of the forest remained important in the Nanticoke Valley,
employing approximately half of the adult men who did not farm.[18]
In addition to two dozen sawmills that turned out standard-
dimensioned building stock, four tanneries utilized hemlock bark to
tan hides for shoe leather. Some sawmills and tanneries were large-
scale enterprises. In Glen Aubrey, George W. Smith's tannery employed at least twenty men. Smith created a company village very
different from the other hamlets in the valley, providing housing for
his Irish workers and a school for their children. The most striking
symbol of Smith's domination is an octagonal house he had built for
his family and business in the 1850s. Three stories tall, it was en-
circled by a colonnaded porch and capped by a cupola. A central
staircase ascended from the workrooms on the ground floor to the
formal parlors on the second, and then on past the unfinished third
floor into the round room above the sloping roof. Here, local residents later recounted, Smith would stand with a spyglass and keep
watch over the tannery and the gangs of men working in the woods
on the surrounding hills. Regardless of whether the story is true, it
expresses how farmers felt about Smith's control over the locality.[19]
Other tanneries were more comfortably integrated into the community, purchasing hides and hemlock bark from farmers and employing their sons as laborers.

Many artisans served farm families. Carpenters, masons, and cabi-
netmakers, shoemakers, blacksmiths and mechanics, wagonmakers
and coopers all had their own shops, where some employed an ap-
prentice or two to assist them.[20] Small manufactories turning out

18. The importance of the lumbering industry to regional economic development has been highlighted by Ross McGuire, "Lumbermen, Farmers and Artisans: The
Rural Economy of the Nineteenth Century," in *Working Lives: Broome County, New
York, 1800–1930* (Binghamton, N.Y.: Roberson Center for the Arts and Sciences,
1982), 1–12.

19. Smith renamed the hamlet, formerly known as Councilman's Settlement, when
he was appointed postmaster. He also had the school moved closer to the tannery and
summarily fired a teacher of whose disciplinary methods he disapproved. The source
of this story was evidently Glen Aubrey resident Mrs. Ernestine Thompson, who owned
letters that Smith's daughter Caroline White wrote to her cousin Della Couse Preston.
The first recorded version is contained in Spencer's manuscript, "Brief History of the
Village of Glen Aubrey"; Spencer described it as "an old and interesting local legend."
The story is repeated in Swan, *Story of the Valleys.*

20. This discussion is based on the specific nonagricultural occupations listed on the
1855 New York State census, when 16 percent of adult men claimed a primary occupation other than farming or general labor, and on the 1880 federal census, when 13
percent did so. There were as many men employed in tanneries and sawmills as there
were artisans. Merchants and professionals comprised only a quarter of those with specific nonfarm occupations in 1855 and a third in 1880.

chairs and agricultural implements enjoyed a brief period of prosperity during the 1870s. The handful of men who owned stores in the villages and hamlets were relatively powerful. Merchants, manufacturers, and large landowners invested in a wide variety of enterprises; over a decade or two, an entrepreneur might finance the modernization of a mill, open a store, construct a commercial building, and expand his farm operation. All of these men had their feet firmly planted in the Nanticoke Valley soil, combining the pursuit of their trade, business, or profession with agriculture.

Most families engaged in farming.[21] Land was widely, if unevenly, distributed. Three out of four households owned enough land to plant a garden, raise chickens, and keep a milk cow or two; half had enough land to pasture six or more dairy cattle, raise their own hay and some feed, and produce a surplus of potatoes or orchard fruits. Farms were relatively small, averaging 104 acres in 1850 and 77 acres in 1880. This was typical of long-settled regions where the scale of farming was limited by the labor and capital that families could supply.[22]

Nanticoke Valley agriculture combined a subsistence base with commercial dairying. Dairy farming was well suited to local conditions. Soils were much less fertile than those in the Genesee country to the west. The rich layer of humus that had been built up under the forest cover was quickly washed away once land was cleared, and the underlying clay soils were acid and difficult to work. The steep slopes also inhibited intensive cultivation. On the other hand, older farms in the valley and on the uplands could supply the abundance of hay and extensive pasture which dairying required. Cows were milked only in the spring and summer, when they could be put out to graze; they were maintained through the winter primarily on hay rather than grain. Dairying did not demand a large crew of workers, except at haying season; the year-round routine of morning and evening chores was most effectively performed by family labor. Fi-

21. The major primary sources of information on the pattern of farming are the manuscript agricultural schedules of the federal censuses taken in 1850 and 1880. The New York State censuses of 1855, 1865, and 1875 also collected information about agriculture. This data has been supplemented by information from farmers' account books and diaries, merchants' business records, newspapers, and town histories.

22. The classic work on the history of agriculture in New York State throughout this period is Ulysses P. Hedrich, *A History of the Agriculture of New York State* (Albany: New York State Agricultural Society, 1933). Neil Adams McNall, *An Agricultural History of the Genesee Valley, 1790–1860* (Philadelphia: University of Pennsylvania Press, 1952), is a model regional study; the southern upland area of the Genesee Valley had much in common with Broome County. McGuire, "Lumbermen, Farmers and Artisans," 18–29, discusses the development of agriculture in Broome County.

nally, dairying provided farmers with a steady, if relatively small, source of income. Although farmers worried that the fortunes of their families depended on the prices of dairy products in distant urban centers, they also welcomed the opportunity to purchase a wide range of commodities with the cash and credit they received. Commercial dairying represented not only an adaptation to local topographical conditions but also an adjustment to the expansion of capitalist market relations during the mid-nineteenth century.[23]

The pastoral character of agriculture is indicated by the use of land on farms. In 1880, for every acre of tillage there were two of meadow and three in pasture; two more remained in woodlot. Arable land was devoted to feed crops, such as oats and corn, in rotation with hay and fallow. Each summer, farmers cut an average of seventeen tons of hay from their meadows. All this, together with the fresh grass of upland pastures, supported dairy cattle. At mid-century there were already more milk cows than people in the Nanticoke Valley. Farmers increased the size of their dairy herds after the Civil War; by 1880 farm families were milking an average of six cows.

Butter was the most important product of local dairies. Farm families churned a total of 430,619 pounds of butter in 1879, six times the amount that would have been consumed in the community.[24] Two-thirds of all farm families made enough butter to sell, and one-third made at least a thousand pounds a year. Most farmers shipped their butter in fifty-pound tubs to New York City, selling it on commission through village merchants; some also sold butter directly in Binghamton. A family that milked seven cows might receive $250 from the sale of butter in a year; this amounted to 40 percent of the total value of their farm produce and as much as 70 percent of their annual cash income.

The culmination of the settlement process and the maturation of the economy were accompanied by the stabilization of the social order.

23. For analyses of the expansion of dairy farming as a response to changing market conditions, see Hedrich, *History of Agriculture*, chap. 17, "Livestock Industries"; Fred Albert Shannon, *The Farmer's Last Frontier: Agriculture, 1860–1897* (New York: Holt, Rinehart and Winston, 1945), chap. 11, "Specialized Agriculture and Eastern Adjustments"; Eric Brunger, "A Chapter in the Growth of the New York State Dairy Industry, 1850–1900," *New York History* 36 (1955): 130–45, and "Changes in the New York State Dairying Industry, 1850–1900" (Ph.D. diss., Syracuse University, 1954); Gates, *The Farmer's Age*, chap. 11, "Dairy Farming"; Paul W. Gates, "Agricultural Change in New York State, 1850–1890," *New York History* 50 (1967): 115–42.

24. The amount of butter that would have been consumed in local households has been estimated on the basis of evidence presented in Fred Bateman, "The 'Marketable Surplus' in Northern Dairy Farming: New Evidence by Size of Farm in 1860," *Agricultural History* 52 (1978): 345–63.

Over time, the people of the Nanticoke Valley developed a common culture. Local residents, who had almost all grown up in the immediate vicinity, were bound together not only by lifelong association but also by ties of kinship and affiliation several generations deep. Like their counterparts in other long-settled rural communities, people valued homogeneity and harmony. The social and political conflicts attendant on the process of community formation, especially in a diverse and dynamic population, had been resolved. Conflicts rooted in structural contradictions within the community were repressed or removed from the public domain; consensus characterized local life.[25]

The social organization of the valley during the late nineteenth century was shaped by the interaction between neighborhood and community-wide forms of association. When groups organized on the basis of economic interests, as businessmen or farmers, community unanimity disappeared and harmony was threatened. Organizing on a neighborhood basis muted class differences but might lead to community disintegration. Balance was attained when community-wide and neighborhood-based forms of organization complemented one another.

Religious institutions continued to be most successful in combining local loyalties with denominational linkages. The balance between sectarian and neighborhood feeling was always delicate, however, and conflicts were generally solved by division. The proliferation of churches in the Nanticoke Valley during the late nineteenth century resulted from dissension and fission as well as from population growth and religious revivals. The church in East Maine, for example, was founded by a group of staunch Scottish Presbyterians who withdrew from the Maine village Congregational Church in 1871.[26] They were joined by people from their neighborhood who had not previously belonged to any religious organization, and they agreed to construct a building at the crossroads with the East Maine Methodist Sunday-school class. This local interdenominational cooperation did not last long, however. According to the history of the regional conference of the Methodist church, the Methodists helped build the church on the understanding that they would share in its use, but after it was completed the Presbyterians "gave the Methodists to understand that they were not wanted, and utterly ignored their

25. Hal S. Barron, *Those Who Stayed Behind: Rural Society in Nineteenth-Century New England* (Cambridge: Cambridge University Press, 1984), chap. 6, describes a similar process in Chelsea, Vermont.

26. The Maine village church, which had belonged to the Tioga Presbytery even though it was congregational in polity, voted in 1871 to join the Susquehanna Congregational Association.

rights."[27] So the Methodists withdrew; East Maine Methodists later constructed buildings with their counterparts in West Chenango and Oak Hill. Small rural churches regularly cooperated with the larger churches of their denomination and with the other churches in their vicinity. In Maine and Union Center the churches pooled their resources to hold union revival meetings and rotating Sunday-evening services. The relationship among established Nanticoke Valley churches was characterized by emulation. One after another, village churches enlarged their buildings, refurnished their sanctuaries, and added prayer rooms, steeples, and bells. Competition and cooperation, like denominational and neighborhood feeling, coexisted in a delicate balance.

The centrality of religious organizations in the construction of community identity is underlined by the Protestant majority's exclusion of the Catholic minority from significant participation in social life. Local residents were quite diverse in their places of origin. According to the 1855 census, one-third of the population of Maine and Nanticoke had been born in the local community; another half had been born in New York State, one-eighth in New England, and one-twentieth in foreign countries. Two-thirds of the foreign-born were Irish, and one-fifth were Scottish; the rest had come from England, Holland, Germany, and Canada. The native-born population included people from a variety of ethnic backgrounds as well. Some of the people who came from eastern New York State were of German or Dutch descent; many of those who came from Otsego County were Scottish; and some of those who came from New Hampshire were Scots-Irish. In the Nanticoke Valley, these groups consolidated into a dominant Protestant majority and an Irish Catholic minority. By 1880, seven-eighths of the population had been born in New York; one-twentieth were foreign-born, and one-tenth were of foreign parentage. More than three-quarters of those of foreign birth or parentage were Irish. The appearance of homogeneity was maintained by excluding the Irish from membership in supposedly community-wide groups. Neither geography nor class alone explains this situation, for both the landowning farmers of New Ireland and the laborers in the villages' lumber mills and tanneries met the same fate; religious prejudice underlay the pattern of cultural exclusion.

New Ireland, the neighborhood in the southeastern corner of Maine composed predominantly of immigrant Irish farm families,

27. A. J. Chafee, *History of the Wyoming Conference,* as quoted in the records of the Maine Methodist Church. This church's formation is also described in Smith, *History of Broome County,* 504.

never became integrated into the larger community. These immigrants resembled the rest of the rural population in many respects:
they had come to Maine as young couples, sometimes to join siblings,
and had large families here. They purchased land and established
farms; indeed, the Irish had the highest rate of land-ownership of
any group in the Nanticoke Valley. The men even became naturalized
citizens. But the Irish remained residentially segregated, and their
native-born children did not intermarry with the Protestants who
lived nearby in East Maine.[28]

The importance of religion in dividing the Irish from the other
residents of the community is illuminated by the contrasting experience of Scottish immigrants. Many Scots settled on Mt. Ettrick, which
they named after their homeland; they formed a large and close-knit
group of related farm households. They even retained the customs
and culture of the Highlands and looked back with nostalgia to "my
ain countree." At the same time, they were not isolated; instead, they
invited their non-Scottish neighbors to participate in their celebrations. The Scots were readily accepted, for they were active in the
local Protestant churches. Their children intermarried with their

28. Records of the Irish who lived in Maine are scanty, probably because the Irish
settlement itself had disappeared by the turn of the century. The manuscript census
schedules document the kinship ties that knit New Ireland together. But it is impossible
to tell what kinds of ties linked this neighborhood with the Irish individuals and families living elsewhere in the valley, such as the domestic servants in Maine village and
the tannery workers in Glen Aubrey. Nor is it clear how Maine's Irish residents were
related to other groups of Irish immigrants in the region. The nearest substantial rural
Irish settlement was just across the Pennsylvania line in St. Joseph's, where the Rose
family had established a Catholic parish and settled a dozen or more families from the
southwestern counties of Ireland on their extensive landholdings during the two decades before the famine. The nearest Catholic church was in Binghamton; its priest
served three counties. Aside from the few wealthy families who erected St. Patrick's
Church, most of the Irish who lived in Binghamton at mid-century were transient; the
men were employed on the canal, in railroad construction, or as casual laborers. There
is no evidence that the Irish who settled in the Nanticoke Valley had formerly lived in
either of these communities. One story of how the Irish came to Maine (remembered
because it pertains to John Casey, the baseball player memorialized in "Casey at the
Bat") suggests that John Pumpelley, an Owego land speculator and railroad investor,
originally sold the first Irish immigrants their farms. This story is reported in a local
newspaper article based on interviews with Casey descendants by Nanticoke historian
Eleanor Swan. Information on the history of the Catholic church in Broome County is
contained in the biography of the Rev. James Francis Hourigan in Smith, *History of
Broome County*, 541–48. For information on the Irish settlement at St. Joseph's, I am
indebted to Ross McGuire, who studied Irish immigration to Broome County during
the early nineteenth century. Robert Hogg was evidently unusual in his favorable opinion of Maine's Irish farmers. The Hoggs had also worked on the Rose estate before
their settlement in the Nanticoke Valley; this direct contact, coupled with a shared
hatred of English landlords, probably inspired his sympathetic attitude.

non-Scottish neighbors and they enjoyed a social status equal to that of the native-born residents. The Irish, on the other hand, were Catholic; they were assumed to be different, and so they remained distinct.[29]

Other Irish immigrants lived in or near the villages of Maine, Glen Aubrey, and Nanticoke. The men generally worked for wages as lumbermen and tannery laborers, and most stayed in housing provided by their employers or in shacks in the woods. Although some may have been kinsmen, relatively few had wives or children with them. Young women worked as live-in domestic servants in well-to-do merchants' households. Few of these Irish workers remained in the Nanticoke Valley for long. Subordinated by class as well as excluded by ethnicity, they were present in the community but did not belong to it. These Irish workers figured in most contemporary descriptions of the local community only as the stock figures of "Paddy" and "Bridget."

Affirming a common Protestant identity through the exclusion of Irish farmers and workers tended to mute class differences among native-born residents of the valley. However, economic interests were not entirely subsumed by ethnocultural identities, and farmers and merchants organized separate associations.

Although the villages served the entire community, they were dominated by the commercial elite. Union Center, Maine, Nanticoke, and Glen Aubrey continued to grow.[30] In Maine, a village green was created and a new residential street laid out after the Civil War. The green was more than a ceremonial space; it became a gathering place for summer Saturday-night band concerts as well as public celebrations. The ornate Gothic Revival houses along Lewis Street, which contrasted sharply with the smaller and simpler Greek Revival buildings on Main and Church streets, visibly expressed the prosperity of the village's entrepreneurs. As an article in the 1878 *Union News* put it, "Every year brings more plainly to view the fact that our village is certainly growing in business and beauty."[31] The Maine Lodge of Free

29. The history of the Scottish settlers of Mt. Ettrick is chronicled in the newspaper series compiled by Garrett, "Early Scotch Settlers."

30. Because none of the Nanticoke Valley villages ever incorporated, reliable population figures are not available. Some totals are available for Maine village; there were approximately 220 residents in 1855, and the population peaked at 335 in 1880.

31. *Union News* 26:50 (10 May 1878), as quoted in Robert J. Spencer, "I See by the Paper" (manuscript, 1957). For information about the development of Maine village during this period, I am indebted to the Preservation Planning Workshop of Cornell University, which surveyed the historic buildings in the village.

and Accepted Masons consolidated the village's commercial elite; its list of officers resembles a business directory.[32] Other organizations were more inclusive, but still village-centered; although they counted residents of the open-country neighborhoods among their membership, they were dominated by villagers, and people who lived in outlying areas had to come into Maine to participate in their activities.

The villages' commercial elite presented their interest as that of the community as a whole, but farmers were aware that was not necessarily so. They founded their own groups which met in open-country neighborhoods. Farmers' clubs existed as early as 1872. According to Child's *Gazetteer*:

> Two "farmers' clubs" have been organized, and periodical meetings are held at the residences of the different members, and the deliberations are participated in by the families of the members. Crops, stock, out-buildings, agricultural implements, & etc., are critically examined and commented upon. . . . Such meetings nurture amicable social relations and afford opportunities for the interchange of ideas, which will tend to stimulate a spirit of generous rivalry and promote the farming interests.[33]

Farmers' jubilees, which were held in district schoolhouses and open to the public, featured invited speakers and debating contests; in addition to agricultural subjects, participants addressed current political questions. Agricultural fairs were established in Maine and Nanticoke in the early 1870s as well. For two days each year, people from all over the valley came to the fairgrounds to view exhibits of livestock and implements, vegetables and needlework; they enjoyed horse and foot races, picnics, and one another's company. The founders of these organizations were not all practical farmers, but most members were. Farmers with little capital or inclination toward commercial agriculture, however, did not join these agricultural societies.[34]

32. For the histories of these and other village organizations, see Earl Ingalls, *A 125 Year History of Maine Lodge, No. 399, Free and Accepted Masons, 1856–1981*, ed. Lawrence R. Rice (Maine, N.Y.: Masonic Lodge, 1981); James C. Babbitt, "The Maine Community Band: A Brief History, 1873–1973," in *A Short History of Maine*, comp. Woodward, 38–41; Smith, *History of Broome County*, 501–2.

33. Child, *Gazetteer*, 121.

34. The activities of the Maine and Lamb's Corners agricultural societies are documented in local newspapers and described in Woodward, *A Short History of Maine*, 18–19, and Spencer, "I See by the Paper," 2–3. The 1876 Atlas included a large sketch of the Maine village fair grounds. The Broome County Historical Society holds copies of programs from the 1880 Lamb's Corners and 1886 Nanticoke Valley Agricultural Society fairs. Further information on activities in Nanticoke is found in the typewritten biography of Charles Johnson in the files of the Broome County Historical Society. I

While farmers and merchants were both interested in the improvement of agricultural techniques, they were divided on other matters of concern to farmers. In 1874, soon after the Patrons of Husbandry was established in Broome County, Nanticoke Valley farmers formed Unity Grange #74.[35] One of their first activities, according to the local newspaper, was to open "a store, or depot, for supplies at Delano's Corners with Marshall Delano as superintendent where all Grangers can get the worth of their money and the right change back."[36] This was a critique, not only of the national market, but also of local merchants and feed dealers; the Grange store represented a direct alternative to their enterprises. The agricultural organizations of the Nanticoke Valley demonstrate the existence of conflict within the community.

The conception of social order that became dominant in the Nanticoke Valley during the late nineteenth century was articulated in a rhymed description of Maine village composed by Harriet E. Tucker for recitation at a meeting of the Good Templars' Lodge in 1874.[37]

We are a peaceable people and live by hard labor,
Each man is as good, every whit, as his neighbor,
Unless he gets drunk, and then he's to blame
And ought not to bear a very good name.
Here, my good friend, pray let me digress
And say I hope the number is less,
Let us work with a will to get them all in
To the Good Templar's fold, where they'll drink no more gin,
And then what a happy people we'll be
When nothing is drunk stronger than tea.

The poem opens by characterizing the community as composed of social equals, but it differentiates people by their moral conduct. By equating drink with sin it holds individuals responsible for their own

---

have benefited from discussion of agricultural societies with Ian Mylchreest; his unpublished paper "Men at Work: Labor in the Nanticoke Valley" describes fairs as public spectacles rather than serious vehicles for agricultural improvement.

35. A second Grange was established in Glen Aubrey in 1887, and a third in Maine village in 1890. Union Center also formed a Grange in 1908. Leonard L. Allen, *A History of the New York State Grange* (Watertown, N.Y.: Hungerford-Holbrook Co., 1934), 192–98.

36. Quoted in Spencer, "I See by the Paper," 3, from a newspaper item published on 4 June 1875.

37. Tucker was a single woman of thirty-six who lived with her mother and her mother's second husband, wagonmaker Jefferson Ransom, in Maine village. In 1890, she married James N. Ingalls, a widower with grown children; his grandson J. Ralph Ingalls copied and preserved the poem.

actions at the same time it exerts social pressure toward their re-
demption. The restoration of the intemperate will realize the vision
of a united community with which the rhyme opens. In these few
verses, the text acknowledges that the characterization of social relations in the opening lines is not a statement of facts but an expression
of values.

The church stands at the moral center of the community. Since the
poem describes Maine village rather than the ideal community, however, there are three churches rather than one:

> Of churches, the number we have is three,
> The pastors are Washburn, Hayward and Lee.
> We've organs and players and choirs that can sing
> Mear, Martin, Old Hundred or any such thing.
> Our school by Miss Rixie Eldred is taught,
> To keep it in order, she has faithfully sought.

Tucker does not name the churches by denomination, for that would
emphasize that Christians were divided among themselves rather
than joining in a universal evangelical Protestant church. Counting
their pastors, organs, and choirs, by contrast, gives the appearance of
a multiplication of the means of grace. Religion and civil society are
closely allied, for the school follows the church as an agent for order
within the village.

The rhyme moves without a pause from Maine's public institutions
to its business establishments. Tucker lists all of the stores and shops
located there in 1874; to have left any out would have been an economic injury as well as a personal affront. She celebrates the diversity
of the commodities available in the village, emphasizing that Nanticoke Valley residents could satisfy all their needs within the local
community. Highlighting the differences in the types of goods carried by the four mercantile stores fosters the illusion that they were
not really competitive, but rather complementary.

There is only one suggestion that business was not simply a matter
of sociable consumption.

> We have farmers, a number, who sell eggs and butter
> If they don't get a big price, O, how they mutter.

Tucker carefully avoids the question of who was responsible for the
prices farmers received, refraining from mentioning that village mer-

chants had anything to do with marketing dairy products. After all, she has already described the largest commission house:

> Of merchants, Taylor Bros. first I will mention,
> To say aught against them, I have no intention.
> They run a fine store, and sell all they can,
> And Henry, their clerk, is a model young man.

The causes of the farmers' dissatisfaction seem to lie outside the local community.[38] Tucker is careful not to represent buying and selling as a transaction in which either party might seek to take advantage of the other.

Although Tucker includes every business proprietor, she does not name all the residents of the village who made their living "by hard labor." While sons in partnership with their fathers are mentioned, women who worked with their husbands and fathers in family businesses are not. Tucker lists the milliner:

> Miss Muzzy, too, is right up the stairs,
> She'll make you a bonnet, in style, she declares.

But she omits herself, even though she worked as a dressmaker. Tradesmen who did not have their own shops are simply enumerated.

Tucker does not acknowledge the presence of Irish workers in the village; they are subsumed by the generic term "hands" and carefully placed under the control of their employer.

> W. H. Sherwood deals in leather and lumber,
> J. Wright is his foreman, his other hands a number.

The Irish could not be assimilated within Tucker's vision. Irish Catholics were not eligible for membership in the universal evangelical Protestant church. They were also excluded from the Good Templars' Lodge, even though they—along with the Germans and all those em-

---

38. Village merchants tried to deny that farmers and merchants might have conflicting interests. Their advertisements in newspapers and business directories present their wholesale and commission trade as a service to farmers. The commission system did tend to defuse antagonism in the relation between merchants and farmers, but it was primarily intended to protect rural merchants against sudden changes in urban commodity prices.

ployed in the lumber industry—had a reputation for drinking.[39] The Irish workers remained anomalous and never found a place in the village's definition of community.

Only once does Tucker suggest that not all inhabitants of the village had to "live by hard labor."

> We have young ladies who live quite at their ease
> They never make bread, butter or cheese,
> And young gentlemen, too, so fine and so gay
> Who have nothing to do but play croquet.

Idle youths undoubtedly belonged to families that were better off than most, but Tucker does not recognize economic and social stratification. The poem implies that these people were irresponsible because they were young, not idle because they were rich. Living on unearned income was not a sign of success; instead, it was a bit ridiculous. These verses, like the rest of the poem, translate differences among people into moral terms.

Differences from others defined the boundaries of community among Nanticoke Valley residents. Harriet Tucker's vision notwithstanding, what people had in common was not a set of abstract values but rather a routine of sharing, a set of activities that bound them together in their daily lives. Those whom they did not regard as similar to themselves were not integrated into these routines and so remained outsiders. Within the community, conflict as well as consensus might reinforce communal values. Differences mattered because people felt that what anyone did affected everyone else. Harmony was regarded as essential, so conflicts were resolved or repressed. While stores competed for customers and churches competed for converts, all presented themselves as servants of the whole community and guardians of its best interests. In vernacular speech, people were plu-

---

39. Men who worked in rural industries and were transient laborers rather than local part-time farmers seem to have been predominantly of Irish, New York Dutch, or Pennsylvania German descent. The work culture of lumbermen involved bouts of intense labor alternating with periods of enforced leisure which were often accompanied by drinking. More settled contemporaries regarded these men as irresponsible and found them threatening to the values of the established community. Occupation, ethnicity, and alcohol were often conflated in their minds. For example, one long-time Maine resident recalled in 1903: "I remember the settlement of Dutch Hill by the Dutch from Albany and Schoharie Counties. They were good to lumber it and get drunk." A. B. Dayton, quoted in "Maine of To-Day," *Whitney Point Reporter*, 29 May 1903. The Irish were generally regarded as especially likely to become drunk and disorderly.

ral, but community was singular. By the middle of the nineteenth century, the community was not simply a place with which Nanticoke Valley residents identified in their dealings with outsiders; it had become a value that people invoked in their interactions with one another.

In the political culture that dominated the valley, even partisan conflict was submerged or denied. The town meeting ceased to be a forum for meaningful debate of local issues; instead, it simply elected officers who made the crucial decisions about the town budget. The towns of Maine and Nanticoke stood firmly in the Republican column in national politics from the Civil War onward, and any dissent was regarded as unpatriotic. Public events became occasions not so much for the affirmation of particular political positions as for the confirmation of civic unity; unanimity itself had become the supreme community value by the late nineteenth century. On Decoration Day (now Memorial Day), when Nanticoke Valley residents commemorated the glorious service of local men in the Union cause, they celebrated the community's own unity as much as that of the American nation.

Consolidation, 1880–1900

At the turn of the twentieth century, the Nanticoke Valley was relatively homogeneous, socially integrated, and seemingly stable. At the same time, it was in the middle of a process of long-term demographic decline and economic transformation. The population of Maine and Nanticoke fell from 3,128 in 1880 to 2,415 in 1890; by 1900 there were only 2,220 people living in the two towns. This loss of population resulted in part from familiar features of life in long-settled rural communities. When farms became too small to subdivide, one son might look forward to inheriting the farmstead, but the others had to leave. Some migrated to Kansas and Nebraska to establish farms. Others learned a trade or found a job in industry. Because the nonagricultural sector of the rural economy contracted sharply during the late nineteenth century, young people who left farming for wage earning had to leave the community as well. After 1880, the steady cityward stream of landless youths was swelled by former farming families. People who preferred the limited hours and regular wages offered by industrial employment to the ceaseless toil and uncertain returns of farming sold or rented their

Ida and Judson Riley, c. 1870. Nanticoke Valley Historical Society.

Ida Riley Davey and Vernon Davey, c. 1879. Nanticoke Valley Historical Society, courtesy of Alleyne Davey Bostwick.

Four generations in the Riley-Davey family, c. 1906. (Clockwise) Ida Riley Davey, Vernon Davey, Lucy Ann Bicknell Riley, Florence Davey. Nanticoke Valley Historical Society, courtesy of Alleyne Davey Bostwick.

land and moved to the city. Even if they migrated only fifteen miles over the hills to Binghamton or to the adjacent industrial village of Lestershire, they entered a different, and clearly distinct, social order.

Those who remained in the rural community adjusted their expectations to local circumstances. Keeping the farm in the family—holding onto the land, struggling to pay off the mortgage, and passing the farm on to a child who could be trusted to carry on—was as much as most families could hope for, and more than many could attain. Couples limited their fertility, balancing their need for youthful labor against their increasing inability to provide for their children's future and to ensure that their children would remain near enough to take care of them in old age. Farm families expanded their commercial dairy operations, relying on the steady income and small

Judson Riley's farm, c. 1908, taken from Ida Riley Davey's farm. Nanticoke Valley Historical Society, courtesy of Alleyne Davey Bostwick.

profits to maintain their farms, while they continued diversified subsistence production to maintain themselves. Their horizons were limited, for the accumulation of wealth was beyond their reach. But there was a certain satisfaction in keeping their place in the local community. Those who chose to stay in the Nanticoke Valley valued the web of relationships which connected them with friends and neighbors.

The process of economic and demographic contraction actually facilitated the formation of stable social networks. As Hal Barron points out in his study of a rural Vermont community, population stagnation, or even decline, did not disrupt the lives of "those who stayed behind."[40] Instead, continuous outmigration enabled the rural community to maintain its traditional way of life in spite of changing

40. Barron, *Those Who Stayed Behind*, chap. 5.

circumstances. The Nanticoke Valley population became more homogeneous, not only through normal aging but also through the differential outmigration of those who did not fit into the dominant culture. By 1900, nine-tenths of the population was native-born and of native parentage; only 3 percent was foreign-born. Most of the immigrants had been in the United States for many years; more than a third had arrived before 1850, and only a fifth had come during the previous twenty years. The Irish still predominated among people of foreign birth and descent, but their numbers had been depleted by the decline of the rural industrial labor force and the departure of the sons and daughters of New Ireland's farmers. Their exclusion from the community, which had been an ideological matter in the 1870s, became a demographic reality in the 1890s.

The homogeneity of the community reinforced residents' sense of stability. People in the Nanticoke Valley were aware of the economic and social changes occurring during the late nineteenth century, but most thought of these changes as taking place in the cities of the Susquehanna Valley rather than along their own Nanticoke Creek. The community itself did not seem subject to historical change. Although that view was, in large measure, an illusion, it was fostered by the kinds of changes taking place in the valley. The community became culturally more homogeneous, more purely agricultural, and more clearly defined as the country in contrast to the city.

The deindustrialization of the countryside was an integral part of late-nineteenth-century economic development. Industries formerly carried on in small workshops throughout the county were centralized in large factories in the cities. Local manufacturing enterprises could not keep pace with the expansion in Binghamton. By the end of the century, most had disappeared entirely; the few that survived became locally oriented service and retail businesses. In the lumber industry, the largest mills shut down; some small sawmills remained, but only as part-time custom operations. The 1900 county history spoke of lumbering as part of the more prosperous and populous past: "Nanticoke once enjoyed prominence as a lumbering town, but with the clearing away of the forests the only remaining mainstay of the inhabitants was general agriculture."[41] Industries that supported agriculture had somewhat more stable histories. Gristmills continued to serve local farmers on a custom basis, but by 1880 they were grinding as much livestock feed as they were meal and flour; some began selling commercial feed as well. Few rural artisans could compete

41. Lawyer, *Binghamton*, 696.

with the highly capitalized urban factories that were rationalizing and mechanizing the production process during the late nineteenth century. Some artisans compromised with their urban competitors by utilizing prefabricated elements within the production process. The Norton wagon shop at Bowers' Corners, for example, purchased carriage hardware from large foundries and made wooden bodies for them. By the turn of the century, Norton held the franchise for several Binghamton carriage companies and used standardized methods to build vehicles to order. This adaptation to changing industrial conditions did not prevent whole stages of the production process from leaving the local community.[42] Other artisans who sought to remain in their trade shifted from manufacturing to retail sales; the transformation of the rural economy involved a transition from "shops" to "stores." As the country and the city became more differentiated, the city monopolized manufacturing and the countryside was left with retail, repair, and service functions.

The construction of the new Wells and Corwin creamery building on the site of the former tannery in Maine village in 1895 signaled the transformation of the economy of the Nanticoke Valley. At the end of the nineteenth century, agriculture became the dominant sector of the rural economy.[43] The processing and marketing of dairy products was mechanized and centralized, and local farmers continued to increase the scale of their dairy operations.

The establishment of centralized creameries relieved farm families of the laborious and exacting tasks involved in butter making. Throughout the nineteenth century, farm families and inventors sought to design improved butter churns, both to decrease the time and energy required in churning and to allow larger quantities of cream to be handled at once. Before 1880, however, improvements in household butter-making techniques and equipment no more than kept pace with increases in the scale of production.[44] It was the inven-

42. The history of the Norton wagon shop is summarized in McGuire, "Lumbermen, Farmers and Artisans," 36–38.
43. Only one in nine men listed a specific nonagricultural occupation on the 1900 federal census. Employment in extractive industries and the artisan trades declined sharply, while the proportion of men employed in commerce increased markedly.
44. For information on patents for churns, see Joan Jensen, "Churns and Buttermaking in the Mid-Atlantic Farm Economy, 1750–1850," *Working Papers from the Regional Economic History Research Center* 5 (1982), 61–100. The most common type of churn used locally during the late nineteenth century was the simple dasher type; barrel churns became more popular by the turn of the century. Some farm families attempted to substitute animal for hand power by hitching the churn up to a treadmill, but it was difficult to get a dog to maintain the steady speed required. The most widely adopted innovation was the large butter-working table that replaced small wooden

tion of the mechanical cream separator that led to the establishment
of centralized "butter factories." By 1880, the DeLaval Company was
manufacturing and distributing machines that processed large quantities of milk very rapidly; they operated by centrifugal force and
could be powered by small steam engines. The churning was done in
a large, rotating barrel and might be steam powered as well. A skilled
butter maker and a laborer could operate a creamery serving dozens
of farms. During the last two decades of the nineteenth century,
creameries were established wherever dairy farms were sufficiently
dense to support them. Although centralized creameries never monopolized the manufacture of butter, they quickly became dominant
in the commercial butter-making regions.[45]

The first creameries in the Nanticoke Valley were established
around 1890; by 1894, six were in operation.[46] Those located in
Maine village, Nanticoke, and Glen Aubrey were private companies.
The East Maine Creamery Association was a cooperative, while the
Crystal Creamery in Union Center was a joint stock operation; although two these creameries were not formally affiliated with the
Grange, they were founded by Grange members. Both the number of
creameries and the scale of their operations continued to increase
through the turn of the century. At the same time, the establishment
of creameries accelerated the trend toward specialization in dairying.
Because farmers were paid according to the butterfat content as well
as the quantity of the milk they brought to the creameries, farmers
began to improve their herds, improve their feeding practices, and
look more favorably on other innovations that promised to increase
the quality and quantity of their milk production.

The relative importance of the commercial villages within the rural
community increased during the late nineteenth century. As the rural

---

bowls and paddles; this was essential for handling the large quantities of butter many
local farms were producing. John P. Corbin, *Practical Hints on Dairying, or, Manual for
Butter Makers* (Whitney's Point, N.Y.: n.p., 1871), advertised the "Eureka Butter
Worker" this Broome County resident patented in 1870.

45. For the history of butter factories and the development of mechanical separa-
tors, see Henry A. Alvord, "Dairy Development in the United States," *Yearbook of the
United States Department of Agriculture, 1899* (Washington, D.C.: U.S. Government Printing Office, 1900), 381–98; T. R. Pirtle, *History of the Dairy Industry* (Chicago: Mojon-
nier Bros., 1926), 75–80; Edward Wiest, *The Butter Industry in the United States: An
Economic Study of Butter and Oleomargerine* (New York: Columbia University Press, 1916),
19–27, 39–42.

46. Creameries are listed in the Annual Reports of the Commissioner of Agriculture
of New York State for 1892 through 1900. The diary of Judson Riley contains many
entries pertaining to the establishment and operation of the East Maine cooperative
creamery, for Riley was a stockholder, member of the board of directors, and treasurer
between 1893 and 1897.

population fell, stores and shops disappeared from such crossroads hamlets as North Maine, and the residents of open-country neighborhoods went into the villages for goods and services. Many farmers made daily trips to the creameries in Maine, Nanticoke, and Glen Aubrey. The second county history, published in 1900, remarked of Maine village: "At the present time Maine has a less number and variety of business interests than were noticeable a quarter of a century and more ago, but those that remain are of a substantial and apparently permanent character."[47] In this respect as so many others, decline and stability complemented rather than contradicted one another.

The churches also became more centralized during the late nineteenth century. Some small crossroads churches consolidated with the village churches of their denomination; others became interdenominational neighborhood institutions. At the same time, church-sponsored organizations proliferated. As outmigration diminished the pool of potential converts, churches adopted a variety of new strategies to sustain the interest of their congregations. Regular religious services were supplemented not only by Sunday-school classes and prayer meetings but also by special events such as concerts, recitations, and Christmas tree parties. Church socials became more frequent and more elaborate. Ladies' aid societies not only provided financial support for religious causes but also conducted social events for the congregation and community.

Civic rituals affirmed the centrality of community by connecting the present with the past. By 1900, the significance of Decoration Day had been enlarged; it commemorated not just Civil War veterans but also the valley's "pioneers." Families that had scattered across Broome County reunited on that day to honor the memory of their ancestors. Even local historical observances celebrated family continuity rather than community change. Continuity with the past and unity in the present went hand in hand; both helped people create a feeling of stability in a time of change.

Over the course of the nineteenth century, the Nanticoke Valley passed through three phases of development. Between 1787 and 1855, settlers and their children cleared and cultivated the land, engaged in small-scale, diversified enterprises, and constructed churches and civic institutions. The contours of the community were shaped by generational and gender relationships, as patterns of prop-

47. Lawyer, *Binghamton*, 715.

erty holding and inheritance, intermarriage and reciprocal exchange governed the formation of households and neighborhoods. Family-level processes generated the distinctive configuration of rural society. During the period between 1855 and 1880, population and resources were in relative balance. Farmers expanded their commercial dairy operations, and artisans and merchants benefited from closer connections with regional markets. Community organizations consolidated, and residents forged a sense of common (although not entirely inclusive) identity. In the years after 1880, as the rural economy deindustrialized and became more exclusively agricultural, demographic decline was accompanied by increased cultural homogeneity. The people who stayed in the valley adjusted their generational and gender relationships to the limits imposed by the local economy, maintaining family continuity in spite of economic and social change. The ways that family relationships shaped and were shaped by the community's history form the subject of the next chapter.

CHAPTER TWO

The Power of Kinship

... talking of our folks and friends.
　　　　　　　　　　　　—George W. Riley, Diary, 1881

On 31 December 1880, George W. Riley wrote in his diary:

today ends another year of our lives and this is my Sixteenth Diara
　am able to give an account of my Selfe every day for the past 16
years or 5840 days. Perhaps I cannot give as good a record as I
ought to be able to give but am glad that things have gon no worse
for us than they have, but on the Contrary have great reason to
Praise the giver of all good gifts that our lives have been spared and
So many blessing have followed us during the whole time of my Diara Keeping together with our whole lives. but Many has ben the *many changes*
Changes, with all its disapointments and trials that this world of *trials*
cares are hier to, during that time our little seven year old girl has
grown to womanhood got married got to be Mother over four years
ago. Juddie has ben Born and grown to be a Man in size and is a
great help to us. and we have ben able to pay all our debts, bought *raised kids*
the Frost place, built a new Barn on it, got Ida and Bert on it and *work farm*
Started. Built our wagon house, an addition on our house, wood *contribute to religion*
mill and shops, Cleared and improved a good deal of our place.
helped to Build a church at Maine and have tried to do what little I
could towards helping the Cause of Religion along. during the sixteen years maney afflictions have befalnus in the loss of my Father,
Lucys Father, one of my half Brothers and one half Sister, together
with Scores of Friends that have gon to there last resting place. but

death has not ben permitted to enter into our little family for which
we cannot be to thankful and with all the rest we have had maney
good times which is pleasant to reflect on . . . it is a fact ever aparent
to me that during all of the quarter of a century that has past in my
Married life The greatest good that this world has afoarded me has
ben my Ever True and faithfull Wife to Stande by and helpe and
encourage doing all in her power to make every thing pleasant to all
around. May God Bless hur guide and direct and keep and save us
all is my earnist & sincere prayer.[1]

This meditation expresses George Riley's sense of what has been most
significant and meaningful in his life. Keeping a diary was in itself an
important act; George's wish to be able to give an account of himself
echoes the Protestant tradition of self-examination, of recording one's
conduct and state of mind in order to reflect on and assess one's spiritual condition. But Riley's stock taking was not primarily individual.
The meditation begins with George himself, but it shifts immediately
from the first person singular to the first person plural, from "I" to
"we." Although Riley kept a personal diary, he did not think of himself separately from his family; his identity was bound up in his relationships with others.

   In describing change over time, George began with the growth of
his children toward adulthood. The passage of time was marked not
by some external chronology but by the development of the family.
George and Lucy Ann's daughter, Ida, had become a woman, wife,
and mother, while their son, Judson, had grown to be able to perform
a man's work. George then described the property that the family
had accumulated and improved during that time. The ideal implicit
in his account is simultaneously economic and familial. George and
Lucy Ann had secured a farm adequate to their family's support, and
they had helped their daughter and her husband get started on a
farm of their own nearby.

   The account moves from birth to death, for while the Riley children were growing up George and Lucy Ann's fathers and George's
older half-brother and half-sister had died. George also mourned the
death of "Aunt Lucy," the friend who had acted as a mother to

   1. All quotations from first-person sources are reproduced exactly as they were written. I have not standardized the spelling, added punctuation, or corrected the gram-
mar. The writing styles of Nanticoke Valley diarists varied markedly, depending not
only on their level of education but also on their choice to write in a spoken or more
literary mode.

George and Lucy Ann since his own mother's death.[2] However, the
losses during those years were tempered by the recollection of the
good times they all had shared. Riley's retrospective mood continued
into the new year, for on 2 January 1881 he wrote: "Lucy and I have
ben doing Chores   She is now getting dinner . . . . eate our Supper
all alone, a thing that happens only acaisingly   dun our Chores and
visitted here in our warm and comfortable sitting room talking over
the events of our childhood of our folks and friends that have gon
sum of them long ago." In the vernacular vocabulary of the late nineteenth century, "folks and friends" signified family and kin, the "ame-
diate Family Circle" (as Riley put it on 10 September 1880) and relatives
by descent, marriage, or affinity.[3] Sharing memories with Lucy Ann kept
the past alive.

Riley's New Year's Eve meditation moves from the family into the
community and from temporal to spiritual concerns. There is no discontinuity in this progression. Helping to build a church was like improving a farm, a concrete and visible sign of an invisible and
spiritual truth. Friends who "have gon to there final rest" were remembered within the context of eternity (10 August 1880). Riley saw
the ordering of human relationships in religious terms. Six years before, he had resolved on New Year's Day: "I hope to cultivate such a
disposition that I may be a good father, a good and affectionate husband, and a reliable neighbor and citizen and above all may set such
an example before my family and a dying world that I may serve the
cause of salvation" (1 January 1874). Riley's consciousness of his responsibilities as a father and husband, as well as a neighbor and citizen, betokens the depth of his familial identification. He concluded
that his closest companion and greatest help throughout the past
twenty-five years was his wife, who stood by him in the difficulties of
earthly life as well as before God. Grateful for the active assistance
and encouragement that she provided to everyone around, he asked
for God's blessing upon her. Riley not only defined his family and
community roles in religious terms; he also carried his familial identity into his spiritual life.

Kinship defined individual identity in the Nanticoke Valley. People
conceived of their lives as constituted by their relationships with oth-

2. Lucy Allen was the second wife of Matthew Allen, Sr.; after her husband's death
she lived with his son Matthew Allen, Jr., who was George Riley's closest male friend.
Aunt Lucy does not seem to have been related to George Riley through birth or marriage; rather, their kinship was a matter of mutual choice.

3. Riley wrote a retrospective entry on 10 September 1880, the twenty-fifth anniversary
of his and Lucy Ann's wedding, which closely resembles that written on New Year's Eve
four months later.

ers. Men as well as women, adults as well as children understood themselves not as autonomous individuals but as participants in ongoing interdependent relationships. Kinship ties were not private. Everyone in the community knew how people were related, and they identified individuals in terms of those relationships: Ida Riley Davey, for example, would be "George Riley's girl, who married George Davey's oldest son, who farms above the Rileys on East Maine Road." They identified unknown individuals through their kinship, however distant, to a person who was familiar. This way of speaking ensured the clear understanding of people's obligations to and expectations of others. For kinship was no more personal than it was private. The mutual obligations of siblings, cousins, and other collateral kin, as well as those of parents and children and husbands and wives, were defined by community norms. Some relationships were flexible, but the degree of personal choice that was acceptable in them was also socially delimited. Although George Riley was exceptionally articulate about the familial dimension of his life history, his sense of self as intimately related to others was widely shared in the community.

This chapter analyzes the meaning of family and kinship in the Nanticoke Valley between 1855 and 1900. It begins by exploring the patterns of household composition, inheritance, and intermarriage which were shaped by intergenerational and gender relations and which shaped the kinship networks in open-country neighborhoods. It then turns to the demographic changes of the late nineteenth century, explaining how migration out of the community, coupled with family limitation, facilitated family continuity amid economic and social change.

Household Formation

Kinship governed the formation of households as well as the conduct of relationships between individuals.[4] The process of household

4. Feminist anthropologist Rayna Rapp has proposed that "family" be defined as the set of normative rules governing household formation in a given culture and social-historical context; Rapp, "Household and Family," in Rapp, Ellen Ross, and Renate Bridenthal, "Examining Family History," *Feminist Studies* 5 (1979): 176. This definition is useful because it calls into question the contemporary assumptions that families are contained within households and that there is some universal, irreducible unit that constitutes the family at the core of every household. My analysis of families, households, and kinship has also been influenced by the critique made in Sylvia Junko Yanagisako, "Family and Household: The Analysis of Domestic Groups," *Annual Review of Anthropology* 8 (1979): 161–205, and the approach outlined in Jane Fishburne Collier and Sylvia Junko Yanagisako, eds., *Gender and Kinship: Essays toward a Unified Analysis*

formation was quite uniform throughout the Nanticoke Valley; farmers and artisans, rich and poor, native born and immigrants all followed similar patterns. It also remained quite stable throughout the late nineteenth century. Three principles underlay local practices of household formation: that each conjugal family of husband, wife, and children should live in its own household; that each household should have an adult male at its head as its representative in civil society; and that people without conjugal families of their own should be included in the households of their kin.

When young people married, they usually established their own households. Between 1855 and 1900, no more than 5 percent of all households included married children of the household head; in half of those instances, the married child was not accompanied by his or her spouse. Newlyweds might stay with their parents for a short time when they were getting started, and daughters might return home if their husbands died or deserted them, but normally young couples lived separately from the households in which they had grown up. Only a handful of local households conformed to the popular twentieth-century image of farm families in the past: an older couple sharing their household with a married son who would eventually inherit the land. The coresidence of two adult men would have raised troublesome questions of authority, both within the household and in terms of its representation in civil society. A son who remained at home, economically dependent on his father and subject to his father's control, would still be regarded as a youth, no matter what his chronological age. Most men waited to marry until they had the resources that independence required.

Coresidence of parents and married children more often occurred when middle-aged couples took in their aging parents. But even this was not customary in the Nanticoke Valley. Between 1855 and 1900, no more than 10 percent of all Nanticoke Valley households contained aging parents of the heads of household. In nine out of ten

(Stanford, Calif.: Stanford University Press, 1987). I share many anthropologists' skepticism about imposing theoretically universal, but often culturally and historically biased, categories on the practices and beliefs of people in other cultures. Accordingly, I have not defined family, household, and kinship abstractly but rather elucidated how Nanticoke Valley residents thought and acted about such matters. This approach follows David M. Schneider, *American Kinship: A Cultural Account* (Englewood Cliffs, N.J.: Prentice-Hall, 1980), which explains why kinship is a matter of meanings rather than rules and describes the meanings of kinship in contemporary American culture. In the following analysis, I have adopted local practice in the use of kin terms, tracing kinship ties through persons rather than using such alien categories as "mother-in-law," although to avoid confusion I have used such generic terms as "husband's mother" rather than personal names when the persons are unknown to the reader.

instances, the household included a widowed parent rather than an older married couple; seven out of ten households of this type contained a widowed mother rather than a father. Older couples maintained their own households as long as possible, often throughout their lives. Furthermore, it was just as common for parents and their married children to divide a dwelling as it was for them to share a household. This seems to have been the preferred arrangement when two married couples were involved. The division of shared houses into separate households implies that people valued the autonomy of each conjugal family at the same time that they valued association among related families. This balance between independence and interdependence in intergenerational relations was a fundamental feature of the kinship system in the Nanticoke Valley.[5]

Older women were much more likely than men to live with their married children, for widows seldom remarried and once their children were grown they could rarely continue living independently. Losing their wives did not affect men's household status in the same way. Widowed men were more likely to remarry, and they often chose younger single women rather than widows of their own age; thus a larger proportion of men lived in the married state throughout their lives. Even if they did not remarry, widowed men continued to head their own households as they grew older. Only when they became infirm would men relinquish head-of-household status and join the households of their married children. An aged man might preside over a household of adult sons, but a woman generally would not, even if the sons were still unmarried and had not yet acceded to the property. The power of gender prevailed over generational position in determining who would be regarded as the head of household. This gender difference in the positions of older people reflects the dominant cultural premise that households were headed by men.

5. Daniel Scott Smith's findings on the living situations of older people in the United States as a whole during the late nineteenth century are quite similar to the findings for the Nanticoke Valley. Although the proportions of older people living in particular types of households differ regionally, the relationships between marital status and relation to head of household are the same in the local community and the national sample. Interestingly enough, more older people were living in three-generation households in the city than in the countryside at the turn of the century. The norms that governed household composition, however, were broadly similar; Smith emphasizes the balance between independence and interdependence as a fundamental feature of the American family system. Daniel Scott Smith, "Life Course, Norms, and the Family System of Older Americans in 1900," *Journal of Family History* 4 (1979): 285–98, and "A Community-Based Sample of the Older Population from the 1880 and 1900 United States Manuscript Censuses," *Historical Methods* 11 (1978): 67–74.

Households readily expanded to include relatives who had no families of their own. Between 1855 and 1900, 5 percent of households included siblings of the heads; half that many included descendant relatives. Orphaned children were commonly adopted by aunts and uncles or brought up by older siblings. Not all young people living with kin had lost their parents, however; some provided assistance and companionship to the older people with whom they lived. Single women usually joined the households of their married sisters and brothers after their parents died, and widowed or single siblings often lived together. Irish farm households were especially likely to include unmarried brothers or sisters of the husband or wife, and sets of Irish American single siblings often continued living together on the family farm after their parents' death.[6]

Two generations of coresidence in the Benton family illustrate these principles of household formation, both in the breach and in the observance. When John W. Benton went off to fight in the Civil War in the fall of 1862, he left his forty-five-year-old wife, Rosella Leadbetter Benton, their sons, Leroy and Charles, aged eleven and eight, and his parents, James and Celinda Snow Benton, aged seventy-five and seventy-nine. Just before his departure, John posted bond that he and his heirs would support his parents:

> furnishing to the said James & Celinda Benton for their own proper use and benefit during the natural life of each and both of them with all proper and necessary Board, Room, fuel, lodging, wearing apparel suitable for the different seasons of the year, and all necessary medical attendance and nursing when sick, and their necessary and proper funeral charges at their death, all of which shall be done in a manner calculated to secure the peace comfort and happiness of the said James & Celinda Benton. . . . [7]

6. Households composed of sibling sets seem to be prevalent when celibacy rates are high and siblings jointly inherit the family farmstead. Strong sibling cooperation has been observed among other Irish-American farm populations. For a midwestern example, see Sonya Salamon's "Ethnic Differences in Farm Family Land Transfers," *Rural Sociology* 45 (1980): 290–308, and "Sibling Solidarity as an Operating Strategy in Illinois Agriculture," *Rural Sociology* 47 (1982): 349–68.

7. This bond probably formalized an arrangement that the two generations had made some time previously. John W. and Rosella Leadbetter Benton lived with his parents in East Maine from their marriage in 1847 through 1855. By 1860, they had all moved to a farm on Ashley Road and John W. Benton had succeeded his father as head of household. John probably assumed responsibility for his parents' support at the same time he inherited their property; the proceeds from the sale of the family

Three generations of Bentons lived on the large farm on Ashley Road in the Gates District of Maine. However, while James stayed with Rosella and the boys, Celinda spent much of her time in Maine village with an older son and his family. In the winter of 1862, when James Benton became physically ill and mentally incompetent, Celinda returned to help care for him. James died before John returned; Celinda remained with John and Rosella until her death a few years later.

In 1865, the Benton household was augmented by Rosella's younger sisters, Jane and Plumah Leadbetter, aged thirty-three and thirty. John and Rosella referred to them as "the girls," for both were unmarried. Since their parents' deaths in 1861, they had lived with their oldest brother and his family on the Leadbetter farm in East Maine, earning money by taking in spinning and weaving rugs on a custom basis for neighbors. They stayed with the Bentons whenever they were needed in their sister's household or found work to do in the neighborhood. Between 1865 and 1880, they spent about half their time with Rosella. By 1880, they had a small house of their own on the Leadbetter land between their brothers' farms, but they visited the Bentons regularly. After Plumah's death in 1888, Jane stayed with the Bentons almost continuously until she died in 1894.

Six weeks after Leroy Benton married Helen Davis in 1878, he brought his wife home to the farmhouse on Ashley Road. His younger brother, Charles, had just married Helen Augusta Dean; they set up housekeeping on the adjacent farm the Bentons had purchased the year before. While Charles and Augusta lived next door, Leroy and Helen moved in with his parents. The two generations shared the house by dividing it down the middle. Rosella Benton took the parlor and the parlor bedroom on the first floor and the bedrooms above them on the second. Leroy and Helen occupied the sitting room, dining room, and front bedroom, as well as the small bedrooms upstairs. They shared the kitchen, pantry, woodshed, and cellar, which were located toward the rear of the house. Rosella ate meals and received visitors on her side of the house. This arrangement was most common where two married couples were involved, but a month after Helen's arrival John W. Benton departed "for the Far West," leaving his wife behind.[8] Except for three brief visits

---

farm in East Maine seem to have been reinvested in the Ashley Road land. The agreement had to be formalized when John W. Benton enlisted so that his promise of support would be binding on his heirs and estate in the event of his death. Benton Family Papers, 1840–62.

8. Helen Davis Benton, Diary, 6 April 1878.

home, he remained in Kansas and Nebraska for the next twenty-one years. Charles and his family joined John W. Benton in Nebraska from 1888 to 1897. In their absence, Leroy headed the household and provided for his mother by farming both his brother's land and the land his father had left him. In this case, coresidence resulted from marital breakdown.

Kinship was a lifelong bond of mutual aid. The balance of help given and received did not have to be even at any given moment or within any particular relationship. Reciprocity among kin extended through the life course; adult children who cared for their aging parents did so because of what their parents had done for them in the past, not in exchange for the future inheritance of a farm. Mutual aid was also generalized throughout the kinship network; families took in dependent relatives because they believed that kin were responsible for one another. Those relatives who were in the best position to provide a home for others without jeopardizing the welfare of their immediate families were expected to do so. People recognized that this was not an economic bargain that might have been made between strangers. When belonging to a family was all-important but conjugal families were fragile units, such practices and beliefs were essential to the common welfare.[9]

The most serious limitation of this social system, as well as its greatest strength, was the fact that it was based almost entirely on kinship. People who were isolated from their relatives by death or distance were particularly vulnerable; if they were suddenly deprived of a home, they might have difficulty finding another.[10] Those of an age to work might seek employment in another household, but elderly people might have no alternative to struggling by themselves. Fami-

9. Families took in relatives of whom they disapproved and with whom they had long ago severed all social contact when those relatives had no other resources. It made little difference whether the persons involved were insane, addicted to drugs or alcohol, dying of consumption, or involved in illegitimate sexual relations, as long as they did not threaten physical violence to themselves or to others. To allow such persons to be sent to the county poor farm was regarded as a mark of shame on the family as a whole.

10. The minimum obligations incumbent on neighbors centered on taking actions to preserve life and property in emergencies: providing rescue and first aid, helping to put out fires, capturing stray animals, and laboring to save crops. These obligations were not dependent on the interpersonal relationships among specific neighboring families; rather, they were regarded by all as essential to protecting the common welfare. Neighbors were also obligated to provide assistance when it was asked for in more ordinary situations, such as small amounts of goods and/or time. Who asked for such favors from whom was clearly shaped by interpersonal relationships among specific families in a neighborhood, but in principle people could not refuse such favors when asked; only by not asking in return could they avoid continuing back-and-forth interaction. Neighbors were not obligated, however, to take in the homeless.

lies were also the most common provider of welfare services to disabled people. They did not do so alone; when it was economically necessary, they received public assistance to care for handicapped relatives in their homes. Disabled people without kin, however, ended up in public institutions.

The Inheritance of Land

In the Nanticoke Valley, inheritance was a process rather than an event. It began when parents provided for children's marriages, and it continued after their death as children consolidated the property. Wills were only one instrument for the passage of property from one generation to another. Deeds were equally important; older children generally received the bulk of their portions while their parents were still alive. Wills might simply confirm or tidy up arrangements made years before. At the same time, old couples' determination to remain independent as long as possible ensured that most had some property to pass on when they died. Those fathers who made wills specified exactly how the residual property was to be divided, while those who did not left it up to the probate courts. In either case, the children often exchanged pieces of land or bought out one another's interests so that they ended up with contiguous farms or cash. The whole process was protracted enough that in some families couples were making provision for their own children at the same time that they were inheriting from their parents.

Families passed down property in flexible and varied ways. Inheritance is a family strategy rather than a custom, a way of achieving desired goals rather than a fixed set of normative practices.[11] The goal of most families was to establish their children on farms in the local community. This goal appears to have been nearly universal among landowning farmers in New England and the mid-Atlantic region. It did not necessarily involve the perpetuation of the family

11. I developed this perspective on inheritance in cooperation with Susan Amussen; Amussen, *An Ordered Society: Gender and Class in Early Modern England* (Oxford: Basil Blackwell, 1988), 76–93. It has also been influenced by Jack Goody, "Strategies of Heirship," *Comparative Studies in Society and History* 15 (1973): 3–20, and by the case studies in *Family and Inheritance: Rural Society in Western Europe, 1200–1800*, ed. Goody, Joan Thirsk, and E. P. Thompson (New York: Cambridge University Press, 1976). For a critique of legalistic conceptions of inheritance and marriage systems, see Pierre Bourdieu, "Marriage Strategies as Strategies of Social Reproduction," in *Family and Society: Selections from the Annales: Economies, Sociétés, Civilizations*, ed. Robert Forster and Orest Ranum (Baltimore: Johns Hopkins University Press, 1976), 117–44.

name on a particular piece of land, as has been suggested for colonial New England. In the Nanticoke Valley, a familistic orientation was combined with the market orientation assumed to be common among American farmers during the nineteenth century. Local farmers were not as speculative in their attitude toward land as many historians have suggested for the mid-nineteenth-century upper Midwest; they did not regard land as a short-term investment made for the sake of individual profit. Rather, they engaged in a myriad of market transactions for familial ends. They subdivided their own land, bought and/or helped their children buy land from neighbors, and even sold land to nonrelatives in order to furnish their children with cash.[12] The financial arrangements that lay behind the transfer of land within the family were also various. Not all sons were simply given part of the family farm; some purchased land from their fathers with money they had earned elsewhere, while others received the parental farmstead on condition that they make payments to their brothers and sisters and/or support their parents in old age.

How many and which of a couple's sons ended up farming land adjacent to that of their parents depended on the number, ages, and sexes of the children, as well as on the amount and nature of the resources that the couple could accumulate during their lifetime. The distribution of property was essentially continuous from the time the oldest children reached adulthood. Provisions made for older children might affect the prospects of younger ones, and changes in the family's economic situation might modify their future. These things could not all be foreseen and planned out in advance. Parents did the best they could to meet the exigencies of the moment in a way that would be compatible with the long-term interests of the parents themselves and all of their children.

Individual family members did not necessarily agree on how their best interests were to be defined or about what strategies would protect them most effectively. Children might contest with one another, overtly or covertly, about their respective shares of the family property. While prevailing ideologies of family relations defined the terms and set the boundaries of such struggles, they did not entirely prevent them. In the Benton family, for example, it was agreed that Leroy and Charles would receive equal portions when they married. Because John W. Benton had been unable to hold onto all the land he had purchased before the Civil War, the family had to buy land

12. In this way, they resemble the farm families analyzed by W. M. Williams in *A West Country Village, Ashworthy: Family, Kinship and Land* (New York: Humanities Press, 1963).

from neighbors to ensure each son a viable farm. When Charles went West, Leroy took over the mortgage payments along with the operation of his brother's farm. Meanwhile John W. Benton helped Charles get established on a farm in Nebraska. When Charles returned to Maine nearly a decade later, he was broke; the drought had bankrupted him, and John W. held title to the unsalable farm he left behind. Charles took up residence on his old farm next to his brother. This put Leroy in a difficult position. On the one hand, Charles had simply resumed his rightful place, and his family was in need; on the other, Charles had received a double portion, in Nebraska as well as in Maine, and Leroy's labor had paid for some of it. Such conflicts were not easily resolved, or even openly discussed. But they were built into the inheritance process.

In some farm families, jealousies might develop among children as they vied for their parents' favor. But parents and children might come into conflict over these matters even when no siblings were involved. Young men would seek to attain the social adulthood that came with establishing their own farms and households as soon as possible, but it was in parents' interest to delay their sons' independence as long as they could, for as long as young people remained at home on the family farm they were contributing to the increase of the parents' property, while when they married they would take away some portion of the parents' resources. On the other hand, parents could not force their children to postpone marriage indefinitely, for the children could simply go off and work for someone else or leave the community entirely. The process through which most children attained their independence involved a delicate, if unstated, mutual adjustment, with parents seeking to make it advantageous for some children to remain on the farm after the others had left, and children seeking to negotiate the terms of their independence in such a way that their parents would support their plans. These contradictory and competing claims shaped the process of inheritance within families.

Amid all these variations, one pattern stands out: sons were given land, but daughters received household furnishings when they married, and the value of these "movables" was considerably less than that of the real property sons received. This gender difference runs through the histories of local families like a theme through so many variations, and was as deeply rooted in the kinship system as the most fundamental conceptions of the mutual obligations of parents and children. The rights of sons as opposed to daughters were rarely contested within particular families or questioned in the common culture. Seldom were a daughter and her husband established on a farm carved out of her father's land. George Riley, who purchased the adjacent farm for his daughter and her husband, was quite exceptional. Riley deeded half of the "Frost place" to Ida and Bert Davey and retained ownership of an undivided half, providing in his will for their inheritance of the rest. Immigrant parents occasionally passed on land to their daughters. The Scottish families of Mt. Ettrick provided some married daughters with small house lots and divided their property equally among all their children when they died. The farmers of New Ireland made their unmarried children joint tenants of the family farmstead. But most parents, including the Scots and Irish, assumed that daughters would go to live on farms their husbands established or inherited. Parents contributed to furnishing their daughters' households, but they did not contribute to the founding of the new family enterprise as they did when sons married.

It made no sense to fathers to give their daughters land because they did not regard women as independent economic agents. To men, the ownership of productive property was an attribute of heads of households and a prerequisite for independence, a quintessentially masculine status. Women were properly the wives of male household heads and subordinate members of farm family economies. This assumption is especially clear in the provisions made for widows. Even when husbands willed more than the statutory "thirds" of their property to their wives, they rarely did so in a way that made women genuinely independent. Widows usually received only a life interest in the estate. They were not free to sell it or to dispose of it among their heirs as they chose; instead, it would be divided among the heirs as their husbands had determined. Men often stipulated that their property should pass to their children as soon as their widows remarried. (This was necessary to prevent the estate from descending to another man's children, for women lost control of their property when they married.) They were careful to specify the duties that the children owed their mother and to link their inheritance to the fulfillment of those obligations precisely because, in witholding from women the power to dispose of the family property, they deprived their wives of the ultimate economic power over the children that they themselves had wielded. While these provisions were intended to ensure that widows would be supported in old age, they were based on the assumption that women were unable to function independently. By incorporating this assumption into their wills, men helped make it come true.[13]

13. For a summary of recent work on the legal status of married women, see Norma Basch, "Invisible Women: The Legal Fiction of Marital Unity in Nineteenth-Century America," *Feminist Studies* 5 (1979): 346–66. The definitive work on New York State

Daughters, like widows, had an acknowledged right to be supported by the family estate, but they were placed in a position of dependence on the male heirs. Those who were single seldom received land in their own right when their fathers died; instead, they were supposed to live with their inheriting brothers. Daughters who married had a residual claim on their families. If they became widowed or separated, they could return to the parental household either alone or with their young children; if their parents had died, they might ask a brother to take them in. But this claim was very different from sons' acknowledged right to land. Indeed, daughters' dependence on their families was a direct result of the initial inequality in the distribution of property. Daughters were supposed to be supported by their fathers, sisters by their brothers, and mothers by their sons, but women were not given the means by which they might support themselves.

Daughters might share equally in the division of the estate after their parents died, for New York State laws mandated equal distribution in cases of intestacy. Yet the laws governing probate preferentially allocated real property to sons and personal property to daughters; only when there was too little personal estate to make up their shares were daughters given land.[14] Equal inheritance did not redress the inequalities in the portions of daughters and sons. Nor did fathers who wrote wills give larger shares to their daughters to compensate for the smaller portions they had received earlier, although most fathers were careful to achieve that kind of parity among their sons.

The difference in the form of women's and men's inheritance was just as significant as the difference in the amount. Daughters received their portions in portable or easily convertible form when they married and established households on their husbands' land. If they inherited a piece of the family farm when their parents died, they usually sold it to their brothers who farmed nearby. Occasionally married daughters bought out their brothers and sisters who had estab-

---

law and practice, including the limitations of the married women's property act, is Norma Basch, *In the Eyes of the Law: Women, Marriage, and Property in Nineteenth-Century New York* (Ithaca: Cornell University Press, 1982). Alex Keyssar, "Widowhood in Eighteenth-Century Massachusetts: A Problem in the History of the Family," *Perspectives in American History* 8 (1974): 83–122, analyzes widows' lack of control over property in the late colonial period.

14. To place the New York State laws in comparative perspective, see Carole Shammas, Marylynn Salmon, and Michel Dahlin, *Inheritance in America from Colonial Times to the Present* (New Brunswick, N.J.: Rutgers University Press, 1987). This study of inheritance practices is marred by its failure to consider *inter vivos* transmission of property.

lished farms elsewhere, but the cash and credit required was provided by their husbands. The way property was distributed at the time children married generally determined the way they readjusted their shares of the estate after their parents died. Inheritance thus perpetuated inequality and asymmetry between daughters and sons. Not only did sons receive more valuable portions than daughters, but sons received land in the neighborhood while daughters took "movables" to their new households in their husbands' neighborhoods.

Intermarriage among Neighbors

In the Nanticoke Valley, relatives were bound together more by neighborhood than by coresidence. Even for aging parents and their adult children, the ideal was to live near, but not with, one another. The clusters of common surnames visible on maps of the community attest to some of the kinship ties among neighbors; fathers and sons, uncles and nephews, brothers and cousins commonly occupied adjacent farms. Kinship ties that followed female lines were less visible, not simply because women took their husbands' names at marriage but also because fewer women than men lived near their relatives. Inequalities in the inheritance of land created asymmetries in women's and men's relations with their kindred. Women sustained other kinds of ties with their relatives; they provided mutual aid in childbirth, sickness, and old age, and at times they took their kin into their households. These forms of sharing were often more intimate and enduring than the property relationships that led men to live near their kin. Women were able to sustain the closest ties with their relatives when they married men who lived in their neighborhoods. Only in that way could women continue living near their families; for them it was a matter of conscious choice, while for men such proximity was customary.

In the Nanticoke Valley, kinship was bilateral—traced through both male and female lines. Husbands and wives took each other's relatives as their own when they married, and children belonged to both of their parents' families. Although wives and children took the surname of the male head of the family, kinship groups did not surrender their daughters and the children their daughters bore to the families into which they married. A married woman was still regarded as belonging to her parents' family, and her children were counted among the kin group as well. The tensions between descent and marriage inherent in bilateral kinship systems were defused by a deliberate blurring of the distinction between the two principles: a person had the same relationship not only with a mother's sisters as with a father's sisters, but also with the wives of mother's and father's brothers. Descent groups were overlapping, claiming the same people in a multiplicity of ways. Ties of affiliation ramified relationships as well: a sister's husband became a brother, a brother's wife became a sister, and the sisters and brothers of a sister's husband and a brother's wife became something like cousins as well. In ordinary social interaction, the practice was to find points of connection, ways that people were kin rather than strangers. Kinship was meaningful even when it was sufficiently distant that it carried only generalized expectations of reciprocity rather than specific obligations of mutual aid.

The neighborhood network of Deborah Allen Marean illustrates the density of kinship ties that a woman might maintain by marrying within the neighborhood in which she grew up. Deborah Jane Allen, the oldest daughter of Ebenezer and Oladyne Spencer Allen, married William Marean in 1855. The youngest son of Joseph and Joannah Bundy Marean, William had grown up across the road from Deborah in Allentown. The newlyweds joined William's parents' household. Deborah was surrounded by her husband's kinsmen; his older brothers lived with their families on the two adjacent farms, and his cousin also farmed nearby. At the same time, Deborah had only to step across the road to call on her mother. The widowed Oladyne Spencer Allen headed a household that included Deborah's five younger siblings, and Deborah's oldest brother and his wife shared the dwelling. Next door, Deborah's father's brother, Matthew Allen, Jr., and his family shared a house with Deborah's grandfather and his wife. With her mother, seven siblings, an uncle and aunt, two cousins, and two grandparents nearby, Deborah was not overwhelmed by the sixteen Mareans living in the neighborhood. Deborah became the mistress of the household when her husband's mother died in 1862, and William inherited the family farm after his father's death in 1866. Deborah's mother continued to live across the road until she died in 1892. Deborah's only sister, Sarah, also married within the neighborhood; her husband, John H. Green, farmed just up the hill beyond the Mareans. Furthermore, John H. Green's sister, Eliza, married Sarah and Deborah's brother, Belden. Belden and Eliza Green Allen raised their family in Allentown, taking over the Allen farm and taking care of the aged Oladyne. At the turn of the century, Deborah still had her brother and his wife, her sister and her husband, a cousin, and two nephews and their wives in the neighborhood, along with her husband's older brother and several of his nephews and their families.

The kin-based neighborhoods in the Nanticoke Valley were established by the transmission of property from fathers to sons, but they were woven together by intermarriage. Their vertical ties followed male lines and were embedded in the land, while their horizontal ties followed female lines of affiliation and were enacted in mutual aid. These intermarriages were not simply the accidental result of propinquity and opportunity; women chose to marry neighbors to enhance the quality of their own lives. Proximity did facilitate courtship, and neighborly relations might dispose parents to look with favor on the young people's inclinations. However, women married neighbors not only because they were available and approved as future husbands but also to remain near their parents and kin, carrying their own family ties into their adult lives. The transition from daughter to wife would be less abrupt, and their situation in their new families less isolated, than if they moved away. They might rely on their kindred not only as a recourse in case of disaster, if their husbands died or deserted them, but also as a resource in their daily lives, people with whom they might share their labor, their leisure, and their difficulties.

Women played a crucial role in creating and sustaining the reciprocity among families which constituted neighborly relations. Men may have seen their wives as mediating the relations between families, but women were not passive objects in this process, mere tokens exchanged among men to cement the bonds between them.[15] Rather, women were active agents, marrying within the neighborhood in order to maintain continuity and connectedness through the course of their lives.

Family Continuity amid Social Change

The patterns of household composition and intergenerational relations which characterized the community at mid-century remained quite stable throughout the economic contraction and demographic decline of the late nineteenth century. Indeed, by alleviating the pressure of people on the land, the exodus of young men and women and of whole families contributed to the maintenance of customary patterns of family formation and the intergenerational transmission of farms in the Nanticoke Valley.

15. Gayle Rubin, "The Traffic in Women: Notes on the 'Political Economy' of Sex," in *Toward an Anthropology of Women*, ed. Rayna R. Reiter (New York: Monthly Review Press, 1975), 171–77, makes a feminist critique of the "exchange of women" from within anthropology.

The overwhelming majority of women and men who spent their lives in the Nanticoke Valley married. Throughout the late nineteenth century, no more than one woman in fifteen remained single through her childbearing period. The proportion of men aged forty-five to fifty-four who had never married was half that of women in 1855, exactly the same in 1880, and twice as high in 1900. Women's limited employment opportunities and lack of expectations for inheritance impelled more young women than young men to leave the valley after 1880. Some young men who remained on local farms with the expectation of inheritance had difficulty persuading young women to remain in or return to the community and become farmers' wives.

Men and women who stayed in the rural community married at much the same ages in 1900 as they had done a half-century before. Women's mean age at marriage remained constant at twenty-two throughout this period.[16] Few women married before they were twenty, but once they had reached what was regarded as an appropriate age most married fairly quickly; more than two-thirds of local women were married by the time they turned twenty-five. Their husbands were generally a few years older. The mean age at marriage for men was 26 in 1855, 25.5 in 1880, and 25 in 1900. There was always substantial variation in the ages at which men married. Men almost never married before they turned twenty-one, but five-sixths had married by the time they turned thirty. Relative to people in other places, men and women in the Nanticoke Valley did not marry young when land was abundant, nor did they have to wait for an extended period before becoming the masters and mistresses of their own households when land was scarce. The slight decline in the mean age of men at marriage is especially significant, for it demonstrates that the contraction of economic opportunity did not result in the postponement of marriage for those who remained in the valley.

16. The singulate mean age at marriage has been computed from census data according to the method developed by H. J. Hajnal, which does not correct for possible changes over time in the age at marriage but allows comparison of cross-sectional data at different points in time. For a broad national comparison of these ages at marriage, see John Modell, Frank Furstenberg, Jr., and Theodore Hershberg, "Social Change and Transitions to Adulthood in Historical Perspective," *Journal of Family History* 1 (1976): 7–32, and John Modell, Frank Furstenberg, Jr., and Dennis Strong, "The Timing of Marriage in the Transition to Adulthood: Continuity and Change, 1860–1975," in *Turning Points*, ed. John Demos and Sarane Boocock (Chicago: University of Chicago Press, 1978), S120–50. See also Peter R. Uhlenberg's "A Study of Cohort Life Cycles: Cohorts of Native-Born Massachusetts Women, 1830–1920," *Population Studies* 23 (1969): 407–20, and "Cohort Variations in the Family Life Cycle Experience of United States Females," *Journal of Marriage and the Family* 36 (1974): 284–92.

The inheritance strategies practiced by local farm families were sufficiently flexible to enable most of them to adapt to land scarcity without disrupting the orderly transmission of farm property or violating commonly understood principles of intergenerational relations. By the last quarter of the nineteenth century, most parents had shifted their objective from helping all of their sons establish farms nearby to ensuring that one son remain on the family farm. The designated heir had to care for his parents in their old age as a condition of his inheritance. This arrangement resembles a peasant stem family pattern but had a distinctly American twist. The notion that family property ought to be equitably distributed among sons was not abandoned when it became impossible to divide farms. Parents would furnish their noninheriting children with an education or with capital to set off on their own, either in the West or in the city. Children who were not already provided for when their parents died would be compensated by the inheriting son. Alternatively, the farm would be bequeathed to all the heirs and one son would buy out the others. The convertibility of land to cash and the involvement in the market required by these "favored-heir-plus-burdens" and "partible/impartible" inheritance strategies clearly distinguish them from a traditional stem family pattern.[17]

Most parents succeeded in passing their farm on to a son. Those who did not were among the poorer farmers in the community. Some had enough land, but none had enough capital, to conduct commercial dairy operations. Their sons knew that the farm would not support two families, and they could not obtain regular nonagricultural employment in the local area. So they migrated to the city, leaving their parents to live out their days alone. When the old people died, the land was sold and the proceeds divided among the children.

17. The best case study of what have come to be called the "partible/impartible" or "favored-heir-plus-burdens" patterns, in which one son took over the farm but the others received a more portable inheritance, is David P. Gagan, "The Indivisibility of Land: A Micro-Analysis of the System of Inheritance in Nineteenth-Century Ontario," *Journal of Economic History* 36 (1976): 126–41. David P. Gagan, *Hopeful Travellers: Families, Land, and Social Change in Mid-Victorian Peel County, Canada West* (Toronto: University of Toronto Press, 1981), relates inheritance strategies to the economic and demographic changes that occurred with the culmination of the settlement process and the transition to capitalist market relations in agriculture. For an analysis of similar patterns in Connecticut, see Toby L. Ditz, *Property and Kinship: Inheritance in Early Connecticut, 1750–1820* (Princeton: Princeton University Press, 1986). Ditz's study documents a shift from partible inheritance to a favored-heir-plus-burdens pattern in the uplands as land became scarce and subdivision became less possible; however, she fails to consider what children made of their inheritances, so her argument that life chances became less dependent on inheritance as capitalism developed cannot confidently be extended to the upland farming areas.

These farms were purchased by wealthier families from the local area. Parents enlarged their farms to make room for their sons or helped their sons buy land to farm on their own. At the community level, then, continuity was maintained; poorer families disappeared and wealthier families multiplied, but native sons took their places on the land.[18]

Only the living situations of widows were significantly affected by the departure of children from the community. In 1900, a larger proportion of widows headed their own households than had done so in 1855. The majority of widows aged fifty-five and above had lived with married children in 1855, but in 1900 the majority headed their own households until they were seventy-five; only 25 percent of those aged fifty-five to seventy-four and 40 percent of those seventy-five and above lived with married children. As many widows aged fifty-five to seventy-four were sharing their households with sisters, nieces, or grandchildren as were living with their married children. But 40 percent of those between sixty-five and seventy-four were living quite alone. Women who headed their own households were not necessarily better off than those who were living with children. Some had enough resources to retain their autonomy and shared their lives with close kinswomen, but others were poor and isolated.[19]

Family Limitation

The most significant change in Nanticoke Valley family patterns during the late nineteenth century was a substantial decline in family size. In 1865, married women between the ages of forty-five and forty-nine had borne an average of 4.9 children; in 1900, they had borne only 3.4. By this simple indicator, completed family size had declined by 1.5 children.[20] The dimensions of this decline are indi-

18. The economic processes through which some families sell out and others enlarge their holdings, as well as the demographic processes through which some families die out and others multiply, are described in detail by Williams in *A West Country Village*.

19. For a discussion of the demographic and social causes and consequences of the long-term increase in the proportion of women living alone, see Frances E. Kobrin, "The Fall in Household Size and the Rise of the Primary Individual in the United States," in *The American Family in Social-Historical Perspective*, ed. Michael Gordon, 2d ed. (New York: St. Martin's Press, 1978), 69–81.

20. Both the 1865 New York State census and the 1900 federal census recorded information on retrospective fertility, asking women how many children they had ever borne. The number of children ever born to women aged 45–49 is an especially reliable measure of completed family size because these women had just concluded their childbearing period and their numbers had not yet been depleted by mortality.

cated by the changes in the distribution of completed family sizes that occurred over time. In 1865, the median number of children borne by women aged forty-five to fifty-four was five; in 1900, the median had fallen to two. This steady decline in completed family size altered the course of women's lives. Women born before 1800 continued bearing children as long as they were fertile, spending twenty years or more in a nearly uninterrupted state of pregnancy and lactation. Those born at mid-century deliberately controlled their fertility, bearing children during their first decade of marriage and ceasing to procreate when they were still in their mid-thirties. The decline in fertility both lightened women's burden of labor and shortened the time span of reproduction.[21]

This was not yet family planning in the modern sense of the term, for Nanticoke Valley couples neither used artificial contraceptives nor attempted to space the births of their first few children. It was, rather, family limitation; once parents had as many children as they wanted, they tried to avoid having any more. While the means couples used cannot be positively ascertained, withdrawal and abstinence were the predominant means of family limitation in rural communities.[22] These methods postponed, although they did not necessarily prevent, a woman's next pregnancy. Periodic abstinence was not always practiced effectively in the nineteenth century, because health manuals did not correct the popular belief that a woman was most fertile right around her menstrual period. Abortifacients

21. For a general discussion of how these changes compare with national trends and what the fertility decline meant for the course of women's lives, see Uhlenberg's "A Study of Cohort Life Cycles" and "Cohort Variations in the Family Life Cycle Experience of United States Females"; Robert V. Wells's "Demographic Changes and the Life Cycle of American Families," *Journal of Interdisciplinary History* 2 (1971): 273–82, and "Women's Lives Transformed: Demographic and Family Patterns in America, 1670–1970," in *Women in America: A History,* ed. Mary Beth Norton and Carol Ruth Berkin (Boston: Houghton Mifflin, 1979), 16–33. For an analysis of fertility levels in other areas of New York State, see Wendell H. Bash's "Changing Birth Rates in Developing America: New York State, 1840–1875," *Milbank Memorial Fund Quarterly* 41 (1963): 161–82, and "Differential Fertility in Madison County, New York," *Milbank Memorial Fund Quarterly* 33 (1955): 161–86. Bash found that rural fertility had declined significantly by 1875, especially among farm families; that native-born families had lower fertility than foreign-born families; and that fertility was negatively related to population density. Mark J. Stern, "Differential Fertility in Rural Erie County, New York, 1855," *Journal of Social History* 16 (1983): 49–63, also found both class and ethnic differentials in fertility.

22. Diarists rarely recorded sexual matters. Most women did not note their pregnancies before they gave birth, although a few did mark their monthly menstrual cycles. None described what, if anything, they did to prevent conception. Accordingly, this analysis of family limitation is based on quantitative evidence and inferences about common cultural practices. For further discussion of sexuality and childbearing, see Chapter 4.

were not unknown, for some were advertised commercially and others were made by local women skilled in remedies, but their effectiveness was dubious at best.[23] Abortions were probably available in Binghamton, but few local women had the requisite urban connections. Self-induced abortion has always been a last resort of desperate women, but only at the risk of their lives; unmarried women were more likely to try it than wives and mothers were. Mechanical means of contraception, such as condoms, diaphragms, and spermicides, were not generally available before the early twentieth century.[24]

Family limitation by means of abstinence and withdrawal required the cooperation of husbands and wives; couples had to decide how many children were enough and control their sexual relations to achieve their goal. This practice accorded with fundamental cultural attitudes toward both sexuality and intergenerational relationships. In contrast to artificial methods of contraception, abstinence and withdrawal did not separate sexual intercourse from reproduction; their reliance on self-control made them compatible with Victorian attitudes toward sexuality. Parents customarily planned for their children's future, and their commitment to helping their children get established in life by providing them with material resources was a strong motive for limiting the size of their families. Their concern for their own security in old age reinforced this motivation, for parents who had fewer children to provide for were better able to induce a son to remain in the community with the expectation of inheriting a substantial farm than parents whose property had to be divided among many children.

Some historians have argued that changes in gender relations were primarily responsible for the nineteenth-century fertility decline. According to this view, women sought to limit their childbearing in order to preserve their health, lighten their burden of labor, and attain greater autonomy. Women's ability to exercise control over sexual relations in marriage increased during the early nineteenth century, both because the ideology of separate spheres granted women a certain power within the domestic domain and because popular images of women represented them as morally elevated, spiritually pure, almost asexual beings. Sexual intercourse became, according to this

23. Advertisements for patent medicines which promised to relieve female complaints, including irregular menses, appeared in newspapers and magazines to which valley residents subscribed. A few local women's and men's diaries contain receipts for homemade medication intended to produce similar effects.

24. For the history of birth control in the United States from the mid-nineteenth to the mid-twentieth centuries, see Linda Gordon, *Woman's Body, Woman's Right: A Social History of Birth Control in America* (New York: Grossman, 1976).

analysis, something women might grant or refuse to their husbands.[25] This view tends to mistake prescription for reality, overstating both the power that women wielded over sexual relations in marriage and the degree to which women internalized images of themselves as innocent of sexual desire.[26] Given the silence about sexual relations that pervades nineteenth-century first-person documents, the evidence for women's control of marital sexuality is indirect, drawn entirely from popular prescriptive literature rather than behavior. In some versions the argument becomes circular, for the only concrete evidence of women's control of sexual relations is the very fertility decline that it is supposed to explain. Furthermore, this argument tends to perpetuate the gender polarities of early-nineteenth-century domestic ideology, assuming that men were driven by physical passion while women sought to avoid intercourse and that if men and women

25. The most influential statement of this view is Daniel Scott Smith, "Family Limitation, Sexual Control, and Domestic Feminism in Victorian America," *Feminist Studies* 1 (1973): 40–57. Smith contended that "the new autonomy of women within the family" involved "sexual control of the husband by the wife." Smith conceded, however, that "economic, instrumental, or 'male' considerations" remained important: "the wife's demand for a smaller family may have been so successful precisely because it was not contrary to the rational calculations of her husband." Smith acknowledged that male cooperation was necessary for withdrawal and abstinence to be effective. Finally, he concluded: "In most marriages, perhaps, these decisions were made jointly by the couple." Acknowledging that these qualifications thoroughly undermine the main argument, Smith has recently given up the position put forward in this early article, preferring explanations based on cultural characteristics and perspectives shared by husbands and wives. Daniel Scott Smith, " 'Early' Fertility Decline in America: A Problem in Family History," *Journal of Family History* 12 (1987): 73–84.

26. On the one hand, most women do not seem to have been able to exercise the power this analysis suggests. While the assertion of women's right to refuse intercourse within marriage was certainly important, it was not universally accepted. Linda Gordon, "Voluntary Motherhood: The Beginnings of Feminist Birth Control Ideas in the United States," *Feminist Studies* 1 (1973): 5–22, makes clear that this was a radical position and that norms of masculine conjugal rights continued to prevail in most sectors of society.

On the other hand, most women do not seem to have internalized the images of themselves as asexual angels which were presented in the popular literature. Nancy F. Cott, "Passionlessness: An Interpretation of Victorian Sexual Ideology, 1790–1870," *Signs* 4 (1978): 219–36, suggests that women regarded themselves as exercising sexual self-control; indeed, their virtue consisted precisely in that moral activity, rather than in their supposed innocence. Cott is careful, however, not to make inferences from ideology to behavior. Ellen K. Rothman, "Sex and Self-Control: Middle-Class Courtship in America, 1770–1870," *Journal of Social History* 15 (1982): 409–25, demonstrates that some courting couples engaged in sexual experimentation despite their belief that they ought to control their passions. For evidence that married women were more active participants in sexual relations than the prevailing ideology suggested was proper, see Carl Degler, "What Ought to Be and What Was: Women's Sexuality in the Nineteenth Century," *American Historical Review* 79 (1974): 1467–90, and Karen Lystra, *Searching the Heart: Women, Men, and Romantic Love in Nineteenth-Century America, 1830–1900* (New York: Oxford University Press, 1989), 56–87.

both wanted to limit the size of their families they must have done so for different reasons, with men being motivated by economic considerations and women by essentially emotional ones. The evidence from the Nanticoke Valley suggests that men and women shared a common perspective on reproduction and that they cooperated to limit the size of their families. Concern for the future of their children was as important to women as it was to men, and men's willingness to exercise self-control was as crucial as women's in the successful practice of family limitation.[27]

Economic explanations of the rural fertility decline, which have been most fully developed by Richard Easterlin, focus on fathers' intention to provide their sons with a start in life equivalent to that which they themselves had received. When land availability was declining and the capital costs of farming were increasing, the model postulates, farmers limited the size of their families to guarantee their sons an adequate portion.[28] This explanation accords with the

27. A number of historians have concluded that self-control was central to masculine identity in the middle class during the nineteenth century. Most emphasize the link between the postponement of gratification in sexual life and the curtailment of consumption required for capital accumulation; a few point to direct analogies drawn in the popular literature of the time between "spending" semen and spending money. For analyses of the popular literature, see Ben Barker-Benfield, "The Spermatic Economy: A Nineteenth-Century View of Sexuality," *Feminist Studies* 1 (1972): 45–74, and Phillip A. Gibbs, "Self-Control and Male Sexuality in the Advice Literature of Nineteenth-Century America, 1830–1860," *Journal of American Culture* 9 (1986): 37–41. For broader surveys of nineteenth-century attitudes toward masculinity, see Charles E. Rosenberg, "Sexuality, Class, and Role in Nineteenth-Century America," *American Quarterly* 25 (1973): 131–51, and E. Anthony Rotundo, "Learning about Manhood: Gender Ideals and the Middle-Class Family in Nineteenth-Century America," in *Manliness and Morality: Middle-Class Masculinity in Britain and America, 1800–1940*, ed. J. A. Mangan and James Walvin (New York: St. Martin's Press, 1987), 35–51. It is not clear whether these definitions of masculinity apply to farmers. Farmers resembled other middle-class men in their concern for property accumulation, but they also differed from urban middle-class men in important ways. Their living was less dependent on the expenditure of money, and their accumulation of property was more dependent on their own productive labor. Physical strength and manual skill, as well as work discipline, remained central to farmers' sense of masculine identity.

28. See Richard A. Easterlin, "Population Change and Farm Settlement in the Northern United States," *Journal of Economic History* 36 (1976): 45–75; Richard A. Easterlin, "Factors in the Decline of Farm Family Fertility in the United States: Some Preliminary Research Results," *Journal of American History* 63 (1976): 600–614; and Richard Easterlin, George Alter, and Gretchen A. Condran, "Farms and Farm Families in Old and New Areas: The Northern States in 1860," in *Family and Population in Nineteenth-Century America*, ed. Tamara K. Hareven and Maris A. Vinovskis (Princeton: Princeton University Press, 1978), 22–84. The relationship between land availability and fertility which this model postulates has been documented for rural regions across America throughout the nineteenth century: Don R. Leet, "Human Fertility and Agricultural Opportunities in Ohio Counties: From Frontier to Maturity, 1810–1860," in *Essays in Nineteenth-Century Economic History: The Old Northwest*, ed. Richard K. Vedder and David K. Klingaman (Athens: Ohio University Press, 1975), 138–58, Don R. Leet, "The Determinants of the Fertility Transition in Antebellum Ohio," *Journal of Economic History*

quantitative evidence from the Nanticoke Valley. The timing of the local fertility decline underscores the importance of declining access to land in the adoption of family limitation. The couples who settled the valley did not limit their fertility. Those who married just as the settlement process reached maturity were the first to limit the size of their families.[29] Fertility declined most sharply among the generation that had to get established in the community after undeveloped land was no longer available and family farms could no longer be divided; these couples must have had a special sense of the importance of parents' provision for their children.

Parents' concern for their children's future was not simply altruistic; it also involved their own security in old age.[30] Parents sought to

36 (1976): 359–78, and Don R. Leet, "Interrelations of Population Density, Urbanization, Literacy and Fertility," *Explorations in Economic History* 14 (1977): 388–401; Gary L. Laidig, Wayne A. Schutjer, and C. Shannon Stokes, "Agricultural Variation and Human Fertility in Antebellum Pennsylvania," *Journal of Family History* 6 (1981): 195–204; R. M. McInnes, "Childbearing and Land Availability: Some Evidence from Individual Household Data," in *Population Patterns in the Past,* ed. Ronald D. Lee (New York: Academic Press, 1976), 201–28; Morton Owen Schapiro, "A Land Availability Model of Fertility Changes in the Rural Northern United States, 1760–1870," *Journal of Economic History* 42 (1982): 577–600, and Morton Owen Schapiro, *Filling Up America: An Economic-Demographic Model of Population Growth and Distribution in the Nineteenth-Century United States* (Greenwich, Conn.: JAI Press, 1986); Mark J. Stern, *Society and Family Strategy: Erie County, New York, 1850–1920* (Albany: SUNY Press, 1987).

29. Census data indicate that the nineteenth-century fertility decline was already underway by 1865 and had been largely completed by 1880. According to the 1865 New York State census of the Nanticoke Valley, women who were born before 1800 had an average of 7.2 children, while those who were born between 1800 and 1815 had an average of 6.0. According to the 1900 federal census, women born before 1825 had an average of 4.9 children, and those born between 1825 and 1845 had an average of 3.8. This retrospective fertility data may be systematically skewed by fertility-related mortality differentials, but it suggests the timing of the fertility decline. Furthermore, the refined child/woman ratio—the number of children under the age of five per thousand married women between the ages of fifteen and forty-five—was 835 in 1855 but had fallen to 545 by 1880 and remained at 548 in 1900. The refined child/woman ratio is a rough indicator of fertility, since it is affected by the level of infant and child mortality and by the age-distribution of married women in the population, but it can be computed from census data and used to compare fertility levels over time. Bash, "Changing Birth Rates," and Stern, "Differential Fertility," both found that fertility had begun to decline by mid-century in rural New York State.

30. For a model of the old-age security motive for fertility, see William A. Sundstrom and Paul A. David, "Old-Age Security Motives, Labor Markets, and Farm Family Fertility in Antebellum America," *Explorations in Economic History* 25 (1988): 164–97. Criticizing the "altruism" of the Easterlin model, Sundstrom and David adopt a "bargaining" framework, suggesting that parents were motivated by concern for their own welfare in old age rather than by the desire to help their children get established. The difficulty with testing this hypothesis directly is that the Easterlin "bequest" motive and Sundstrom and David's "old-age security" motive would result in empirically identical behavior; fertility would respond to changes in the costs of establishing children on nearby farmland, for children would have to live nearby to be counted on to support their parents. This hypothesis is potentially more useful in explaining changes over time. It predicts that parents would loosen their controls over children's marriages

ensure that at least one child remained in the community and would
be available to care for them when they were no longer able to live
independently. During the late nineteenth century, having many children was no guarantee that any would stay in the Nanticoke Valley.
Women had special cause for concern about their security in old age,
for it was mothers rather than fathers who generally became economically dependent on their adult sons.

Economic relationships between parents and children did not remain static during this period. At the same time that economic opportunities for young people contracted and sons became more
dependent on their fathers for access to land within the local community, the potential power of young people in relation to their parents
also increased, for they had viable alternatives to remaining in the
valley. Those who decided to stay might agree to do so because their
parents enabled them to marry relatively young and provided fairly
well for them. The balance of resources and opportunities available
to both parents and children, then, affected the conduct of intergenerational relationships.[31]

when they feared that the children might depart rather than wait for their inheritance,
and that couples would limit their fertility when young people could find alternatives
to working on and inheriting their parents' farms. Although Sundstrom and David did
not test the first inference, it is confirmed by data from a number of communities in
New England and New York State. Sundstrom and David did test the second inference
and found that the growth of the local nonagricultural labor market was related to
fertility decline. There are problems with Sundstrom and David's approach. First, both
declining fertility and the expansion of the rural nonagricultural labor market may be
indications of the commercialization of the economy; as the price of farmland rose, the
number of landless laborers also increased. Second, the existence of local nonagricultural employment opportunities for young people acted to keep them within the community and thus available to help their parents in old age. Migration to less-developed
farm areas or to urban centers clearly functioned as an alternative to family limitation
in some situations, yet according to Sundstrom and David's logic this should have led to
an even greater fertility decline since children would no longer be around when their
parents were old. Furthermore, there were alternatives to family limitation when the
bargaining power of children was raised relative to that of their parents. For example,
parents could favor the son(s) who agreed to remain nearby and support them in their
old age, increasing inequality among sons rather than curtailing family size. Finally,
Sundstrom and David fail to consider gender differences. Women were more likely
than men to become dependent on their adult children in widowhood and old age, yet
women did not control the property central to intergenerational bargaining. Sundstrom and David's framework is interesting because it does not assume that family
members all shared the same interests, but it is not sufficiently informed by a noneco-
nomic understanding of the ways older and younger generations conducted their relations with each other.

31. For a general theory of fertility decline that analyzes the total flow of resources
between the generations over the life course, see John C. Caldwell, *Theory of Fertility
Decline* (New York: Academic Press, 1982). Caldwell hypothesizes that fertility will remain high as long as parents benefit from children but decline when children become
a net drain on parental resources. The costs and benefits of children are, in this frame-

Economic considerations alone cannot explain intergenerational relations, and parents' and children's negotiations about inheritance and old-age security should not be evaluated in strictly economic terms. Farmers had not uniformly adopted the calculus of the marketplace and applied it to their family relationships in the nineteenth century, so it is not appropriate to apply the calculative model of classical economics to their behavior. Cultural norms defined the standards by which parental and filial conduct was judged and the processes through which intergenerational tensions and conflicts were mediated. Deeply held ideals about relationships in farm families supported the adoption of family limitation in response to changing economic conditions. The mode of thinking that planning for the long-term accumulation and transmission of farm property involved was extended to the matter of reproduction itself. Family limitation was an adaptive strategy, drawing on and preserving elements of the traditional family system at the same time that it involved new family practices. The stability in the ages at which young people were able to marry as land became a limited resource and the continuity in the intergenerational transmission of farms which most families achieved during the late nineteenth century testify to its success.

Women's life histories were profoundly altered by the decline in fertility, and many women must have welcomed the relief from continual childbearing. But it was primarily intergenerational, rather

---

work, dependent on the power relationship between fathers and young people; changes in this relationship, as well as in the economy, will affect the balance between costs and benefits. Not all costs and benefits are evaluated in terms of their market equivalents. Caldwell argues that in transitional societies, where families reproduce themselves through subsistence production even though they also produce commodities for sale or send individuals into the wage labor market, resources will continue to flow from children to parents even though the children do not earn wages or produce commodities. This model is certainly applicable to nineteenth-century America.

The empirical analysis of fertility decline most consistent with this theoretical framework is advanced by Nancy Folbre's "Patriarchy in Colonial New England," *Review of Radical Political Economics* 12 (1980): 4–13, and "Of Patriarchy Born: The Political Economy of Fertility Decisions," *Feminist Studies* 9 (1983): 261–84. Folbre argues that the expansion of capitalist relations, as well as the culmination of settlement, shifted the balance of power between fathers and sons. When sons had alternatives to waiting for an inheritance, fathers had to grant them autonomy and property at earlier ages to ensure that they would remain on the family farm, and the terms of the intergenerational bargain became less favorable to the older generation, leading to declining fertility. Folbre's analysis implies (though she does not suggest) that fathers might be able to make better bargains with one or two sons than with twice that many, so they might see family limitation as a way of shoring up their relative position. Folbre concludes that although some young women in New England enjoyed new labor-market opportunities, women's position was not improved relative to that of men in the way that young men's was relative to their fathers'. The shift underlying the fertility decline, then, was related more to intergenerational than to gender relations in New England.

than gender, relations that led to the adoption of family limitation by Nanticoke Valley couples. At the same time, cooperation between husbands and wives in planning for their children's future and in conducting their sexual relations was a necessary precondition for the practice of family limitation. Nanticoke Valley couples acted as coparents of children for whose future they were jointly responsible and with whose welfare their own security was inextricably bound up.

Remembering the Ancestors

Toward the end of the nineteenth century, people in the Nanticoke Valley began holding family reunions. Relatives who had moved away returned to celebrate their grandparents' wedding anniversary or birthday. As members of the settler generation passed away, their descendants recalled the stories they had told about the past. Some reunions became formal annual events; speakers recounted the family history, while participants recited poetry and sang old familiar songs.[32]

The histories recounted at family reunions were almost always nostalgic. Elizabeth M. Riley Newton, George Riley's youngest sister, began her address to the 1898 Riley reunion:

> My dear friends, my own kindred: How these gatherings make my thoughts go back to the past. There comes to me visions of Home, when our large family was unbroken save through very small ones who were called away before the brothers and sisters had time to learn their names. There were six brothers besides us two girls, all of our Mother's children, all strong and well. I think I again see them scattered a little to homes of their own . . . until the new homes numbered more than half a dozen. Then I see changes, oh so many changes, in every one of these homes. Some of these changes brought joy and made these homes very sacred but others such dark clouds that we who are left can feel them yet, and because of these changes I have written what I have—not for the older ones for they have heard what I will tell you and perhaps very much more from

32. Although most of the speeches given at family reunions remained in the oral tradition and perished with those who heard them, a few were written down and have been preserved. For information on family reunions in New England and the upper Midwest during the late nineteenth and twentieth centuries, see Robert M. Taylor, Jr., "Summoning the Wandering Tribes: Genealogy and Family Reunions in American History," *Journal of Social History* 16 (1982): 21–38, and Millicent Ayoub, "The Family Reunion," *Ethnology* 5 (1966): 415–33.

Dyer-Pier family reunion, Glen Aubrey, 1898. Nanticoke Valley Historical Society, courtesy of Jennie Whittaker.

our own dear Father and Mother's own lips—but for the younger ones who never had this privilege. For many of them know very little or nothing of their grandfather or grandmother Riley—and when I think how soon all we of the first family will be gone, then who can tell you of them? No one. . . . [33]

Elizabeth Riley Newton thought of herself as a transmitter of tradition, responsible for conveying to the younger generation the stories she had heard from her parents. In the act of retelling their stories, she imaginatively recreated the time before the family circle had been scattered by marriage and broken by death. Those changes made the past all the more precious to her and lent a special urgency to her mission to pass on her parents' memories.

33. Elizabeth M. Riley Newton, speech delivered at the Riley family reunion at Ross Park, Binghamton, N.Y., 20 August 1898, copied by Leroy Bostwick.

The stories told at family reunions focus on the first members of the family to come to the Nanticoke Valley, describing their migration to the region and their determination to make a home in the wilderness. Stories typically exalt parents' self-sacrificing labor for the sake of their children's future, treating the suffering they endured as unavoidable and presenting their perseverance as morally uplifting. Belden Allen's history of the Spencer family typifies this genre. The son of Ebenezer and Oladyne Spencer Allen, Belden was nine years old when his father died.

> In 1846 she was left a widow with seven children, the oldest being fifteen years old and the youngest about three months. Then there was the debt left on the farm and she took charge of the business, both in and out of doors, the children helping all they could. Finally the debt was paid and another small farm was bought and paid for. Very few mothers would be able to endure what she did.[34]

Some tales went untold at reunions because they were more traumatic, lacked a triumphal ending, and pointed to adults' responsibility for children's suffering.[35] For example, in 1914 Fitch Hyatt Marean wrote down what his father, Jason, and his aunt had told him about their childhood.

> When the oldest [child], a girl, was sixteen, the father had an injury that caused him to be insane and he had to be kept chained to the floor three years in order to protect the children from his violence. His wife kept the family together as best she could, but they had hard times. I heard one of the children tell of seeing the tears run down through her mother's fingers as she asked the blessing over the potatoe and salt she had for them. The same girl told of trying to eat grass because of hunger. The youngest boy, Jason, when about ten, worked for a man at Newark [Valley] and told of lying down in the cow path and holding his breath in an effort to kill himself be-

34. Belden Allen, *The Spencer Family* (Glen Aubrey, N.Y.: privately printed, 1900), 23. In the preface, Allen says that he was elected "historian" at the 1896 family reunion and gathered information at the 1899 reunion, which was attended by 113 people from both sides of the family.

35. My understanding of the way that stories describing the apparent abuse of children by parents are often embedded in narratives praising the sacrifices pioneer parents made for their children's sake has been deepened by discussions with Elizabeth Hampsten, author of *Read This Only to Yourself: The Private Writings of Midwestern Women, 1880–1910* (Bloomington: Indiana University Press, 1982) and editor of *Homesteading on the Knife River Prairies* by Pauline Neher Diede (Bismark, N.D.: Germans from Russia Heritage Society, 1983).

cause he was so tired; it seemed he could not go another step after
the cows. He remained there for three years and then ran away because of fear of the man. He did not grow any more until he was
seventeen.[36]

The histories recounted at family reunions suppressed memories of
human cruelty, neglect, and conflict, for their telling would have disrupted the sense of solidarity such stories were intended to create.

Many of these family histories are curiously timeless; they present
the past less as a former time than as a different place, a changeless
world quite disconnected from the present. Narrators seldom confronted the "oh so many changes" that had occurred since their childhood. Rather, they recreated in memory the unbroken family circle
they had lost or left. In the Hogg family, however, stories about the
original immigrants' departure from Scotland became a vehicle for
their descendants' expression of regret about their own departure
from Mt. Ettrick for the cities of Broome County. There were clear
generational transformations in the Hoggs' tales of emigration.[37]
Over time, the parents' critical political perspective became submerged in the children's sentimental idealization of Scotland; the
next generation identified the Scotland of their grandparents' past
with their own remembered childhood on Mt. Ettrick. The Hoggs
published in the popular press both verses they had memorized
as children and elegies they composed as adults. Geordie Hogg
("Sawney") wrote a series of poems to commemorate the family's history. The last six stanzas of "Sawney's Girlies' Sentiments," which are
addressed to the poet's granddaughters, describe Mt. Ettrick at the
turn of the century.

> Let me tell you of the early Scots
>   That lived on Ettrick Hill;
> 'Twill bring to mind some vacant spots,
>   I would they were occupied still.

36. Fitch Hyatt Marean, Letter to the Editor, 18 July 1914, in "Historical Sketches of
Maine," *Whitney Point Reporter,* 23 August 1914. Lewis Marean was injured in 1827,
when Jason was nine years old, and died in 1830. Fitch Hyatt Marean waited to tell this
story until all the people directly involved were dead.

37. Seena B. Kohl has pointed out that these recollections, which contain stories
heard from parents and grandparents as well as memories of childhood experience,
are simultaneously first-, second-, and third-person documents. The older generation's
stories are likely to undergo a symbolic transformation as they are retold by the
younger one in their own old age. Seena B. Kohl, "Memories of Homesteading and the
Process of Retrospection," *Oral History Review* 17 (1989): 25–45.

The old log house at the end of the lane
  Where Uncle Paisley and dear Aunt Belle
Reared Elizabeth, Frank and Jane
  And lastly Johnnie and Nell.

The little old house of cousin Will's
  With Beardie has gone to decay;
And stranger folk the doorway fills
  Of Robbie's red shop, down the way.

Little Jimmie has sold his farm away,
  And strangers pass in at the door;
Uncle Robert keeps his farm today,
  But his farming days are o'er.

Uncle William's empty house and place
  Speak volumes as we pass along;
We call to mind his kindly face
  And seem to hear a quaint Scotch song.

These changes since the long ago
  Point us to the home on high;
Let us strive to forget life's care and woe
  And live for the "sweet by and by."[38]

This poem was ostensibly written "of Scotch folks, for Scots to read," but it recapitulates the experience of many rural families. The world the original settlers had created was vanishing. As the older generation passed away, reciting the names of the ancestors and revisiting the places where they had lived ensured that they remained alive in memory. Neither family histories nor family reunions prevented the world from changing; instead, they reaffirmed people's relationships in the present by recreating their connections to a shared past. Remembering their ancestors at family reunions helped dispersed kin groups maintain a sense of their rootedness in the rural community.

38. James George Hogg, "Sawney's Family," in "Early Scotch Settlers of West Chenango," ed. Garrett, 1902. The Hoggs took pride in their family's rich literary and cultural tradition. At Mt. Ettrick they customarily celebrated Robert Burns's birthday with a program of recitations, speeches, and ballads which combined traditional, published, and improvised compositions. There were also published poets in the family on both sides of the Atlantic; the American Hoggs took special pride in their Scottish kinsman James Hogg, known as the Ettrick Shepherd.

For those who remained in the Nanticoke Valley, reunions and recollections of the past validated the choices they had made in the present by stressing their continuity with family tradition.[39]

Nanticoke Valley residents' sense of historical time, like their sense of personal history, was founded on their place in the local community and bounded by kinship networks. For women and men alike, identity was defined more familially than individually. Families, too, were characterized by their persistence over time; as they gained in generational depth, their kinship ties also ramified. This web of interconnections joined the present to the past and the individual to the community.

While kinship was central to both men's and women's life histories, women and men occupied distinct places within the kinship system. Women were integral members of the farm households that controlled the productive property on which the rural economy was based, yet they were formally subordinated to men and gained access to land only through their fathers and brothers, husbands and sons. At the same time, women were not isolated within male-dominated households. Although cultural norms prescribed that conjugal families should maintain separate households, people sustained substantial and continuous ties with their relatives and took them in when the need arose. Because property was transmitted from fathers to sons, many people lived near their kin and open-country neighborhoods were formed around clusters of related families. The vertical links in such networks, which were formed by inheritance, usually followed male lines, while the horizontal ties, which flowed from intermarriage among neighbors, were forged by women. When coresidence did occur, too, it involved women and their relatives as often as it did their husbands' relatives. Kinship was a crucial resource for women, and women played a central role in the provision of mutual aid. There was a distinct asymmetry in men's and women's places in the kinship system, however. While men were tied to their male relatives primarily through the inheritance of property, women were tied to their kin primarily through the sharing of labor and the provision of care. Women's kinship bonds were more direct, if less substantial, than those of men.

39. Family reunions, along with local historical celebrations, exemplify what Eric Hobsbawm called the invention of tradition; such public rituals "seek to inculcate certain values and norms by repetition" and by linking them with the past. See Eric Hobsbawm, "Introduction: Inventing Traditions," in *The Invention of Tradition*, ed. Hobsbawm and Terence Ranger (Cambridge: Cambridge University Press, 1983), 1–14.

Four generations of women in the Haskins-Dudley family, c. 1902. Nanticoke Valley Historical Society.

PART II

RURAL WOMEN'S LIVES

Courtship

We understand each other, I hope, better than ever.
—Judson Riley, Diary, 1894

In the Nanticoke Valley, the gender system simultaneously structured women's lives in terms of their relationships with men and defined a distinctly feminine life course. Even in the most gender-marked aspects of their lives, women were directly and powerfully linked to men. Marriage was central to women's life histories; women attained social adulthood when they married and set up households with their husbands, not through the achievement of individual independence. Marriage and motherhood were inextricably interconnected. Childbearing was a familial as well as a feminine experience, for the reproduction of the farm family concerned men as well as women. Fathers were intimately involved in the rearing of their children. The position of single women, deserted wives, and widows underlines the crucial importance of marital ties to women's welfare. Most women were dependent on men for access to the land and other resources required for productive labor; brothers and sons customarily took the place of nonexistent, absent, or deceased husbands in the lives of older women. The differences between the life courses of women and men did not create disjunctions between them but rather bound them together in gendered relationships.

Rural women did not create a separate subculture around their gender-specific experiences. Although kinswomen assisted one another in the critical transitions of adult life, especially childbirth and bereavement, they also shared those experiences with men. The

Fred and Martha Warner Marean and their daughter Grace, c. 1891. Photograph by Gilmore Studios, Binghamton. Nanticoke Valley Historical Society, courtesy of Leigh and Dorothy Ames.

(*Facing page*) Marean and Ames families, c. 1901. (Front row, left to right) Mr. and Mrs. Dyer; William and Deborah Allen Marean; child; Mr. and Mrs. Dyer. (Middle rows) Leigh Marean, Grace Perry Marean, and their son Floyd Marean (in Leigh's arms); Alonzo and Mary Slack; Clarence and Grace Marean Ames; John and Ina Smith Marean; Mrs. Junius Warner. (Back row) Arthur Ames; Martha Warner Marean and Fred Marean; Laura Ames; Clayton Ames; Junius Warner and child (in his arms). Photograph taken in Fred and Martha Warner Marean's parlor, Glen Aubrey. Nanticoke Valley Historical Society, courtesy of Leigh and Dorothy Ames.

Marean family, c. 1891. (Front to back, left to right) Fred and Martha Warner Marean; John, Grace, and Leigh Marean. Photograph by Wm. Dyer and J. A. Ames, Allen Settlement View Co., Glen Aubrey, N.Y. Nanticoke Valley Historical Society, courtesy of Leigh and Dorothy Ames.

support systems on which women relied included their fathers and brothers, husbands and sons, as well as their mothers and sisters, daughters and nieces. They treated kinsmen much as they did their women friends, calling upon them for assistance in matters of birth and death as well as in the daily difficulties of family life. Rather than allow themselves to be segregated from or subordinated to their husbands on the basis of sexual difference, women sought to sustain a familial culture based on gender integration and mutual aid.

The informality and directness of courtship enabled women to assess prospective husbands' character and to attempt to establish marital relationships on a basis of intimacy and understanding. Women chose to include their husbands among their childbirth attendants, emphasizing shared parenthood rather than gendered parturition. Women and men tended the sick and watched over the dying together. In all of these transitions, women sought to interact with men not simply as a different sex but also as members of a common family.

In the Nanticoke Valley, the conditions of late-nineteenth-century life sustained gender-integrated kinship patterns. Not all men were like George Riley, who attained a genuinely bifocal vision of the gendered world, understanding women's point of view as well as his own. Some men persisted in seeing others from the perspective of their own position and asserting the prerogatives of masculine status. But women's definition of the meaning of kinship was especially powerful in the crucial transitions that marked the life course. Women nurtured mutuality in their relationships with men by sharing those life experiences with them and integrating men into the networks of reciprocity that extended from those transitional moments into the ordinary activities of family, neighborhood, and community life.

The following three chapters consider these transitions, exploring the ways in which women nurtured their ties with men as well as with other women. They focus first, in this chapter and the next, on courtship and childbearing, which defined the normative female life course, and then on the experiences of women without husbands.

Marriage was the crucial event in young women's transition to adulthood. Young men's transition to adulthood was a more multidimensional process.[1] Men could move toward independence before

1. For a discussion of the changing definition of youth during the nineteenth and early twentieth centuries, see Joseph F. Kett, *Rites of Passage: Adolescence in America, 1790 to the Present* (New York: Basic Books, 1976). Kett's analysis, like the popular literature he studied, takes the masculine experience as normative. John Modell, Frank Furstenberg, Jr., and Theodore Hershberg, "Social Change and Transitions to Adult-

they found a wife; indeed, they were not supposed to marry until they had a solid economic foundation for the new household they would form. Marriage confirmed the independence men had achieved through the accumulation of property. Women never became autonomous individuals in that sense. Their status in the community flowed from their family position; they became adults when they married, rather than marrying as a result of becoming economically independent. Married women were no longer subordinated on the basis of generational position, but their subordination based on gender continued. Marriage defined women's adult identity.

The choice of a husband was the most important decision most women could expect to make. Wives were formally subject to their husbands' authority and were virtually represented by them in civil society. Women might be accepted as respectable members of the community because of their kinship ties and personal conduct, but their economic position depended on their husbands' property and occupation. Their labor might make a family comfortable, but it could not ensure them security, much less prosperity. Young women were advised to choose a husband who was skilled in a trade and husbandry and had steady habits. Given the powerful role husbands played in women's lives, men's consideration for their wives' welfare was seen as the primary ingredient of women's happiness.

At the same time, women were supposed to be the passive parties in courtship, accepting or rejecting men's proposals but not free to propose marriage themselves. Women's prescribed passivity in so crucial a process made courtship fraught with tension. In the Nanticoke Valley, women's power in courtship was enhanced both by the presence of women's families and by the young people's gender-integrated social life. Furthermore, courting couples were granted substantial freedom to develop an "intimate acquaintance."[2] Women used the period of courtship to probe a prospective husband's character and to establish a pattern of communication they hoped would continue through the marriage.

Most courtships began within the active social life that young people conducted in the community. Youths were not segregated from adults during the late nineteenth century; they lived and

---

hood in Historical Perspective," *Journal of Family History* 2 (1976): 7–32, show that the transition to adulthood has become more uniform and temporally compressed during the twentieth century for both men and women.

2. Many of the terms of this analysis of courtship are based on the framework developed by Ellen Kate Rothman, who studied the correspondence of middle-class couples during the nineteenth century.

worked with people of all ages, and they participated in the shared sociability of their households and neighborhoods. At the same time, they carried on their own group-oriented social activities. Sometimes these involved only other youths; equally often, young people planned activities for wider community organizations. The most striking characteristic of young people's social life was the degree to which the sexes mingled. Nanticoke Valley society was characterized by its inclusiveness; family and friends, adults and children, men and women socialized together. When young people associated with one another, they did not become exclusive either. The participants in their activities were constantly shifting; groups formed and reformed around particular events as one activity flowed into another. Within the young people's society, relationships between women and men remained informal and fluid. Young men and women met, not on the basis of gender difference, but as relatives and neighbors; they interacted, not as opposites in a formalized ritual of acquaintance, but as friends and companions.

Young women and men were allowed considerable freedom to socialize with their friends independently from their families. Parents do not seem to have been especially protective toward their daughters. George Riley's acceptance of his eighteen-year-old daughter's relative autonomy is typical; late one night George noted in his diary, "Ida has not got home yet—we are going to bed" (7 February 1875). Parents' anxiety was allayed by the fact that they knew where their children were and were well acquainted with their companions.

Most activities did not require young people to couple off. Many events, such as the musical, oratorical, and theatrical exhibitions that young people organized, were by definition group affairs. Other more spontaneous gatherings, such as sleigh rides and berry-picking expeditions, involved groups of siblings and friends rather than couples. Even suppers and dances, which paired up young men and women, did not require them to come as couples. Young women often went with a female friend or were escorted by a brother. At box socials and in country dances, women and men were forced to shift partners as part of the fun. It was not unusual for a young woman to be accompanied to a party by one young man and return home with another. The diaries of young people show a flexible pattern of relationships between women and men.

Courtship was marked by the same informality. Young men and women who became attracted to one another amid the swirl of parties, visits, and expeditions could spend time together at such gatherings without attracting much attention. Exclusive pairing was not expected, so couples could explore their mutual interest without pressure from their peers. Indeed, the group did not allow coupling-off to interfere with or inhibit the participation and enjoyment of everyone who attended its activities. If a young man and woman chose not to pursue a relationship further, they could simply disappear back into the group. Courtships began, and often ended, within a context of friendship.

When a young man and woman formed a particular attachment, they began to see each other outside of the group. They went out walking or riding on Sunday afternoons or evenings, visited one another's homes, and spent as much time as they could together. Their courtship was well known to their peers and to their families, for it followed predictable patterns. When a youth called at a woman's house and was polite to her family but seized every opportunity to see her alone, he was declaring that he had taken a special interest in her; if she encouraged his attentions and accepted his invitations, a courtship would begin. Equally important, when a young woman invited a man to join her family for Sunday dinner or to attend a special evening service at her church, she was expressing a desire to get to know him better; if he consented, they assumed the status of a courting couple. The rituals of courtship had commonly understood meanings. These conventions allowed women as well as men to take the initiative in the early stages of a relationship, as well as allayed women's uncertainties about men's intentions.

The public character of courtship, which flowed from its integration with group and family-oriented social activities, gave parents and friends opportunities to exert influence over young people's choice of marriage partners at a fairly early stage. Once a couple were courting, however, they were comparatively free to associate with each other. Young women were neither chaperoned nor bound by strict rules about when they had to return home; indeed, parents and siblings were likely to vacate the family sitting room so that the young woman could be alone with her beau. Courting couples enjoyed a significant measure of privacy.

No customary forms dictated when a courting couple might approach the subject of marriage or how they should act once they came to an agreement. Within the general terms prescribed by community moral standards, young people themselves determined the meaning of their relationship. At the same time, once they were courting they were involved in a process that was presumed to lead toward marriage. A formal proposal was not always necessary. Some young couples found that everyone else expected them to get married before they themselves had discussed the subject; others never explicitly agreed to marry but simply assumed that they would and acted on that basis. The conventions governing courtship allowed young people considerable latitude in decision making but also helped them to avoid ambiguity. Courtship could be broken off at any point, not only by outright rejection but also by a willful violation of its conventions. A young man who became less regular in his visits or a young woman who began to encourage other suitors would signal a change in their relationship. As long as young women and men acted according to the canons that governed the conduct of courting couples, the simple continuance of their relationship involved a *de facto* progression toward marriage.

Marriage was the culmination of courtship, the consequence of young people's own choices and commitments. At the same time, it was part of the process of generational transition in both of the young people's families, so the timing of marriage and the arrangements that young couples made to start their life together were affected by their family situations. The formation of a new household usually depended on provisions made by parents. Most couples had to wait to marry until the young man had negotiated the terms of his independence with his father and the young woman's parents had granted permission to marry. Thus the freedom from parental control that courting couples enjoyed did not extend to marriage itself. Couples who married in opposition to the wishes of their parents forfeited the parental contributions their new household would have otherwise received, a cost few could afford. Most new families were founded when young couples' parents accepted them and helped them get established.

Lala Ketchum Marean

The courtship of Lala Ketchum and Henry Marean demonstrates both the initiative young people took in selecting a spouse and the controls parents exercised over the timing of marriage. Lala and Henry became engaged in July 1862, when she was fifteen and he was twenty, but they had to wait for almost three years before they could marry. Five months later, Lala died in childbirth. Lala and Henry had both grown up in Maine village; her parents kept the hotel, while Henry worked as a store clerk. He spent much of the time before their wedding working in Binghamton and Syracuse. Lala wrote to him often, sent him her poetry, and kept a diary she intended him to read. The front cover of Lala Ketchum's diary is inscribed "Respectfully dedicated to Henry," and it begins: "My precious pet. For want of something to busy myself about I believe I'll keep a diary of my thoughts and feelings while you are gone so you may know how I get along."

When Lala and Henry promised to marry, they were aware that they were not ready. They decided to wait two years and told no one of their intentions. In the spring of 1863, Lala wrote to Henry: "Wouldn't some of the girls stick their eyes out if they knew I was expecting to be a married woman next year? Well, they don't know it nor won't yet awhile if I can help it. I shall be nothing more than a girl then, my darling, but I will try oh! so hard to do a wife's duty" (27 April 1863). A year later she saw her youth as one reason to postpone their intended wedding: "In regard to getting married, I hardly think your mother would think it proper for a girl of sixteen. Well, I'll wait till I get my dresses long anyway. Hadn't we better?" (13 March 1864). Henry agreed, waiting until the next fall before writing to the Ketchums asking for permission to marry their daughter.

Mr. and Mrs. E. Ketchum

You must have known that the intimacy long existing between Lala and myself meant something more than friendship. Therefore you will not be surprised when I tell you that I have ardently loved her for more than three long years. . . . We plighted our troth in 1862 and set the date of our marriage at two years from that time, but those two years which seemed almost an age to wait rolled quickly around and we concluded to wait a little longer. In all that time we have been true to each other, never regretting the step which was taken nor wishing to be free, and we are satisfied that in "our union" only will our greatest happiness be secured.

You may have fears in trusting the happiness of your only daughter to my keeping, but I promise you, that my greatest care through life shall be to make her life pleasant and happy.

Stating, as I have our experience in the past and hopes for the future, I now earnestly ask you to give me "Lala" for my wife and urge that our marriage may take place on the first of January next.

You may think us too young to take such an important step, but do not, I entreat you, object on that account for we have waited so long already, that our constancy cannot be doubted and at that time Lala will lack but a few months of eighteen, while I shall be nearly twenty-three.

I shall call this evening to hear your reply. I hope that you will
carefully consult the happiness of your only child in your answer.
Hoping that our wishes will meet with your approval I am yours

Very Respectfully

Henry Marean

Although Henry formally requested Lala in marriage, he clearly
spoke for both of them.

Lala's parents insisted that the wedding be postponed until Lala
turned eighteen but offered no other opposition to the young
couple's plans. Lala was more apprehensive about Henry's family's
reaction. In the summer of 1863, Henry's sister and brother had discovered their understanding. Lala wrote:

> I should think Minnie and Arthur were quite badly alarmed about
> our being married. Perhaps your folks would have felt as bad if they
> only believed it. I am afraid Minnie won't like the idea of your hav-
> ing a wife for fear she would not get so much of your attention.
> Darling little sister, it shall be my care never to wound her feelings,
> and of course I shall be willing for you always to love her as fondly
> as now. (6 July 1863)

Lala also worried about Henry's mother's attitude to her: "The trouble with your mother was just about what I imagined it to be. I'm
very sorry if I am the means of causing any disturbance but I don't
know as it can be helped" (12 March 1864).

Lala and Henry's primary concern during these years was how to
get established in life. Henry never considered volunteering for mili-
tary service in the Civil War; at one point he and Lala discussed
whether his father might pay for a substitute, but that proved unnec-
essary. Economic concerns predominated in their correspondence.
Lala felt confident that they could make their way even if they began
with very little.

> What difference does it make if we don't have much capital to start
> on? We are both young, and willing and able to work.... There
> is no danger of our starving, and to live and be with you "my own"
> will be true happiness, let the surroundings be what they may. (19
> July 1863)

Lala did not want to delay their marriage until Henry had saved
more money or secured a better position. During the last six months

before their wedding, when Henry was weighing job offers in Bing-hamton, Syracuse, and Oil City, Pennsylvania, Lala considered not only the salary Henry would be paid but also the opportunities for earning money that would be open to her.

I've been thinking that . . . I'll coax Henry to hire enough rooms so we can keep about four boarders. I could easily do the work for six and I should want something to occupy my time while Henry was away. It would not perhaps be quite so pleasant at all times as living alone, but I think we could stand it—if it paid. Or perhaps if he would go into a dry goods store and I had "gumption" enough he could get me a chance too. Perhaps Henry will think this an extrav-agant idea but I guess I shan't consent to be a burden to him but a help-meet as well as help-mate. (19 January 1865)

Lala's emphasis on the biblical term "help-meet" stressed the woman's duty to contribute to the family's support. She consciously rejected the middle-class ideal of a woman's proper role:

One great reason for my deciding in favor of this is that in such a place I would be sure to have something to do. I know that I couldn't be contented to sit stil and do nothing while my husband worked night and day to keep me in idleness. That is not the kind of wife that Henry needs, and he is not going to have such an one. (23 January 1865)

In the end, Henry accepted the position that Lala favored, even though it paid a lower salary than he had hoped for.

While Lala and Henry debated where they would live, she worked in her parents' hotel and tried to prepare for her wedding. That was not easy, as she confided to her diary:

I've worked pretty hard and am some tired. . . . there are so many here that I have to do housework, and it seems as if I should fly when I think that I am to be married in May and of the pile of sewing that ought to be done. If I knew for certain that Henry would go into business here I shouldn't care so much, for I shall have time to make my necessary clothing, but housekeeping articles, it is impossible the way things are now. If he stays here, we can stay at my father's house until I get prepared, but if not, it won't be so nice for I shall want to be with him. . . . I thought that I should have an abundance of time to do all sewing, and I should if I were any where else, but there are a thousand things every day for a "Lala" to do, and it seems as though every day slid along without accomplishing anything for myself. (17 January 1865)

Eager as she was to be married, Lala was somewhat apprehensive about leaving her parents' home. When her mother went away during the summer of 1864, Lala wrote: "I imagine now that I'll have 'the blues' some, for Mother left this afternoon. I suppose I've got to live without Mother sometime, but that I can do when you are with me." Lala hoped that Henry's companionship would compensate her for the family closeness she would be giving up.

Lala and Henry were separated for four months following their May wedding; he worked in Syracuse while she stayed at her father's house until she was ready to furnish their household. Lala joined Henry in the fall. At the end of October, she died immediately after giving birth to a daughter. Named after her mother, Lala Marean was raised by the Ketchum family in Maine village.

Helen Davis Benton

While Lala Ketchum actively planned for the future, Helen Davis passively awaited it. Her diary reveals the tension such a situation might involve. Helen did not marry until she was twenty-one; her husband, Leroy Benton, was twenty-six. Helen and Leroy had grown up in the same neighborhood in Maine; their families visited back and forth and helped each other with their work. By the time Helen was nineteen, she and Leroy had a special relationship, but they were unable to see their way clear to marry for several years.

In 1877, Helen went to work as a servant in a nearby community. The day after she arrived, she wrote in her diary: "I have spent one night. It seems a long time to look forward but I suppose will soon pass. I feel a little lonely but will soon feel like home I hope" (2 March 1877). A week later: "I feel a little more at home than I did but Oh for a home." Helen rarely underlined in her diary, but in this entry she underlined the word "home" with a long stroke that curved clear off the page. Feeling at home and having a home were different matters; she might adapt to a temporary living situation, but that was not the same as having a home of her own. Helen was quite lonely. Sometimes she attributed this to being away from her sisters, and sometimes she missed her mother. Generally her melancholy was more diffuse: "How quickly the weeks pass, another one is almost passed. I cannot enjoy the future, I mean present, but am looking for something to be enjoyed, so like a little child trying to grasp something beyond our reach" (6 April 1877). Helen felt powerless to shape her future but could not rest in the present. She tried to convince herself that everything would work out and admonished herself: "If I could 'leave those things of the future to fate' and enjoy the present I would be happier" (7 June 1877). But neither the uncomfortable present nor the uncertain future provided Helen with much consolation. "We can't have everything in this world just as we would like and it is better so," she reminded herself, "although we would often wish to have them so" (18, 20 September 1877). Helen's unfulfilled wishes had the last word.

Helen returned to her father's house in the fall of 1877 because she became seriously ill. When she resumed writing in her diary, she expressed discouragement about how long it was taking her to recover; at times she gave way to what she called "the blues." Helen's physical collapse and emotional depression were evidently brought on by the stresses of her situation. Separated from her intended husband and her kin, working as a servant in a strange household, and unable to foresee how she and Leroy could marry, Helen was in an impossible position. Her illness hastened her return home and forced some resolution of the problem. Helen's strength gradually increased and her spirits slowly revived. On 16 January 1878, she and Leroy were married.

For six weeks after the wedding, Helen remained at her father's house while Leroy remained at his parents' house up the hill; then she joined him there. Although she was not going far and was already familiar with her new home, Helen was still nervous about making the transition. She noted "the last Sunday I shall stay at Father's most likely" (3 March 1878). The next day she remarked: "I picked up some of my things, but I could not set myself about any of consequence." When Helen actually moved, she recorded: "started for my new home. I felt a little bad at first" (5 March 1878). The next day she reflected: "I feel almost like a stranger in a strange place. I tried to put away some of my things." The strangeness Helen experienced at the Benton's arose from her new position as a wife; the places and people were the same as before, but her relationship to them had changed.

Chauncey McIntyre and Judson Riley

Two young men's diaries describe courtships that ended in separation as well as those that culminated in marriage. Their successful courtships progressed swiftly, for both men were already prepared to marry. Chauncey McIntyre and Myrtie Durfee were wed when he was twenty-four and she was seventeen. First, however, Chauncey had courted Cora Lewis. Her name appears in his diary when Allie, his younger half-brother, was married: "Cora and me stood up with them" (2 August 1885). Chauncey and Cora began courting, and by November Chauncey was spending his weekends with Cora's family rather than with his own newly widowed mother. At Christmas he and Cora exchanged gifts. Soon, however, things began to go awry. Finally: "I went up to see Coe. Coe and me settled up. I took what things I let her have and let her have what she gave me and called it all square" (20 March 1886). The gifts Chauncey and Cora had exchanged were tokens of their mutual affection; returning them dissolved their obligations to each other.

Chauncey began courting Myrtie Durfee three months later. They may have known each other before, for Myrtie had grown up in the McIntyre District of North Maine. In the summer and fall of 1886 they went out riding every Sunday evening. On 27 October, Chauncey "bought a suit of clothes, coat, ring and undershirts" at Whitney's Point. Three days later, "I went to see Myrtie at night. Took her the ring. We went to meeting." Chauncey and Myrtie's wedding took place on 18 December 1886; they had courted six months.

Chauncey McIntyre was already independent when he began courting. His mother's second husband had died in 1884, when Chauncey was twenty-two and Allie was seventeen. In December 1885, a few months after Allie married, Chauncey got his mother to make over the deed to his parents' farm to him, mortgaged the land, and gave his brother the money to rent a farm, thus sharing the inheritance with his brother without dividing the land. After Chauncey and Myrtie were married, they lived with and worked for his relatives for a season while Allie worked Chauncey's farm on shares. Chauncey's widowed mother lived on the farm until 1887, when she remarried again and so was provided for. Chauncey and Myrtie finally moved to their own place a year after their wedding.

Judson Riley's first serious relationship with a young woman began when he was nineteen. He had been acquainted with Carrie Knapp in childhood, for she had grown up in the Nanticoke Valley; but her family had moved away. In 1887, when Carrie was twenty-two, she returned to teach school in Nanticoke during the summer term. Judson accompanied her to ice-cream socials and oratorical exhibitions and went out riding with her after church. When she returned to teach the next summer, they spent every Sunday together. At the end of the term, Judson wrote sadly: "Carrie is going home next week, so tonight is my last night" (31 July 1888). Judson and Carrie kept up a regular correspondence for two years. Eventually Carrie's name simply disappears from the diary; evidently the relationship could not be sustained over such distance. Judson's first courtship ended when he was twenty-two.

Judson did not pay special attention to another young woman until he was twenty-six. On 16 December 1893, Judson wrote: "I received a letter from someone that has grown dear to me within the past three or four weeks." On New Year's Eve he went to visit Lillie Pope, who lived in the village of McDonough in Chenango County. Lillie's father was a Methodist minister, and it is likely that Judson met Lillie at a regional religious gathering. They "watched the old year out and the new one in right enough" and attended church with her family the next day. What happened later that evening is recorded in three different places in Judson's diaries for 1893 and 1894. At the end of the 1893 volume, Judson wrote simply that he "had a better visit tonight than last night with Lillie." At the beginning of the 1894 diary, he remarked that "Lillie and me had a visit in the parlor and a talk about some things and understand each other, I hope, better than ever." The nature of their understanding is suggested by the entry Judson made after he returned to Maine the next day: "I had a very good time up there and I hope and pray that something may come of this visit some time that will make my life happier some day, and perhaps an other life too." The young couple had decided to marry.

Their courtship progressed rapidly. In mid-January 1894, Lillie spent almost two weeks in Maine. First she stayed with a mutual friend, and then she moved to the Rileys'. Judson wrote: "Lillie came home with me. We did not retire very early this evening." He then crossed out the word "evening" and replaced it with "morning"; evidently they did not retire until morning had come (13 January 1894). "Bert's folks"—Judson's older sister Ida, her husband Bert Davey, and their children—came over to meet Lillie as well. Following this exchange of visits, the couple prepared for their wedding. Judson noted, "Got me a suit of clothes today that I intend for my wedding suit"; and he took one trip to McDonough to make the final arrangements. On 28 February, Judson and Bert went to Lillie's home. "Lillie and me were married this evening at 6:30 pm by her father. There were quite a company of neighbors present." Judson was twenty-seven and Lillie was twenty-three. Their courtship had lasted four months. Evidently both were ready to marry and had only been waiting to meet the right person.

Judson Riley's father was dead by the time Judson married. In his will, George Riley had provided that Ida Riley Davey would inherit the other half of the farm that he had bought for her and Bert after their marriage. He had left his widow Lucy Ann the sum of five hundred dollars, all their household furniture, and an undivided half of his real and personal estate for her lifetime. All the rest of his property went to Judson, who would inherit his mother's share of the estate after her death. Taking over the farm and providing his mother with a home was an implicit condition of Judson's inheritance.

Judson brought Lillie home with him when he married in 1894. For a few months the young couple and Judson's mother kept house together. In August, however, Judson recorded that "we are going to get some things to keep house by ourselves. Mother is going to have the kitchen for her room and we will have the sitting room for our kitchen" (15 August 1894). The Riley house was divided into separate households. Lucy Ann evidently found it easier to live with her daughter than with her son's wife. In December 1894, Judson noted that they "did not have a very pleasant Christmas today. Everything went wrong." The next day, "Mother is up to Ida's." Lucy Ann decided to make the change permanent. On 30 December, "Mother went up to Bert's tonight to stay. She is going to stay up there right along I guess." Judson's marriage led to a change in both his mother's and his sister's living situations.

Ina Smith Marean

The 1899 diary of Ina Smith illuminates how a courtship was conducted within the context of family relationships. Ina Smith was eighteen years old in 1899; the next year she married John Marean, who was twenty-three. They had grown up on adjacent farms near Glen Aubrey; their families were very close, sharing work and visiting back and forth daily. Ina's diary does not record any explicit agreement that she and John would marry, but he enjoyed the status of an accepted suitor. Ina and John consistently acted toward each other in a way that was understood by their families and neighbors to lead toward marriage. What remained to be settled was not whether, but when, they would marry. John lived and worked on his family's small farm. His father was relatively young and active, so John could not look forward to inheriting the land in the near future; he had no property or prospects of his own. If Ina and John wished to remain in farming, they might have to wait some time to marry. In Ina's diary, their courtship seems not so much a process as a state of being.[3]

Throughout 1899 Ina and John's relationship followed a set pattern. John came over to visit every Sunday, they went out together on Friday or Saturday evening, and they managed to see each other at least once in between. When John visited Ina at home, he was usually integrated into her family's activities, such as reading aloud or playing pedro. What might happen if they were left alone is suggested by one entry: "Mother seen me set on John's lap today, it was the first time she ever did" (21 February 1899). Ina did not have to record her mother's disapproval. Later that year, after "John came up a little while in the afternoon," "Mother got awful mad at me" (3 December 1899). Ina's mother held her, rather than John, responsible for their lapse from propriety. At the end of the year, however, Ina noted a significant advance in the amount of privacy she and John were accorded: "First time I every set up with John to home, my folks went to bed for a wonder" (2 January 1900). Ina was finally allowed to entertain John after her family had retired.

When Ina and John went out together, they generally spent their time in the company of other young people. They had considerable freedom of movement. Dances held at friends' homes often lasted until the small hours of the morning: "John and I went down to Mont Walters to a dance surprize for Jen Walter, got home half past four. Father and Mother went to Glen this afternoon. Went to bed and took a little nap when they were gone" (13–14 April 1899). Although most of the social events they attended took place in the local community, Ina and John occasionally traveled further; for example, on the Fourth of July they went with two other young couples to the Casino, an amusement park in Union.

What is most striking about Ina and John's social life, however, is not their independence but rather the way they conducted their courtship in the context of the relationship between their families. "Father, Mother, Kerney and I went down to Fred's to spend the evening. After we got down, made up our minds to go to the dance at Henry Marean's, John and I. Stayed all night with Grace" (8 March

3. Ina Smith wrote her diary for herself, but she allowed John Marean to read it. She went to the trouble to keep her diary in mirror-writing so that it could not be read without her permission, but one day "John came up this afternoon, and he read this book all through" (24 September 1899). After Ina and John were married they moved to Sidney, N.Y., where John ran a livery stable, and then to Binghamton, where he drove a streetcar. Marean Family Papers; Leigh and Dorothy Lawton Ames, interviews with author, April and May 1982.

1899). Kerney was Ida's younger brother; Fred was John's father, and Grace was his sister. Ina and Grace were especially close friends. Grace did what she could to further the courtship between her friend and her brother. At the same time, John and Ina's relationship facilitated Grace's courtship with Clarence Ames, whom she eventually married. The four young people were often together. On a typical summer day: "John, Grace and Clarence came this evening. John went home at eight o'clock, Grace and Clarence stayed till ten" (22 July 1899).

John's older brother Leigh and his wife, Gertie, also played an important role in Ina and John's courtship. Ina and John stayed with them on their farm in Smithville Flats for several days in midsummer. Ina noted that "the boys" drove the stage to Greene and went fishing, while "Gertie and I churned" and "I ironed John's shirt" (25, 28 July 1899). Ina and John enjoyed this foretaste of domesticity. After Gertie had a baby in the fall, John and Grace went to stay at the farm so that Leigh and Gertie could visit their parents. Ina missed John intensely, filling the margins of her diary with such phrases as "Oh John" and "I thoughts are away." After vowing that "I would do almost anything to see John," Ina went to Smithville Flats to visit him. "Today is Grace Marean's birthday, she is sweet sixteen. George Vandeburg and I went to Smithville to surprize John and Grace" (2 November 1899). They stayed from Thursday until Sunday, when the young people all came home together. This time, the four young people were alone on the farm without the supervision of a married couple. Ina enjoyed managing the household: "Grace and I did the work this forenoon. This afternoon we went to Greene with the boys. Had clams for dinner" (3–4 November 1899).

Ina Smith and John Marean were accorded an extraordinary degree of freedom by their families; they went away and kept house together for a few days. On the other hand, they did this within a familial setting. Whatever Ina and John made of these visits, it is unlikely that their families would have allowed them the same privilege in any other situation. The way in which courtship was embedded in relationships within and between families made it possible for young couples to enjoy so much intimacy. If their courtship had been less public, less enmeshed in the networks of kinship and neighborhood, it would also have been more formal and more distant.

The Transition to Marriage

Nanticoke Valley courtships resemble those described by Ellen Kate Rothman for white Protestant middle-class couples in the North during the mid-nineteenth century. Rothman found that most courting couples were allowed a substantial degree of freedom from adult supervision. Courtship was quite informal; rigid Victorian conventions did not dictate how young women and men might interact and create distance between them. Within the local community, women and men could enjoy the privacy that publicity made possible. Rothman did discover a shift toward more formalized modes of interaction between men and women during the late nineteenth century, especially in urban areas. In the rural Nanticoke Valley, however, the kin-based and gender-integrated modes of sociability which facilitated informal courtship continued.[4]

The informality of courtship helped women protect their interests as they approached marriage. Women were well aware of the risks marriage involved. Before entrusting their future to a man, they sought assurance that he was trustworthy, scrutinizing his habits and probing his opinions. Women observed a prospective husband as he went about his work, in his relationships with his mother and sisters and her own, and in his conduct toward their neighbors and friends. Good character alone was not enough, however; women needed to have confidence in a man to marry him. So they engaged in confidential talks and shared their private thoughts and feelings. Courting couples valued candor, directness, and honesty as well as respect, faithfulness, and friendship.

Women hoped the intimacy that courtship engendered would set the tone for their marriage as well. When they were courting, women had the power to accept or deny a suitor and to hasten or delay the wedding. They were surrounded by their kin and protected by the community. Although some women hesitated to relinquish these advantages and take the final step toward matrimony,[5] most tried to nurture the kind of relationship during courtship that they wanted

4. Rothman, *Hands and Hearts: A History of Courtship in America* (New York: Basic Books, 1984), 204–9. Karen Lystra found a similar freedom from parental supervision in the courtship of white, middle and upper class, largely urban couples. Lystra, *Searching the Heart: Women, Men, and Romantic Love in Nineteenth-Century America, 1830–1900* (New York: Oxford University Press, 1989), 164–65.

5. In contrast to the men's diaries, which describe a direct approach to matrimony, these women's diaries dwell on protracted courtships. But it is impossible to base generalizations about differences between men's and women's approaches to courtship and marriage on such a small sample. Participants' records of a dozen courtships have survived for the late–nineteenth-century Nanticoke Valley. All the documented instances of courtship (with the partial exception of Lala Ketchum and Henry Marean) conform to the pattern Rothman found in her study of courting couples. Rothman suggests that men were reluctant to make a commitment but moved toward marriage swiftly once they decided to marry and found a possible partner, while women, who experienced less ambivalence in the early stages of courtship than men did, wished to prolong the courtship and approached marriage itself with a certain apprehension. Rothman,

after marriage.[6] Women integrated the two families and social networks, minimizing the disruptions that the transition to marriage involved. The open and direct, simultaneously personal and public quality of relationships between courting couples in the late nineteenth century was a foundation for the marital partnerships women wanted.

Hands and Hearts, 68–75, 157–65. Lystra interprets such "courtship crises," precipitated by the woman after the couple had promised to marry, as tests of the man's commitment. Lystra, *Searching the Heart*, 166–91.

6. Lystra argues that the emotional identification and intimacy developed during courtship helped to blur the boundaries between masculine and feminine separate spheres in marriage as well. Lystra, *Searching the Heart*, 121–56.

Childbearing

I done nothing today   only attend to Lillie.
—Judson Riley, Diary, 1894

M arriage marked women's sexual initiation. In the Nanticoke Valley, the consummation of marriage was celebrated by a popular ritual known locally as a "horning." When the newlyweds retired to bed on their wedding night, they were greeted by what Judson Riley called "quite a salute"; people assembled around the house and created a commotion until the couple appeared and treated their friends. Older residents of the Nanticoke Valley remember hornings, although the custom has declined since World War II. According to their accounts and to the descriptions participants recorded in their diaries, the point of the horning was to prevent the young couple from going to bed. When the light in their room was put out, or when a bell tied to the bed began to ring, the group gathered around the house blew horns, beat tin pans, set off firecrackers, used noisemakers, and even fired shotguns. Young people organized the event, but married couples and their children participated. The newlyweds had to get dressed and come out or invite their friends and neighbors in; if they were slow in responding, their friends might burst into the bedchamber. The couple treated the crowd with cider and taffy or whatever else was handy. Often there was music and dancing. After a round of toasts filled with thinly veiled allusions to masculine potency and feminine fertility, the group dispersed and the couple could return to bed.

People in the Midwest called this a "shivaree." There the ritual directly expressed the notion that a couple had to pay tribute to their neighbors in order to consummate their marriage; if they refused to do so, the crowd might play tricks on them.[1] Some people disapproved of hornings; their profane character, association with alcohol, and sexual explicitness made them improper by some standards. Yet most people, however proper their ordinary behavior, participated in hornings. According to one local resident, a young couple who were not greeted with a horning would have been disappointed, for they would believe that they "didn't have any friends." A horning was disorderly and a bit ridiculous, but it was also exciting, a ritualized way for the community to recognize the sexual dimension of marriage.[2]

The horning, like the wedding, was a rite of passage. The contrasts between these two rituals are as striking as their commonalities. The wedding ceremony itself was short and simple. If the couple or their families had a religious affiliation, a clergyman usually officiated; if

1. The term "shivaree" was used in the Midwest and on the Great Plains during the late nineteenth and early twentieth centuries. Sometimes the tricks the crowd played on couples became rather rough; midwestern accounts include stopping up the chimney to fill the room with smoke and fixing the bed so it would fall apart. Such tricks do not seem to have been common in the Nanticoke Valley, although at least one local bridegroom was kidnapped, blindfolded, taken into the woods, and then set free to make his way home as best he could.

2. The word "shivaree" is clearly a variation on the French term "charivari." In early modern France, masked or costumed groups of young unmarried men directed the charivari against people who had transgressed the community's norms governing marriage and family life—by failing to produce a child within a year of marriage, by remarrying someone distant from them in age, or by committing adultery, for example. In England, during the same period, people who violated sexual norms were subjected to the public shaming of "rough music." In the "skimmington ride," for example, adulterers and wife beaters were subjected to symbolic punishment and ridicule. It is not clear just how these rituals were transformed in their transatlantic passage. In the seventeenth century, incidents resembling the charivari took place in Quebec, while others resembling rough music occurred in New England. But there has been little systematic study of the development of these rituals over two centuries in North America. In the nineteenth century, the horning or shivaree was not associated with deviant behavior; it celebrated legitimate sexual relations. At the same time, it did symbolize the community's power over young people's sexual conduct. E. P. Thompson has argued that such rituals should be seen not as a unified form but as a mode for the expression and enforcement of various ideologies of gender and power relations. For the French case, see Natalie Zemon Davis, *Society and Culture in Early Modern Europe* (Stanford, Calif.: Stanford University Press, 1965), 97–123; for the English case, see E. P. Thompson, " 'Rough Music': Le charivari anglais," *Annales* 27 (1972): 285–313. A comparative discussion of these rituals was held in Paris in 1977 by the Ecole des Hautes Etudes and the Centre Nationale de la Recherche Scientifique, and its proceedings appear in Jacques LeGoff and Jean-Claude Schmidt, eds., *Le Charivari* (Paris: Mouton, 1981); see especially E. P. Thompson, " 'Rough Music' et charivari: Quelques reflexions complementaires," 273–83.

they did not, a justice of the peace presided. The ceremony was generally held at the bride's home in the afternoon, and only the families and close friends of the couple were invited. When the groom came from another community, his family might be represented by one or two members; as long as he had a kinsman to "stand up with him," his mother and sisters were not expected to attend. Most weddings were followed by a supper, but there was no reception. The horning, in contrast, included the entire neighborhood; equally important, it was organized by friends rather than by the couple and their families. The horning did not focus on the sacred character or civil consequences of marriage but rather on the sexual license it granted.

This communal and convivial celebration of the consummation of marriage was based on the assumption that a woman remained a virgin until her wedding night. Although not all courting couples waited so long to have sexual intercourse, premarital chastity was accepted as normative.[3] Only when those norms were violated (although not always then) was there explicit discussion about sexuality among the unmarried people of the community. Still, transgressions were common enough that young people as well as old discussed instances of illicit sexual behavior. The silence about sexuality which pervaded urban middle-class culture in the Victorian period was not complete in the rural community, even among its most respectable members. Gossip remained an important mode of social control in the Nanticoke Valley.[4]

Courting couples enjoyed enough privacy that they could engage in sexual exploration with little fear of discovery. As young people walked home from dances or visited in the parlor after the woman's parents had gone to bed, their affectionate gestures might lead to passionate embraces. The pregnancy that was regarded as the inevitable result of sexual intercourse, however, was impossible to conceal.

3. In the Nanticoke Valley, as in other places, the norm of premarital chastity applied in principle to both sexes, but in practice there was a double standard. Men were generally regarded as less capable of controlling their sexual passions than women were; popular literature described men as having stronger sexual passions as well. Among men, premarital sexual experience was regarded as normal, although regrettable. There is some evidence of a sexually explicit masculine subculture in the valley. A few young men's diaries contain the words of bawdy songs and stories that turn on illicit or deviant forms of sexual relations. "Dirty pictures" and books circulated among some curious youths as well as among their more experienced elders. But this subculture was associated with such exclusively masculine environments as lumber camps and railroad towns, rather than with family farming communities. Local men took care that other men did not expose their wives, sisters, and daughters to such materials.

4. Susan Dwyer Amussen, *An Ordered Society: Gender and Class in Early Modern England* (Oxford: Basil Blackwell, 1988), 98–117, 129–31, analyzes gossip and reputation as means of exercising control over sexual behavior.

Couples who had promised to marry were accorded more latitude
than those whose commitment to each other was less certain and less
public. People often overlooked the fact that a baby was born less
than nine months after its parents' wedding. As long as premarital
conception occurred within a long-standing, socially recognized relationship and the bride was not obviously pregnant when the wedding
took place, nothing was said about the "early baby." According to local "old wives' tales," women were especially likely to conceive on their
wedding night and first children were prone to arrive prematurely.
Sometimes everyone knew and no one said anything; women might
even discuss how well developed an infant was for a "six-months
baby."

Young unmarried women sometimes became aware of early babies.
Lala Ketchum recorded in 1865: "It is reported that Abe Clark's folks
(or wife) has a 'great big boy.' It seems to me that they have been in
something of a hurry, but probably its all right." Lala added a cryptic
but suggestive comment: "I am willing however" (19 February 1865).
If Lala condoned the arrival of a full-term baby less than nine
months after its parents' wedding, she might also have consented to
sexual intercourse with Henry Marean before their long-awaited marriage. The birth of Lala's daughter, not quite six months after the
wedding, might have been premature, but the infant's survival, especially after the death of her mother in childbirth, suggests that the
baby may not have been a full three months premature.

Lala Ketchum's discussion of sexual matters is unusual among
young women's writings, especially in its oblique reference to herself.
Ina Smith recorded hearing gossip about a premarital pregnancy:
"John got a letter from Leigh and he said Matie Payne has got in a
fix. In high company. I should think I don't know how true it is
though" (7 January 1899). Ina was careful not to give credence to
such rumors, for she knew that another woman's reputation was at
stake. A month later, Ina reported that "Matie Payne was married
today" (7 February 1899). This woman's putative pregnancy was discussed by other young women and their future husbands. Such gossip
served as a warning to them.

In the Nanticoke Valley, the treatment of illicit sexual relations
depended on how much they disrupted the family system. Illegitimacy was regarded quite differently from prenuptial conception. The
stories young women heard about unwed mothers were vague, communicating only the community's condemnation of sexual immo-
rality and its assumption that the woman was to blame, and implying
that "ruined girls" simply vanished from their families and neigh-

borhoods.⁵ Not all unwed fathers escaped scot-free: a few fathers sued their daughters' "seducers" for breach of promise and paternity. But this action did not save the woman's reputation, and it involved a humiliating public admission that the man had refused to marry the mother of his child. People understood that such suits had more to do with feuds among men than with the fate of women. Most men suspected of fathering illegitimate children, finally, did not belong to the local community. This view was not simply a matter of projecting local failings on strangers.⁶ Nanticoke Valley men who impregnated local women were usually compelled to marry them before the child was born. Indeed, the pressure that could be brought to bear on local men was so strong that some fled the community when they feared that a young woman might put them in a compromising position. The community upheld the principle that sexual intercourse was permitted only in marriage by insisting that illicit sexual relationships be legitimated. When that was not possible because the man was an outsider, the community expelled the offending woman instead.⁷

Except on the occasion of a horning, Nanticoke Valley residents were more reticent about socially sanctioned sexual relationships than they were about illicit ones. In their private writings, married women and men seldom even alluded to their sexual lives. A few diaries, read with an ear attuned to their muted tone, do speak of the sexual aspect of marriage. Helen Davis Benton, for all her apprehensions about the future, evidently welcomed her sexual relationship with Leroy. After their wedding, when she was still living at her father's, Helen noted which nights she spent with him: "I staid with Leroy all night" (21, 23 February 1878). Conversely, she felt lonely when he was not with her: "I had to sleep all alone" (25 February 1878). A few entries suggest that they made love on Sunday afternoon: "Went to meeting. After dinner I went to bed, Leroy also. We laid till chore time. I went after the cows and helped milk" (30 June 1878). In the Gates household, too, the relative leisure of the Sabbath evidently provided an opportunity for lovemaking. One Sunday when Velma

5. For a discussion of the situation of unwed mothers in the region, see Joan Jacobs Brumberg, " 'Ruined Girls': Changing Community Responses to Illegitimacy in Upstate New York, 1890–1920," *Journal of Social History* 18 (1984): 247–72.

6. Only in some cases of incest did families unite to blame outsiders. The baby born to a young woman who had been sexually abused by her father or, more commonly, her stepfather was usually passed off as the child of the wife in the family.

7. The assumption was that "fallen women" moved to cities and ended up as prostitutes. More often, however, they went to visit relatives somewhere else and were passed off as young widows.

Leadbetter Gates had just returned after a two-week absence, her husband Russell noted that he "stayed at home and enjoyed myself" (19 March 1893; also 26 March 1893). There was no necessary contradiction in people's minds between Christian piety and marital sexuality, for the Old Testament they read on Sundays included the fulfillment of conjugal love among the blessings of the Sabbath.

Childbirth

To Nanticoke Valley women, bearing children seemed to be an inevitable consequence of marriage, not a matter of deliberate choice. Knowledge of how to prevent pregnancy was confined to married people, rather than taught to young women as they grew up or passed on to brides on the eve of their wedding. Indeed, some women were ignorant even of the "facts of life" when they married. While sexuality was seldom discussed even in private, however, childbearing was an acceptable topic of public discourse among women and men alike.

Relatively few Nanticoke Valley women recorded the fact of pregnancy in their diaries, and fewer husbands mentioned their wives' condition. This is typical of nineteenth-century American diaries. Rural people said little about pregnancy, not so much because it was an improper topic of conversation as because it was considered a normal state rather than a "delicate condition."[8] Pregnant women continued to engage in social activities until the day they gave birth; pregnancy was not a period of seclusion. Pregnant women also continued to perform their ordinary work. Not only was their labor needed on family farms, but physical exercise was regarded as beneficial. Rural residents believed that women who remained active had an easier time in labor than women who did not. Only if a woman became ill would her work routine be modified, and then it was her illness, and not her pregnancy, that was remarked.

The fullest descriptions of childbirth in the Nanticoke Valley diaries were written by George Riley. On 26 October 1866:

8. In this regard, rural people appear to have had more in common with eighteenth-century couples than with the middle-class women and men who began to define pregnancy as an illness in the early nineteenth century. For a discussion of changing attitudes toward pregnancy based on personal documents, see Jan Lewis and Kenneth A. Lockridge, "'Sally Has Been Sick': Pregnancy and Family Limitation among Virginia Gentry Women, 1780–1830," *Journal of Social History* 22 (1988): 5–19. Lewis and Lockridge suggest that the acceptance of this definition of pregnancy as illness might have led Virginia gentry couples to adopt family limitation.

Got up at twelve o'clock midnight and routed Aunt Lucy   At nine
o'clock in the morning our boy was born   Nine in eve got all
Things straightned out   Lucy Ann and the Baby is adoing well.

Once his wife went into labor, George Riley summoned the family's
closest female friend to come to her aid. It was understood that Aunt
Lucy would attend Lucy Ann in childbirth and care for her and the
baby afterward. She stayed for ten days and then visited almost daily
for the next month. Nevertheless, George was also involved in running the household during his wife's confinement:

Staid at home all day   Aunt Lucy went down home with Jas & Har-
riett So we had to be Chief cook.   We Ida & my selfe dun up
chores in a workman like manner according to our calculations. (28
October 1866)

Childbirth did not require medical attention as a matter of course.
Experienced women were regarded as competent to deliver babies
and to care for the new mother and infant under normal circumstances. In childbirth, as in illness, medical consultation was reserved
for situations that people felt were life-threatening or were uncertain
about how to handle themselves. Four days after his son's birth,
George came home to find that his wife had taken a turn for the
worse and that a doctor had been called. She soon improved, however; her relatives came for Thanksgiving, and in early December she
went visiting for the first time. "The Baby grows nicely," George remarked (2 December 1866).

George Riley also recorded his daughter's confinements. The births
of her first and third children are noted quite laconically, in spite of
the fact that one took place in the Riley's house: "Ida's Boy was born
today about seven o'clock" (28 November 1876). Ida's second child
was born after she and Bert had moved up to the adjacent farm. On
26 January 1881, George wrote:

A little after twelve o'clock last night Birt came down and routed
Lucy Ann and went after his mother   got back just after two o'clock
and there girl was Born before they got in the house—no one there
but Lucy Ann.

Lucy Ann Riley and Hannah Davey continued to care for Ida and her
baby during the next few weeks. Bert hired a woman to stay with
them, but she was responsible for running the household; taking care

of the new mother and infant remained the responsibility of Ida's older kinswomen. On 1 February, George remarked that he

> got Mrs. Davey brot hur up to Ida's to stay tonight. Lucy Ann was up there   fetchd hur back   She is allmost used up with a cold and sore throat   threatens to go to her lungs

Two days later, George complained:

> Lucy Ann has ben up to Bert's all afternoon and is gon again this evening to Stay all night   leaves us all alone   Seems lonesome Wish this world was not so full of Cares and trials as it is   Especially with hur fur she never thinks of her own Comfort or welfare but is ever ready to Sacrifise hur own fur others (3 February 1881).

George's concern for his wife's health was mixed with his own loneliness; he was not accustomed to separation from Lucy Ann and felt it keenly. Still, George recognized and respected the bonds of mutual aid that united women. Equally important, he assisted his wife in caring for their daughter and grandchildren. "Lucy and I staid at home   dun chores & etc. Lucy went up to Birt's awhile   I got supper" (6 February 1881). "Set up at Birt's with Lucy—helped to take care of Ida and the Baby" (18 September 1881). When Ida's family fell ill shortly after the birth of her third child, George and Lucy Ann took turns as caregivers. First "Lucy is staying up at Bert's tonight—they all have got the measles" (23 May 1883). Then George "stayed with Bert's folks last night all night   they are quite bad of and terrable uneasy" (26 May 1883).

George Riley was involved enough in his wife's and daughter's experiences of childbirth to record the entire series of events in his diary. Women's diaries seldom record more than the dates of their children's births. There is one account of childbirth from the mother's point of view among the Nanticoke Valley diaries, however. Helen Davis Benton had her second child on 29 January 1893. She wrote:

> Sunday. I shall never forget it   it rained hard all the forenoon, sun came out in the afternoon   Baby was born at half past eleven. Mrs. Doolittle and Mrs. Leonard were here, Mrs. Leonard stayed.

Helen was attended by a number of women after her confinement. Aunt Jane Leadbetter came for a few days, her niece stayed for a week, and a neighbor did the washing. Finally Helen's older sister came. The day she arrived, Helen wrote: "It seems good to have

Roena here. She goes right to work and I lay back and do not have to worry about work and baby" (9 February 1893). This simple sentence eloquently expresses the meaning of kinship to women at this time in their lives. Two weeks later, when Roena had to return to her family, she was replaced by a hired woman who ran the house while Helen made a slow recovery. Helen and both of her daughters came down with the measles when the baby was six weeks old, so the assistance Helen had received in childbirth continued through her illness. "I have a good many to help me, different ones," Helen remarked (17 March 1893). Soon she was well enough "so I can see to baby a little" (7 April 1893).

Most childbirth accounts in Nanticoke Valley diaries describe similar patterns.9 When a woman went into labor, her husband notified the woman who had agreed to attend her. Sometimes more than one woman came, although usually only one stayed on after the birth. Generally the women most directly involved were related to the new mother, although neighbors stepped into the role when kin were not available. In the Nanticoke Valley, there were no midwives who made a specialty of delivering babies. Instead, older women shared their expertise with their younger relatives. Doctors did not attend births as a matter of course, although some women did choose to have a doctor on call. Those families who could afford it, or who had no female kin available to help out, often hired a woman to keep house for the first week or two following the birth. Most women had a period of convalescence after childbirth; they worked right up until they went into labor, but they were not expected to resume work for a week or two.

Childbirth was often followed by a series of ceremonial visits to the mother and her infant. Women and men, adults and children, friends and neighbors all called on the new mother, even while she was still confined to bed, to congratulate her and take a look at the baby; girls and boys went to see new babies by themselves. The first time a mother and child ventured forth from the house was also a special occasion. In many cases, they made their first public appearance in church about six weeks after the birth.10

9. There are 123 accounts of childbirth in the diaries I studied, most written by women who attended the mother. The diaries include many more birth announcements.

10. This may have been an unconscious survival of the early modern English practice of "churching" a new mother. Baptism was not an elaborate event in the local Congregational and Methodist churches; it took place privately any time from a month to a year after the child's birth. No notation of the ceremony was made in diaries. The records of baptism kept by the churches do not mention the names of godparents.

Husbands were directly involved in childbirth. Most men, like George Riley, were present at the birth of their children and remained at their wife's side as much as possible for a day or two afterward. Not all men's diaries contain detailed descriptions of their children's births, but some men said even less about their own weddings, so their silence cannot be interpreted as a lack of involvement; rather, they seem to have been too preoccupied to write more than a formal record after the event. Most women who attended relatives and neighbors in childbirth mentioned that husbands were present, and a few described the assistance they provided: carrying and heating water, tending fires, supporting the laboring woman as she walked about, and attempting to soothe her pain. This was a more important role than going to fetch women to help; indeed, if there wasn't time to get anyone else, a husband might stay and assist his wife as she gave birth.

The accounts of childbirth in Nanticoke Valley diaries establish that women controlled childbirth. Experienced laywomen, not male physicians, presided over parturition. Husbands were present because women chose to include them. No men other than prospective fathers were involved so directly, but no taboos prohibited men from being in the birth chamber. Husbands felt confident that their wives welcomed whatever help they were able to provide.

Nanticoke Valley fathers' participation in childbirth during the second half of the nineteenth century raises significant questions about the social history of childbirth. Historians of women have emphasized the feminine character of the birth experience when midwives, rather than male physicians, presided over delivery.[11] In their enthusiasm for documenting women's control of childbirth, however, few historians have stopped to ask who else was present in the birth chamber besides the laboring woman and her female attendants; the possibility that women may have welcomed the supportive presence of their husbands has not, evidently, occurred to most of them. Yet scattered evidence from other communities and kinds of sources suggests that the Nanticoke Valley was not unique. J. Jill Suitor noticed that many nineteenth-century medical manuals mentioned husbands among birth attendants.[12] Suitor suggested that male physicians acceded to

11. See, for example, Judith Walzer Leavitt, *Brought to Bed: Birthing Women and Their Physicians in America, 1750–1950* (New York: Oxford University Press, 1986).

12. J. Jill Suitor, "Husbands' Participation in Childbirth: A Nineteenth-Century Phenomenon," *Journal of Family History* 6 (1981): 273–93, argues that "many husbands attended the births of their children during the nineteenth century to provide emotional support to their wives, even when a medical attendant and female friends or relatives were present." In a survey of manuals on marriage and health and on mid-

women's requests that their husbands be present because that would help resolve the problem of "delicacy" raised by their own role. In the Nanticoke Valley, however, husbands did not begin attending child-births when male doctors began presiding over deliveries; rather, it was already customary when women themselves controlled childbirth. Men's participation in childbirth may have reinforced their sense of themselves as coparents of children and facilitated the adoption of family limitation. It certainly reflected women's choice to draw their husbands directly into this most distinctly feminine of experiences.

Infant Mortality

The possibility of loss was part of the meaning of pregnancy and childbirth during the late nineteenth century. Many pregnancies ter-minated in miscarriage, and a few in stillbirth. Some infants died within a few days.

Miscarriages, like pregnancies, were rarely identified in women's or men's diaries. Judson Riley's diary for 1894, however, contains an ex-plicit description of his wife Lillie's miscarriage seven months after their marriage. Judson recorded:

> Oct. 3rd. This p.m. I went after the Dr. for Lillie. She was taken real sick this forenoon and grew worse. When the Dr. came he said it was mis-carriage Same as we had thought.
> Oct. 4th. Lillie was real sick all night. She did not sleepe nor me either much. I done nothing today only attend to Lillie . . . Lillie is better tonight I think.

For the next two days, Judson "staid by Lillie" except when he had to do chores. Neighbors came to help out, and then Lillie's father and mother arrived from McDonough. Her recovery was slow at first, and ten days after the miscarriage Judson "saw the Doctor about Lillie. She does not seem to get along as she ought to." A fortnight later, however, she was well enough to go about her usual work. The diaries

---

wifery and obstetrics, Suitor found that a significant proportion of those published between 1830 and 1910 mentioned husbands among birth attendants. Referring to medical manuals in particular, Suitor states: "Many of the authors did not specifically encourage the practice, but permitted it when wives requested that they do so." Suitor concludes that the presence of husbands during childbirth coincided with a trend to-ward mutual affection in relations between husbands and wives and was probably re-lated to the decline in marital fertility.

of married women and men contain a number of similar instances. Families handled miscarriages much as they did childbirths, except that they called the doctor right away. Women were expected to recover from a miscarriage in about two weeks.

The deaths of infants who had been born alive were generally recorded in diaries. Some tiny babies were never really expected to survive. When Ida Riley Davey had a premature baby in 1892, both Judson, her unmarried brother, and Vernon, her fifteen-year-old son, recorded its birth and death. Judson wrote:

> May 1st. Ida unwell.
> May 5th. Ida had a little child last night. Weighed 2 1/4 pounds.
> May 6th. the little baby up to Berts died today and I made a box to bury it in.
> May 7th. I went over to the Abbott Church to get W. A. Johnson to come over to Berts and make a prayer at the house this p.m. for the babys funeral at Berts. they buried it on our lot in the cemetary.

Vernon wrote:

> May 1. Ma is sick.
> May 5. I staid down to Granp Rileys and when I came home I found a baby boy here. he weighed 2 1/4 pounds.
> May 6. This afternoon I went down and got Gma Davey   The baby died this afternoon.
> May 7. The baby was buried down in the Allen settlement graveyard.

Because the baby was born alive, it was accorded a simple funeral.

Although some babies "were called away before the brothers and sisters had time to learn their names," infant deaths were regarded as especially sad.[13] Nanticoke Valley diarists described them more fully than they did the deaths of adults; rather than simply noting the date and time of death, they usually made a sympathetic comment about the bereaved family.[14] Parents were understandably anxious about their children's health during the most vulnerable period of infancy.

13. Elizabeth M. Riley Newton, speech delivered at the Riley family reunion at Ross Park, Binghamton, N.Y., 20 August 1898, copied by Leroy Bostwick.

14. Infant deaths must have been widely discussed, since they were noted by diarists who were neither relatives nor neighbors of the bereaved family. Only suicides and homicides were recorded as universally throughout the community, appearing in all the diaries that cover the dates on which they occurred.

When infants' lives were in danger, mothers called on the same system of mutual aid on which they relied in childbirth. Women sat up with the mother or cared for the baby themselves so the mother could get some rest. If the child died, they stayed to help the family. Helen Davis described one such death:

> I got up at half past five and found Mrs. Ketchum up to Mrs. Ward's. Their baby sickened and died. She helped lay it out, then came home to breakfast.... Two ladies came in and helped make a shroud for the Baby. (28 July 1877)

The next day, Helen and Mrs. Ketchum attended the funeral. Men were also involved in caring for critically ill infants. In addition to tending their own children and grandchildren, men were drawn into the assistance their wives offered neighboring families. For example, George Riley recorded: "Nat Coopers Baby died this morning ... aged 5 Months. We went over this afternoon and called on them and went down to Oak Hill to let the relatives know" (21 September 1884).

Most women who miscarried or lost an infant were able to bear healthy children afterward. The course of family life was not usually deflected for long by the loss of a child. For some parents, however, the experience could be devastating. Byron and Lydia Buck Gates lost their first two children to diphtheria during the Civil War. Their daughters Minnie and Jennie, aged two and four, died the same week. Louise Gates Gunsalus, Byron and Lydia's granddaughter, was told that after the funeral

> Grandmother was just beside herself, she just about lost her mind. Grandfather didn't know what to do. So he sent a telegram to Dan, her brother. He thought that if he could get her out of these surroundings and somewhere else it would be good. And it was. She was pregnant then, for my father. So they went West and shut the house up tight, sold everything.

They lived in Michigan with Lydia's brother and his family for almost a year, returning only after their son had safely weathered the first months of life. "Grandmother was mentally sound when she came back," Louise continued, "but very depressed. And Grandfather was depressed. He was just crushed by the loss of those two little girls." The family never recovered economically either, for they had to start all over again, buying livestock and farm implements at inflated prices. Their fine Greek Revival house fell into disrepair. "Lydia Buck could have been a very emphatic individual," Louise concluded. "Then all of this fell in on her, and she just lacked the initiative to do anything further."[15] Byron, too, mourned his daughters' deaths until the birth of his granddaughter nearly three decades later.

The familial and feminine dimensions of childbearing were balanced in the Nanticoke Valley. As a crucial part of the female life course, childbirth was an experience women shared with one another, and their mutual assistance made this a truly common, rather than simply parallel, experience in their lives. At the same time, childbirth was a familial event that linked women with their husbands. A man's presence at the birth of his child affirmed his fatherhood at the very moment of motherhood. The familial aspect of childbirth was integrated with its specifically feminine meaning by women's choice to have both husbands and female kin with them. Gender joined, rather than divided, the family at the moment of reproduction.

15. Louise Gates Gunsalus (1894–1983), interviews with author, 20 March, 12 July 1981.

CHAPTER FIVE

Women without Husbands

Some of the most womanly women I ever saw are unmarried.
—Lala Ketchum, Letter, 1863

The experiences of women without husbands illuminate the meanings of gender beyond marriage and maternity. On the one hand, single women and widows were not free from the restrictions of womanhood. Although in principle they were able to act independently in civil society, in practice most controlled little property and were represented by the male heads of the households in which they lived. On the other hand, women without husbands were not isolated. They remained integral to their families and often played central roles in the households of their kin; even aged women were seldom entirely alone. Equally important, women without husbands did not form a separate feminine society but interacted with family and friends across as well as along gender lines.

Single Women

Single women were anomalous in the Nanticoke Valley, not just because most women who remained in the rural community married, but also because unmarried women's status was indeterminate rather than clearly defined. Staying single did not require any positive public act on the woman's part; rather, it followed simply from her not doing what women were expected to do. The range in the ages at which women married was wide enough that there was no set age at which a single woman was deemed to become unmarriageable. Although the vast majority of local women had married by the time they were thirty, at least half of those who were still single at that age would marry before they reached the end of their childbearing period. Single women were generally regarded as women who had not yet married, rather than as women who would not marry, throughout their thirties. Some single women continued to engage in social activities with mixed groups of young people until all their contemporaries had married; as long as they could still attract young men, they might hope to marry one of them. Other single women withdrew from the young people's circle very quickly and so were less likely to marry. Nonetheless, an older single woman might still become a widower's second wife.

For most women, remaining single was the result of both voluntary and involuntary factors. At first, an unmarried woman could discourage suitors she did not find appealing with the expectation that others would be forthcoming. After a while she began to face the choice between accepting a man who was less than ideal and remaining single for the rest of her life. How she responded to this dilemma depended, in large part, on her family, for fathers and mothers, brothers and sisters helped shape women's sense of what they could and should expect in a husband, as well as their sense of what their lives would be like if they did not marry. Considerations of social class might figure substantially in this matter, encouraging unrealistic expectations and discouraging attachments thought to be unsuitable. The impoverished but genteel "maiden lady" living alone or with her widowed mother was a figure of fact, as well as fiction, in the Nanticoke Valley.

More often it was parents' expectations that daughters would remain at home to take care of them in their old age that prevented women from marrying. The last daughter living at home often found it difficult to leave. Parents sometimes regarded one daughter as less marriageable than the others and placed her in the role of family caregiver, which made this a self-fulfilling prophecy. Brothers and sisters also conspired to keep one sister at home. Although some women might not have chosen this role for themselves, most became accustomed to it. As they grew older, they became the family mainstay, running the household and managing business affairs. This gave them some of the adult responsibility they would have assumed had they married.

Nanticoke Valley residents rarely presumed that a woman had chosen to remain unmarried. Instead, they idealized single women who cared for others as paragons of feminine self-sacrifice. At the same time, stories of self-willed women who refused to marry circulated in the community. For example, Lamont Montgomery Bowers recalled "Sail" Pollard, who was "smart and independent as her father. When quite a young girl, she would drive a team with a load of lumber from their saw mill to Union and unload it as well as any man. Except for her skirts, she would pass for a big boy anywhere; in later years in a western state, she dressed like a man and run a large farm for years."[1] These stories' assumption that such women had to go somewhere else to find an adequate field of action was well founded.[2]

Plumah and Jane Leadbetter both lived out their lives as single women. Neither expected to remain unmarried; after all, their sister Rosella did not marry John Benton until she was thirty. During the Civil War, when "the girls" were staying with Rosella, John wrote to his wife: "Tell Jane to keep up good courage, for all the boys say that they are a going to marry as soon as they get out of the Army" (27 March 1863). Jane was just thirty at that time, while Plumah was three years younger. There was some concern about Jane's marital prospects, but the possibility of marriage had not yet been ruled out either by her family or by Jane herself.

At the age of forty, Plumah did marry—or so she thought. As her grandniece Louise Gates Gunsalus told the story, Plumah met a man named Vost who came to East Maine on lumbering business from time to time.[3] He brought his twelve-year-old son with him and left the boy with Plumah while he worked in the woods with her brothers. Plumah was quite taken with the boy, and eventually his father proposed and was accepted. Plumah Leadbetter and Ephraim Vost were married in 1873.[4] Shortly thereafter, one of Plumah's brothers happened to meet Vost's legal wife in Ithaca and returned with the news that his sister was not actually married at all. As soon as the truth was discovered, Vost and his son disappeared. The marriage was treated as though it had never been, and Plumah died single fourteen years later. Some women remained single, then, because of failures in their relationships with men.

1. Lamont Montgomery Bowers, Memoirs.
2. Lee Virginia Chambers-Schiller, *Liberty, a Better Husband: Single Women in America: The Generations of 1780–1840* (New Haven: Yale University Press, 1989), discusses the life histories of white, middle-class women who chose not to marry and changing cultural attitudes toward single women.
3. Louise Gates Gunsalus (1894–1983), interview with author, November 1981.
4. The marriage was formally recorded in the town of Maine. Paul Gunsalus provided additional information about the Leadbetter-Vost marriage in an interview with the author on 13 March 1983.

The life of Plumah's niece Velma Leadbetter Gates, who married
relatively late, contrasts with this story of marital misfortune. Velma
Leadbetter was the seventh of eight children in her family, the youngest of five daughters, and the last one to marry. She grew up knowing
that she would be responsible for her own support. Her father had
helped her oldest brother buy land in the West, and her younger
brother was destined to inherit the family farmstead. (Each of the
daughters received fifty dollars when their father died.) Velma was
determined not to be dependent on her family, so she learned dressmaking, and her business took her away from the Nanticoke Valley
for many years. Still, Velma was not autonomous from her family.
Her daughter Louise Gates Gunsalus described how Velma's obligations to her parents continually interfered with her pursuit of an independent career:

> The maiden woman in a country family belongs to everybody in case
> of illness. The married sisters had their homes, their children, and
> they lived on farms; they couldn't leave. But the unmarried sister
> was always available; call on her and she'd come home and take care
> of the mother or the father who was ill. So Mother would have to
> hang a sign out, saying "I'm sorry but I've gone up to my fa-
> ther's". . . . They thought *nothing* of calling her out like that.

Louise said that while her mother was "annoyed" by the assumption
that she had nothing else to do, "she always went."[5]

When Velma married Russell Buck Gates, the only son of Byron
Chandler and Lydia Buck Gates, she was thirty-eight and he was
twenty-five. According to her daughter, Velma did not regard marriage and motherhood as "the height of her ambition." Still, she was
never anxious that she would be unable to marry and have children
when she chose. Velma enjoyed an active social life and "there was
always someone in the offing who was interested in her." She preferred younger men who wanted to have fun to men her age who
were looking desperately for a wife. Velma and Russell met at the
home of Leroy and Helen Davis Benton, their mutual relatives, when
she was visiting her family and he had just returned from the West.
They did most of their courting at the Bentons', rather than in either
the Leadbetter or the Gates households. Velma's father was convinced
that she married to escape the obligation of caring for him in his old
age. The death of Velma's mother just six months after the wedding

5. Louise Gates Gunsalus, interview with author, 20 March 1981.

did not improve his attitude, although Velma came home for a month to care for her mother in her final illness and comfort her father in his bereavement. Velma and Russell always believed that her father's demands were unreasonable, and although she did what she saw as her duty to her father she defended her right to live her own life. First Velma enjoyed the independence that was available to single women only in urban areas, and then she assumed the position of a wife and mother in a respectable farm family.

Some women married relatively late in life after fulfilling their obligations to their parents. Mary Delano, the daughter of Marshall and Lucy Jane Mooers Delano, married her lifelong friend Lot J. Emerson in 1900, when she was thirty-seven and he was thirty-nine. Mary waited until both of her parents were dead before marrying. She cared for her widowed mother for almost a decade in their house at Delano's Corners. Lot worked on his parents' farm just up East Maine Road. When Mary and Lot married, his mother had recently died, so Mary assumed the obligation of caring for her husband's father. She did not give up the house she had inherited, however; she and Lot lived at Delano's Corners and Mary went up the hill to Emerson's several times a day. Although Mary's life was more bounded by the claims of kin than Velma's was, it also had greater continuity; marriage was an extension, rather than a reversal, of the direction of her previous adult life. Many women who married after losing their parents were not so fortunate as Mary Delano, for no one was waiting for them to be free. They married to have a home, and their marriages were often unhappy.

For every single woman who married between the ages of thirty and forty-five, there was another who did not. The diary of Nellie Paisley demonstrates that a woman who did not marry might nonetheless occupy a central position in her family. Nellie Paisley was forty-five years old in 1891. She lived with her aged parents, William and Isabella Paisley, and her thirty-nine-year-old brother John, who was also unmarried. John managed the family farm on Mt. Ettrick. Nellie ran the household, playing much the same role that she would have done if she had been John's wife rather than his sister. In February 1891, John married Grace Howard, a twenty-seven-year-old dressmaker from West Chenango. This event might have threatened Nellie's position in the household, but as things worked out it did not. Nellie and Grace divided the work: Grace took over the indoor labor, such as sewing and cooking, which she enjoyed, and Nellie did the outdoor labor, such as poultry-raising, which she preferred. The sisters—for so people would have called them—papered and painted the house and furnished it with the things Grace had brought with her. Nellie took as much pleasure in the refurbishing as Grace did. In her first months in the Paisley household, then, Grace made a place for herself without usurping Nellie's place.

On 17 November 1891, Grace gave birth to a daughter. Nellie's diary reads: "Grace did not feel good. She was sick in the night. Dr. came half past two, got here just after baby was born. Did not go to bed—got the washing out and got dinner." Nellie assisted at the birth of her niece and took care of the new mother and child. On Thanksgiving day, she "washed and dressed baby for the first time." Grace's maternity did not displace Nellie any more than her marrying into the family did. Two years later, Grace died after giving birth to a second daughter. Nellie raised the two girls as if they were her own.

When William and Isabella Paisley died, Nellie was able to go on living with her brother and nieces on the family farm. Single women who had no brothers at home were not so fortunate. The deaths of their parents created a crisis in their lives of the same magnitude as widowhood did for married women, for they had to find a new home while they mourned the people whose lives had so strongly shaped their own. The most fortunate were able to join the household of a married brother or sister, where they played the role of aunt in a young family. Others went to live with an aged aunt or uncle, where they played a role very similar to the one they had played in their parents' household. Farmers who remained single throughout their lives often had a single kinswoman keep house for them. For example, Thomas Marean shared his household with his older unmarried sister, Esther; when she died, his unmarried grandniece, Cora A. Dayton, took her place.

Women like Cora Dayton exchanged their work in the household and on the farm for a home. They were more fortunate than those who made a similar arrangement with nonrelatives, for kinship gave them a claim on the people with whom they lived in sickness as in health and they were included in the household's social as well as work activities. Yet single women's lives were often disrupted by changes in the families with whom they lived. Women who resided with kin might be passed from one household to another, depending on where they could be most useful. As Louise Gates Gunsalus put it, single women in a family "were just handy, and otherwise a burden."

It was these older single women, who were no longer daughters but had not become wives, who were commonly regarded as "old maids" in the Nanticoke Valley. Harriet E. Tucker's characterization of them as "cross, whimsical, queer" typifies the general attitude.[6] Lala Ketchum defended old maids against such calumnies. The terms of her defense demonstrate that the problems single women faced were based on the combination of their gender with their marital status. During the years of uncertainty about when she and her intended husband would be able to marry, Lala wrote to Henry Marean: "If anything should happen to prevent our union (may the God above forbid though) I am positive I shall never marry, but shall be what is commonly called an old maid" (28 April 1863). This was little more than a way of declaring the true and constant nature of her love. Henry evidently objected, for in a later letter Lala explained: "No, I don't detest all 'old maids,' neither do I fear of being one, but if I am I promise you, I will be a good one not one of the meddlesome kind. A woman no need to be sneered at just because she is single, and I think some of the best and most womanly women I ever saw are unmarried" (undated, 1863). To be womanly, in Lala's eyes, meant to care for others. Yet it was precisely this womanly behavior that made single women vulnerable to the charge of being meddlesome. Single women were expected to help out with the family affairs of their relatives, friends, and employers; there was almost no way they could escape intimate involvement in other people's lives. At the same time, they had no realm of legitimate action of their own and no clearly defined position in the households in which they lived. If they overstepped the boundaries of what others regarded as their proper role, or even so much as exercised their own judgment or expressed their own opinion, they could be seen as interfering where they had no right to do so. If they lived with relatives they might have a firmer basis for involvement than if they lived with nonkin, but jealousy might make their actions more suspect as well. No matter where they found a home, single women occupied a position full of contradictions.

The situation of single women in the Nanticoke Valley highlights the significance of familial definitions of women's roles as well as the centrality of marriage to the normative female life course. Unmarried women were an anomaly in the community; without husbands

6. Harriet E. Tucker's rhymed description of Maine village closes with these lines:

Of old maids, we have some, let me whisper in your ear,
They're just as they are everywhere, cross, whimsical, queer.
Of old bachelors, likewise, we have our full share,
Though to mention their names I never would dare.
And last though not least, henceforth you will know it,
Maine is possessed of a remarkable poet.

Tucker herself was thirty-six and unmarried when she recited these verses for the Good Templars' Lodge.

and children of their own, they did not really belong anywhere. At the same time, they were an indispensable institution; single women took special responsibility for the care of the elderly and the young. Remaining single did not enable women to achieve autonomy as long as they remained in the rural community; unmarried women's family relationships controlled their lives just as strongly as other women's marriages controlled theirs. On the other hand, single women's family experience was often as broad and rich as that of their married sisters.

Deserted Wives

Not all marriages lasted "till death do us part." Conflicts between husbands and wives sometimes led to estrangement and separation. Divorce was possible only when one spouse had flagrantly transgressed the laws of marriage, for example by leaving a spouse to live openly with someone else. Although during the late nineteenth century a few Nanticoke Valley residents who had been deserted by their spouses took legal action to terminate their marriages, many more simply lived alone for the rest of their lives. Separation was much more common than divorce. So, too, temporary or partial estrangement was more common than permanent or total separation. Sometimes a couple continued to share a household and farm without sharing a bed or even speaking to each other for many years. Within certain broad limits, the preservation of families was the supreme value in local society.

People customarily appealed to their kin for support when their marriages broke down. Women who grew up in the Nanticoke Valley might look to their families for concrete as well as symbolic support in case of serious disagreement with their husbands, although people did not always side with their kin. The claims of kinship were not unconditional; at least in principle they were subordinated to accepted universalistic moral standards. Pressure from kin, in fact, helped to enforce marital duties on individuals. A woman unfaithful to her husband might be condemned just as harshly by her relatives as by others—or perhaps even more harshly, for her family might fear the damage to their own reputation that appearing to condone her behavior would invoke. Nor did sympathy within families always flow along gender lines. Although women might be expected to understand one another's predicaments and men to uphold one another's prerogatives, people were often critical of the conduct of relatives of their own sex. However, an abused wife could appeal to her kin without publicly disclosing the details of her situation. If her family backed her up, she could separate from her husband without fear of censure from the community. A woman who left her husband under such circumstances was generally regarded as justified; people assumed she would not take so disruptive a step unless her situation was impossible. Kin provided both moral and material support to women seeking to escape intolerable marriages.

Some marriages were regarded as failures even though the couple never separated. George Riley's diary describes the funeral of "one of our old and esteemed neighbors" as an especially sad event, "perticular So on account of the circumstances attending hur Sickness and death if being as reported so ill treated by hur husband ever since hur marriage that life had become a burden and she longed for death to come and relieve hur of hur troubles" (4 July 1881). This woman, "once the fairest of hur sex," had become a figure of pity among her neighbors. She never appealed to her friends for help, although she would have received their support had she asked for it. Nanticoke Valley residents were willing to intervene in marital conflicts, but only when the wife asked them to do so. This woman did not desert her husband; she waited for death to release her. Her predicament was no secret, but the sympathy that circulated at her funeral did not help her while she lived.

Patterns of marital breakdown reveal the conflicts that occurred in many marriages. Family problems were often attributed to alcohol. Residents regarded drinking as an almost exclusively masculine vice, and women and children as its victims. Not only did excessive drinking waste money and time, leading to neglected families and slovenly farms, but it was commonly understood to increase the danger of wife beating. Some women complained that their husbands did not allow them to spend money and appropriated the small sums they were able to earn. Women also complained that their husbands confined them to the farmstead and did not permit them to visit the neighbors or attend social gatherings. Isolation made it difficult for a troubled woman to seek help. If a man refused to allow his wife to visit her kin, people suspected that something was terribly wrong in the marriage, for this denial was a serious transgression of local norms. Women and men alike commonly considered all these problems as the result of an excessive exercise of masculine authority.

Marriages were most likely to break down either within the first year or after the children were grown. Timothy S. McGowan Wheaton and Olive Emmeline Sanford McCleary separated a few months after their wedding, but were reconciled the next year. Their difficulties arose over Timothy's relationship with his wife's children by her previous marriage. When they married, he was eighteen, and his wife was twenty-eight and newly widowed; her daughters Lucy and Addie were six and three years old. Timothy and "Em" (as he called her) had not been married long when Timothy wrote in his diary: "Dear wife—me and your children can't live together any longer, you know yourself." Timothy copied a letter he was writing into the back of his 1868 diary: "To whom it may concern—I am about to bid you all good bye. All I have to say is that I have got tired of living   two children who is too nasty to live   I could live if it was not for those children   But to live with them any longer I can not stand it   So I will not stay any longer than this week." Timothy loved his wife deeply, writing an elegy "In memory of one most dear to me; I shall always think of her till my last days, and then it will be hard for me to give her up." But he was unprepared to become part of an established family.

During the period that Timothy and Emmeline were separated, he was often melancholy. One meditation written in the back of the 1868 diary expresses his loneliness:

> As I sat me down to think, I thought that I would write as I feel. I feel as if I had not a friend in the world. I feel like an outcast. Who cares for me, who would ask me in out of the bitter cold nights, who would speak a kind word to me when the winds would blow this hurricane and me a poor outcast shivering with cold? No friends to think of me as they used to in childhood day   I thought that I would be a happy man someday. But that cheariest hope has passed me like a dream. There is no more happy days for me. I have not a friend to ask advice from.

Timothy drafted letters asking his wife to take him back, and they were reunited in 1869.

The birth of Timothy and Emmeline's son sealed their reconciliation. Six months after the child's birth, Timothy wrote:

> To whom by chance may read this—This day has been a dark and gloomy day to me. I have not a friend in this wide world, alas not one. I work by day and by night in order to be a noble and upright honest and industrious man. But oh, to do it and live the life that I live is harder than I can bear. Twice I have wished that I had not been born. But such is my lot and I must bear it. It is not for ever

that I have to live. . . . If it were not for my little Son I would leave for parts unknown to any one . . . the love one has for your first and only child! I went to him to kiss him for the last time. But he looked up to me, so innocent, and I will not and could not leave, with his bright eyes and little dimpley hands and golden hair . . . So I will yield (17 April 1870).

Timothy and Emmeline had a daughter two years later, and he never again considered leaving his family. His difficulties with his wife's daughters continued throughout his life, but his commitment to the family he had formed with his wife outweighed his antagonism to her children.

The marriage of John and Rosella Leadbetter Benton broke down during John's protracted residence in "the Far West." John may have left to explore the profitability of farming and land speculation in Kansas, but his prolonged absence amounted to a separation from his wife. In 1881, when John had returned to the Nanticoke Valley, his sister Harriet wrote the Bentons she was glad to hear "that John come back to you all once more." "I hope, John," she admonished her brother, "that you will think it best to stay there the rest of your life . . . or if you think it best to go again to Kansas take your wife with you if she is able to go."[7] But John Benton did not heed his sister's advice. He returned to Kansas the next summer and remained in the West until 1897. Letters from Benton's friends and business agents in the West confirm that John had taken a special interest in a married woman. She had left her husband but was involved in a long series of lawsuits about the family property; Benton himself was named as a corespondent in one of them. Stories passed down in the Benton family say that the two were living together and that Leroy and Charles went West in an attempt to break up the relationship. John Benton returned to Maine only when drought made it impossible for him to remain on his western farm. Rosella Benton spent a total of twenty-one years living without her husband. Although Leroy supported her as he would have done had she been widowed, they all knew that John's absence was the result of deliberate choice. Her descendants recall her as "an embittered woman."

As these examples suggest, the customary form that marital breakdown took was the husband's desertion of his wife. Although a few women sought refuge from violent husbands with their relatives, many more men simply left the community. Whether they went to

7. Harriet L. Plumb to Brother and Sister Benton, 18 June 1881; Benton Family Papers.

Kansas like John Benton or to an upstate New York lumber camp like Timothy Wheaton, men had the freedom of movement and independence of action that allowed them to escape from unhappy marriages. Women, with fewer options, generally remained in broken marriages unless and until their husbands deserted them; then they assumed the position occupied by widows in the community.

Widows

A woman's life was transformed when her husband died, for widowhood usually brought dependence. This sudden shift in status was more significant for older women than the gradual diminution of capacities accompanying the aging process. In the Nanticoke Valley, most widows joined the households of their married children. Older women generally knew where they would go when their husbands died well in advance of the event. Even if a man's will did not specify which child was supposed to provide the widow with a home, aging parents and adult children had a clear understanding of their mutual obligations. In most cases, the two generations were actively involved in mutual aid even when they lived in separate households. The disruption that a change of residence entailed was minimized if the two generations already shared a house.

Although older women were less likely to maintain their own households than older men were, they were also less likely to live alone. If from one point of view women's residence with relatives signifies their lack of control over economic resources, from another it represents their relatively greater access to kin. Older men retained the dignity and position that flowed from the ownership of property and residential independence, but older women held an equally strong place in the kinship system.

Women shaped the kinship system to meet their needs as they defined them. Inheritance practices that favored sons over daughters presumed that widows would live with sons, for men inherited the obligation to support their mothers at the same time that they inherited the family farm. But some widows lived with their adult daughters rather than with their married sons. Over time, there was a gradual shift in the gender relationship between married couples and the aging parents who shared their households. In 1855, 61 percent of coresident parents were related to the male head of household. In 1880, as many households included the wife's parent(s) as the husband's. By 1900, 58 percent of coresident parents were related to the wife; many widowed women chose to live with their daughters. The obligation to provide personal care to the elderly devolved disproportionately on women, and it was incumbent on both older people's own daughters and their sons' wives to care for them.[8]

The Riley family history exemplifies the interaction between inheritance patterns and a widow's preferences. Lucy Ann Riley moved next door to her daughter's household a year after her son Judson brought his wife home. When Ida and Bert moved to Binghamton two years later, Lucy Ann moved back in with Judson and Lillie; after all, she still owned half of the house and farm. But by 1900 she had gone to Binghamton to live with her daughter. Lucy Ann preferred living with Ida even when she had to leave the Nanticoke Valley to do so.

When sons inherited land but daughters assumed the obligation of caring for their widowed mothers, gender inequalities in intergenerational relations were magnified. But neither mothers nor daughters seemed to think of it this way. Daughters sometimes resented having to care for aged fathers when the family property went to their brothers, but they never voiced such complaints about their mothers, perhaps because they recognized that women had no control over decisions involving property. Indeed, the absence of a property relationship between mothers and daughters may have simplified their interaction. Some older women may have chosen to live with daughters rather than sons in order to neutralize the power their sons might exercise over them; it must have been troubling to mothers to assume a position subordinate to their sons after their husbands died. Generational relationships between mothers and daughters were not complicated by gender inequalities as relationships between mothers and sons were. This preference for living with daughters balanced the predisposition for coresidence between mothers and sons that property arrangements created.

Women without husbands sustained significant ties to their mothers, aunts, sisters, daughters, nieces, and granddaughters. At the

8. Historical demographers have observed that in agricultural communities intergenerational coresidence is most common between parents and sons, while in urban communities it is most common between parents and daughters. Most account for this difference by explaining that it is sons who inherit land but daughters who provide care for the elderly; in urban communities where inheritance is not a factor, daughters will assume the burden of providing a home for their parents. However, this explanation does not account for the shift over time in the Nanticoke Valley. For the conventional explanation, see Dorrian Apple Sweetser, "The Effect of Industrialization on Intergenerational Solidarity," *Rural Sociology* 31 (1966): 156–70, and Daniel Scott Smith, "Historical Changes in the Household Structure of the Elderly in Developed Countries," in *Aging: Stability and Change in the Family,* ed. Robert W. Fogel, Elaine Hatfield, Sara B. Kiesler, and Ethel Shamas (New York: Academic Press, 1981), 91–114.

same time, they did not create a "female family" in isolation from their fathers, uncles, brothers, sons, nephews, and grandsons.[9] Women not only maintained lifelong links with their own kinsmen, but they also forged strong ties with the men their kinswomen married. While the masculine property system followed lines of descent, the kinship system women maintained encompassed affiliation as well. Fathers may have thought of daughters as marrying out of the family, but women thought of themselves as marrying into other families and, equally important, they thought of men as marrying into their own. Women's version of kinship was inclusive rather than exclusive in terms of gender. Women claimed their sisters' husbands as their brothers and their daughters' husbands as their sons. The inclusive and gender-balanced character of the kinship system becomes especially visible in the experiences of women without husbands, perhaps because it was so vital to the quality of their lives.

9. This phrase was coined by Marilyn Ferris Motz, who studied women's relationships with their female kin. This bias in the study of nineteenth-century kinship is currently being corrected by Annette Atkins, who is doing research on brother-sister ties; Annette Atkins, "Brothers, Sisters, and Shared Spheres," paper presented to the Pacific Coast Branch of the American Historical Association, San Francisco, August 1988.

PART III

WOMEN'S WORK ON FAMILY FARMS

CHAPTER SIX

The Gender Division of Labor

She helped me hay it as good as a man.
—George W. Riley, Diary, 1875

On 21 July 1875, George Riley wrote in his diary that his wife "helped me hay it as good as a man," a phrase epitomizing George's attitude toward Lucy Ann's participation in the work of the farm. It assumes a clear division of labor by sex: haying was defined in principle as men's work. But it also asserts that the allocation of tasks between women and men was flexible: in practice, women and men stepped out of their conventional work roles when the good of the farm seemed to require them to do so. On that summer day, George had been unable to hire extra male help, so Lucy Ann put aside her usual work to join him in the fields, raking and turning the hay, loading it onto the wagon, and drawing it into the barn. In her husband's eyes, she had done that work "as good as a man"; the standard was masculine, but Lucy Ann had attained it. The opposite phrase—"she done a good job, for a woman"—would have diminished her achievement by maintaining a double standard that presumes that women's labor is generally inferior to men's. George Riley's comment, in contrast, is entirely positive. While it assumes a division of labor based on sex, it recognizes that women are fully capable of performing tasks generally assigned to men, even those requiring substantial strength and skill. George Riley recorded the event because he found it remarkable, but his diary is filled with notations of instances when he and Lucy Ann worked together. The labor women performed on family farms was so integral to the agricultural economy that their husbands and fathers had to recognize its reality and significance.

How did Lucy Ann feel about her labor in the hayfield? Did she offer to do it, or did her husband ask her? Did she resent having to do "a man's work," or did she take pride in her skill and stamina? Without Lucy Ann Riley's record of her own life and labor, it is impossible to compare her perspective with that of her husband. But other Nanticoke Valley women mentioned haying in their diaries. Helen Davis Benton participated in haying both in her youth and as an adult. When she was nineteen, she wrote: "I got breakfast and did up the dishes and then went to washing, I had quite a large washing. I had to help Pa with his haying. At night I was tired" (17 July 1874). The language suggests that Helen regarded haying as a task that properly belonged to men; she referred to "his," not "our," haying. It also suggests that Helen did not have any choice about whether or not to help her father. George Davis did not seem to consider that she had already done the laundry before making this extra demand on her time and energy. Fifteen years later, Helen "went down and raked a while" in the afternoon (11 July 1891). She recorded the event primarily because it was the first time she had used the new rake her husband Leroy Benton had bought the day before. The task itself was quite unremarkable to her, for Helen had "gone down and helped rake" almost every other day of haying season for the previous two summers. Helen did not regard this task as men's work; she wrote neither that she "helped" with the haying nor that she "had" to do it. That evening, she wrote simply: "it tired me dreadfully." The task was not gendered; she spoke of it, as she did of most other tasks, in terms of the time and energy it required.

Interpreting the meaning of women's work on family farms involves placing particular tasks such as raking hay both within the context of the rest of women's labor and in relation to the labor performed by men. Did Helen Davis Benton find haying any more tiring than washing? Did she prefer working outdoors? How often did Helen and Leroy work together, and how did Helen's participation in such crucial farm tasks as haying affect her relationship with her husband? Equally important, did Leroy share the domestic tasks? The relations into which women and men enter through their labor constitute a crucial dimension of the gender system.

The fact that women in the Nanticoke Valley worked in fields and barns, as well as in houses and gardens, clearly contradicts contemporary assertions that American farm women were exempt from field work. Nineteenth-century observers regarded women's supposed absence from the fields as a sign that white American women enjoyed a status superior to that of African American or European peasant women, who were expected to work alongside men. Alexis de Tocqueville regarded this rural gender division of labor as integral to the entire system of gender distinctions in American society:

> In no country has such constant care been taken as in America to trace two clearly distinct lines of action for the two sexes and to make them keep pace one with the other, but in two pathways that are always different. American women never manage the outward concerns of the family or conduct a business or take part in political life; nor are they, on the other hand, ever compelled to perform the rough labor of the fields or to make any of those laborious efforts which demand the exertion of physical strength. No families are so poor as to form an exception to this rule. If, on the one hand, an American woman cannot escape from the quiet circle of domestic employments, she is never forced, on the other, to go beyond it.[1]

Alexis de Tocqueville's limited experience in rural America made his description factually inaccurate, but he correctly understood that the division of labor was connected with other aspects of gender relations.

The fact that farm women worked in the fields does not demonstrate the opposite of de Tocqueville's contention, that because women's work was integral to family farming rural women necessarily enjoyed a higher status within the family or a broader field of action in civil society than women who were confined to "the quiet circle of domestic employments." Some twentieth-century historians of women initially asserted that since rural women's work was recognized as essential to the survival of their families women must have enjoyed equal power in family decision making. Most have acknowledged, however, that this formulation oversimplified the complex and contradictory character of gender relations.[2] The assumption that the distribution of power within the family was based on each person's relative contribution to the family income fails to consider the possibility that patterns of authority within families determined the allocation of tasks among family members. Work and authority relations shaped each other dialectically within the gender system. Hierarchies

1. Alexis de Tocqueville, *Democracy in America*, trans. Henry Reeve and Francis Bowen (New York: Random House, 1945), 2:223. This observation was originally published in 1840.
2. For an early statement of this view and its modifications over time, see the successive editions of Mary P. Ryan, *Womanhood in America from Colonial Times to the Present* (New York: Franklin Watts, 1975, 1979, 1983), especially chap. 1.

of gender affected perceptions of the value of labor as well; work might be devalued simply because women customarily performed it.

Finally, farm people's notions of value were affected by the transition to capitalism in the countryside during the nineteenth century. Capitalist ideology and practice challenged traditional rural conceptions of the value of labor and habits of interdependence. But farm families did not passively adopt the values of the market; many opposed the changes capitalism brought to social life.[3] Customary notions of value provided the basis for resistance to capitalist conceptions, not only in the marketplace but also within the family; indeed, farm people's resistance to capitalist relations may have been stronger in the household and neighborhood than it was in the larger community. This resistance had significant implications for gender relations as well. Not only did farm people retain a notion of the value of various types of labor, but they also espoused values of mutuality that shaped relationships between women and men. Noncapitalist conceptions of the usefulness of work, coupled with traditional practices of variability, flexibility, and integration in the performance of labor, provided a basis for continued interdependence in the working lives of women and men.

"A farmer's wife . . . is a laboring drudge"

In an article subtitled "The Hardships of Farmers' Wives," included in the 1862 report of the U.S. commissioner of agriculture, Dr. W. W. Hall asserted: "In plain language, in the civilization of the latter half of the nineteenth century, a farmer's wife, as a too general rule, is a laboring drudge." Hall judged the condition of farm women according to his middle-class conception of woman's proper place and found it wanting. While praising the "affectionate and steady interest, the laudable pride, and the self-denying devotion which wives have for the comfort, prosperity, and respectability of their husbands and children," he lamented the "melancholy and undeniable fact that, in millions of cases," women's loving self-sacrifice "fails to be recognized or appreciated by the very men who are the incessant objects of these high, heroic virtues." In his opinion, "It is perhaps safe to say, that on three farms out of four the wife works harder, endures more,

3. The most comprehensive recent account of resistance to the rise of capitalism in the countryside is Steven Hahn and Jonathan Prude, eds., *The Countryside in the Age of Capitalist Transformation: Essays in the Social History of Rural America* (Chapel Hill: University of North Carolina Press, 1985).

than any other on the place; more than the husband, more than the 'farm-hand,' more than the 'hired help' of the kitchen." "Many a farmer's wife is literally worked to death in an inadvertent manner from want of reflection or consideration on the part of the husband," he concluded.[4]

Hall was not solely concerned with rural women's burden of physical labor; indeed, he entirely ignored the work farm women did outside the house. He did not mention milking and doing barn chores or participating in haying and harvest, even as examples of what ought not to be expected of women. He criticized household arrangements that forced women to go outside to fetch water, wood, and vegetables, but he seems more concerned with the sudden changes of temperature that going outdoors involved than with the physical strain of carrying heavy buckets. Hall was most alarmed by what he saw as the prevalence of insanity among farmers' wives and daughters. Mental depression and disturbance, in his view, resulted from the lack of consideration farm women received from the men in their families, coupled with women's physiological vulnerability to hysterical disorders.

Hall focused on the position women occupied in relation to their husbands, their children, and the hired help. In his view, the fundamental problem was that farm women were treated disrespectfully. "Many a farmer speaks to his wife habitually in terms more imperious, impatient, and petulant than he would use to the scullion of the kitchen or to his hired man." Men mistreated their wives through their actions as well as with words, by sins of omission as well as commission. Hall's litany included neglecting to repair the house, keep the woodshed well stocked, or procure cheap but invaluable little domestic conveniences; making no allowances for the demands of infants and sick children that might disturb a woman's rest; finding fault with her for the slight disorder that might arise from unavoidable accidents in the kitchen. "It is in such ways as these . . . that the farmer's wife has her whole existence poisoned by those daily tortures which come from her husband's thoughtlessness, inconsideration, hard nature, or downright stupidity."[5]

Men's disrespectful behavior undermined women's position in the household: "The man is naturally the ruling spirit of the household, and if he fails to show to his wife, on all occasions, that tenderness, affection, and respect, which is her just due, it is instantly noted on

4. Dr. W. W. Hall, "The Health of Farmers' Families," in *The Report of the Commissioner of Agriculture for the Year 1862* (Washington, D.C.: U.S. Government Printing Office, 1863), 462–63, 469.
5. Hall, "Health," 463, 465.

the part of menials, and children too, and they very easily glide into the same vice, and interpret it as an encouragement to slight her authority, to undervalue her judgment, and to lower that high standard of respect which of right belongs to her."[6] The primary cause of the hardships farm women faced, then, was not simple overwork but rather lack of respect and power. Hall's remedy for this problem was the clear separation between the household, over which the wife should be given full authority, and the operations of the farm, which the man controlled.[7]

At the same time, it was up to the man to grant authority to his wife; he delegated power to her and defined the limits of her domain. Hall cautioned the farmer that failing to act respectfully toward his wife and undermining her domestic authority would interfere with the orderly operation of the farm: "And as the wife has the servants and children always about her, and is under the necessity of giving hourly instructions, the want of fidelity and promptness to these is sufficient to derange the whole household and utterly thwart that regularity and system, without which there is no domestic enjoyment, and but little thrift on the farm."[8] The difficulty Hall was wrestling with is inherent in all hierarchical family systems in which women are subordinated to men on the basis of gender but superordinate to children and servants on the basis of age and family membership; an excess of masculine authority can undermine other forms of domestic and economic order.[9]

Hall's list of positive injunctions to farmers concludes with the assertion that it is in a man's own best interest to treat his wife with due consideration.

> Let the farmer always remember that his wife's cheerful and hearty co-operation is essential to his success, and is really of as much value in attaining it, all things considered, as anything that he can do; and, as she is very certainly his superior in her moral nature, it legitimately follows that he should not only regard her as his equal in material matters, but should habitually accord to her that deference,

6. Hall, "Health," 463.

7. For this insight, I am indebted to Jody Seitz, "The Origins and Importance of Farm Women's Flexible Labor: Focus on Midwestern Dairy Farms," paper presented at the conference on American Farm Women in Historical Perspective, Madison, Wis., October 1986. Seitz concurs that such a separation did not exist on most nineteenth-century farms.

8. Hall, "Health," 463.

9. For a brilliant analysis of this dilemma as it was discussed in homilies on domestic relations in seventeenth-century England, see Susan Dwyer Amussen, *An Ordered Society: Gender and Class in Early Modern England* (Oxford: Basil Blackwell, 1988), 44–45.

that consideration, and that high respect which is of right her due, and which will never fail to impress upon the children and servants, who daily witness it, a dignity and an elevation of manner, and thought, and feeling, and deportment which will prove to all who see them that the wife is a lady, and the husband a man and a gentleman, and large pecuniary success, with a high moral position and wide social influence will be the almost certain results.

The same mix of material inducements and moral imperatives pervades his final exhortation:

Let the farmer feel that his wife is an equal partner on the farm, and as such is entitled to as high consideration as he claims for himself. He should have a jealous care for the "good name of the house." Let him feel that what degrades his wife degrades himself, that whatever weakens her authority weakens his own power of success, and that in the great struggle of life they must of necessity rise or fall together. But while he cherishes these views as a business matter, as a practical thing of profit and loss, let him make an effort in another direction, not considering his wife merely as his partner in business, but as the love of his youth, who having, in a perfect abandon of trustfulness, thrown herself into his strong arms to be guided, protected, and sustained through life's long journey, has claims on him for these stronger than any tie other than that which binds man to Divinity.[10]

Hall's convoluted attempt to persuade farmers that they and their wives had a common interest attests to the strength of cultural assumptions of gender difference. These assumptions undermine Hall's own argument; as soon as he turns from pecuniary to sentimental considerations, the notion of woman as equal partner is replaced by the image of woman as dependent bride.

Hall had to go to such rhetorical lengths to persuade farmers that their wives should be equal partners in the enterprise not only because he shared the dominant culture's assumption that men are the ruling parties in family relationships but also because the value of women's contribution to farm enterprises was not obvious within the terms of capitalist economics. Hall defined success as the achievement of security and social position through the accumulation of property, and he regarded profit and loss as the determining criteria of eco-

10. Hall, "Health," 469, 470.

nomic value. There is real confusion in his application of economic terms to matters of gender relations on family farms. This arose not only from Hall's desire to reconcile God and Mammon, which led him to shift back and forth between moral and monetary definitions of value, but also from the fact that the domestic labor to which Hall assumed women should restrict their efforts did not produce commodities for sale in the market. Hall was forced to argue that showing due consideration for his wife would increase a farmer's profits precisely because the farm's balance sheet did not always demonstrate that truth. The value of a wife's labor, as well as the cost of neglecting her welfare, was not evident from most farmers' system of reckoning, which took only the sale or exchange of commodities into account. In discussing this question, Hall assumed that men, rather than women, controlled the farm family's decisions about spending and that men did not recognize women's direct and indirect contributions to the family income. In Hall's analysis, the hardships of farmers' wives resulted in large part from their husbands' lack of understanding of the value of their work.

Hall's article exhibits the contradictions that defined the position of American farm women during the second half of the nineteenth century. It does not describe the actual lives of women on Nanticoke Valley farms; not only did few women have hired help in the household, but also, and more important, most farm women actively participated in income-producing labor. Hall's analysis, however, does express the dominant ideology with regard to women's work in mid-nineteenth-century American society. With its notional distinction between farm and household, enterprise and family, it applied the urban middle-class division of the world into masculine and feminine domains to rural conditions. In extending domestic ideology to rural society, Hall stumbled on an important truth: the gender division of labor was inextricably intertwined with relations of authority in farm families. Hall did not get it right, for he was unable to break free of the gendered assumptions of his middle-class model; from the image of the farm woman as laboring drudge, he moved to the image of the wife as downtrodden by her husband. Yet in a distorted fashion Hall recognized the connection between work and authority; even more dimly, he understood that both work and authority were related to prevailing economic conceptions of the value of labor and commodities.

Hall's analysis makes clear, regardless of his protests to the contrary, that the confinement of women to domestic labor, coupled with the adoption of a capitalist calculus of value, would result in the devaluation of women's work and the erosion of women's position in the family. The integration of gender and economic relations was especially transparent on family farms. The connections between the family and the enterprise that were carefully concealed in urban middle-class culture could not be hidden in rural agricultural communities. In the Nanticoke Valley, the family was the primary unit of both labor and property ownership, and relations of authority in work were, first and foremost, relations among husbands and wives, parents and children. Notions of gender and of value were not abstractions but were expressed and embodied in the concrete labor of women and men.

"Women must necessarily have some share in the work of life"

In the Nanticoke Valley, as in other rural communities, farm families organized their work according to a conventional division of labor between men and women. Work itself was gender marked; certain activities were regarded as the responsibility of men, and others as the responsibility of women. At the same time, women and men routinely coordinated their labor. Not only did husbands and wives synchronize their work on a daily basis, but farm processes often began in men's domain and culminated in women's; many farm products had to pass through women's hands before they could be used or sold. Norms of cooperation were designed to ensure both that work flowed smoothly and that no individual saw his or her interest as opposed to that of any other family member. All family members owed allegiance to "the good of the farm," which appeared to them as a matter of immediate and visible necessity. When circumstances seemed to require it, men and women crossed over the boundaries of gender to assist each other.

The pattern of work that had become customary in the valley by the mid-nineteenth century involved both separate and shared responsibilities for men and women. Here, as on most "yeoman" farms in the North and West, men were responsible for plowing and planting the fields, cultivating and harvesting the field crops, and preparing the hay and grain for use as animal and human food. Women were responsible for tending the vegetable garden, processing and preserving the year's supply of vegetables and fruits, and preparing meals. Men were responsible for the construction and maintenance of the house, barn, and outbuildings, for the provision of fuel for heat and cooking, and for the repair of farm and household equipment.

Ames family, c. 1911. (Front row, left to right) Hattie Ames Strong; Laura Deitz Ames (seated); Maggie Ames Audibert. (Middle row) Fred Ames; George Ames. (Back rows) Clarence Ames; Hiram Ames; Arthur Ames; Clayton Ames. Nanticoke Valley Historical Society, courtesy of Leigh and Dorothy Ames.

Johnson family, c. 1895. (Front to back, left to right) Eliza Whiting Ellis Johnson and George Johnson; their daughters Laura Irena Johnson and Alice Johnson Loomis; family friend William Bronk (seated); Eliza's brother John Ellis (leaning on porch). Nanticoke Valley Historical Society, courtesy of Leigh and Dorothy Ames.

Women were responsible for cleaning the house, tending the fires, and sewing, laundering, and mending the family's clothing and household textiles. While these operations divided fairly neatly into a masculine domain centered in the fields and forest and a feminine domain centered in the house, other operations brought women and men together in the barnyard. Men and women shared responsibility for caring for farm animals and processing their products. They did not simply divide the chores between them, although customarily men cared for the horses and women saw to the chickens. Nor did they engage only in occasional bouts of closely coordinated labor, as when men slaughtered livestock and cut up the meat while women preserved it in brine, made sausage, and rendered the fat. In the Nanticoke Valley, dairying involved husbands and wives in a significant amount of joint labor on a daily basis. Barn chores, milking, churning, and packing butter all were performed by women and men together and in various combinations; women and men had a common interest in this most essential farm operation.

The allocation of tasks between men and women was flexible. It varied from one family to another, and within families over time, depending on that mix of choice and necessity we call custom. In some families, women hoed corn and dug potatoes; in others, men cultivated the vegetable garden. Sometimes women did what was generally regarded as men's work because there weren't enough men in the household to complete the task and the family could not afford to hire labor. But other families seem to have departed from the conventional pattern simply as a matter of personal preference or family tradition. Responsibility for particular operations was divided more clearly and consistently than was the actual performance of tasks. Being responsible for the field crops did not mean that men did all the work involved; similarly, the fact that women were not responsible for field crops did not mean that it was regarded as inappropriate for them to work in the fields. No matter how strictly a family maintained the gender division of labor, all were willing to readjust in case of emergency—when frost jeopardized the winter vegetable supply, bugs took over the potato patch, or rain threatened the hay. On those occasions, all available hands would be pressed into service.

The allocation of tasks between women and men was most flexible in the dairy process, perhaps because dairying was conducted in a domain between the fields and the house and involved a myriad of time constraints. It was generally accepted that men cared for the cattle and did the barn chores, both men and women milked, and women skimmed the cream and churned the butter. In some families, however, women helped with the chores as well as milking; in others,

Pitcher twins taking milk to the Niles Creamery, Maine village, c. 1902. Nanticoke Valley Historical Society.

men did all the work in the barn and even churned. Just as women and men shared responsibility for the dairy, so they performed the tasks it involved in flexible and varied ways.

Two families that engaged in dairying on the same scale illustrate divergent patterns in their allocation of labor. The Bowers and the Gates families occupied a similar status in local society and shared roots in New England culture; furthermore, they lived within two miles of each other along the Nanticoke Creek and were related through intermarriage. Yet these two families conducted the dairy process very differently. According to the Bowers's grandson, Clement G. Bowers, Achsah Taylor Bowers

> used to have the proceeds of all poultry that was on the place and she would take care of it. She would market the eggs and make butter, used to take butter into Sisson's store [in Binghamton]. . . . She used to trade the butter off for yard goods to make dresses out of

and clothes for the entire family. The eggs would be shipped to New York and the local storekeepers would also take them.[11]

In the Bowers household, the wife was responsible for making and marketing the butter. In the Gates household the husband conducted the entire dairy operation himself. When Frederick Taylor Gates spent several summers on his grandfather's farm during the Civil War, he observed Louis's daily routine.

> He rose at the first streak of day, skimmed the dairy milk, did the churning, worked the butter, took a nap of an hour after lunch . . . repeated the milking at night, went to bed early and was contented with his monotonous life. . . . His "money crop" and main dependence was the dairy. He made a fancy article of butter and himself shipped it to New York in tubs usually as soon as made, and as prices went, always secured a high figure. . . . He always expected and got a little more for his butter than his neighbors, and making it himself was gratified to get a price nearly or quite equal to the "Orange County Pail," then in the New York market the fancy article.[12]

To their descendants, the divergent arrangements in the Bowers and Gates families seemed appropriate in terms of gender and economically advantageous.

Men's and women's joint responsibility for the dairy is documented by a "manual for butter makers" published in 1871 in Whitney's Point, the commercial village just a half-mile northeast of the town of Nanticoke. John P. Corbin's *Practical Hints on Dairying*, published to advertise the "Eureka butter worker" Corbin had patented, included a discussion of the economics of "the dairy business" and a comprehensive description of the "art of butter making" as well. Throughout the seventy-seven-page text, Corbin assumed that both women and men performed the work of the dairy. In the preface, Corbin assured his readers that the information contained in the manual was based on his own practical experience and "observations made in visiting many of the most noted dairymen" in the region, referring to dairy farmers in the masculine gender, but he went right on to refer to butter makers in the feminine gender in his description of the advantages of the Eureka butter worker: "With it, any dairy-woman can wash, salt, and work hard butter, easily, expeditiously, and perfectly."

11. Clement G. Bowers, interview by Robert J. Spencer, 7.
12. Frederick Taylor Gates, *Our American Ancestry* (Montclair, N.J.: J. J. Little and Ives, 1928), 78, 71–72.

Corbin spoke of "dairymen" and "dairywomen" almost interchange-ably, sometimes separately and sometimes together, and he spoke of butter making as a "family" task. According to the custom of the country, dairying involved both women and men.[13]

Corbin's description of the dairy process is not highly gender marked. There are some suggestions that Corbin followed tradition in seeing the care of livestock as a masculine responsibility, milking as a shared activity, and butter making as a feminine task. Corbin as-sumed that in some families women had primary responsibility for processing—skimming the milk, churning the cream, and washing, salting, and packing the butter. Descriptions of the advantages of the Eureka butter worker emphasize that it is adapted to women's physi-cal capacities, "a good and convenient butter worker, one that any dairywoman can use easily." Working butter was "an operation re-quiring much skill to do it properly, and great strength of muscle if done with a hand ladle, also much time." The Eureka, Corbin prom-ised, would yield high-quality butter in less time and with less expen-diture of physical effort than working butter by hand; this ease was of special importance to women, whose labors would be considerably lightened. When Corbin addressed his remarks specifically to men, he did so in order to remind them of the work that women per-formed and to convince them of the need for such labor-saving de-vices as the butter worker.

> Is it politic for men to buy all labor-savers for their outdoor work, while their wives have to toil away amid the multiplicity of household cares and duties of the dairy-room, working butter with an old-fashioned hand ladle and fatiguing way of lifting, holding and drain-ing the butter-bowl?
>
> Men ought to consider more how many steps women are obliged to take to execute the many and fatiguing labors that necessarily have to be performed daily about dairy work; also amid the thou-sands of duties of housekeeping. The daily duties of dairy women are of a kind that require great physical strength and power of en-durance, also demand watchfulness, with perseverance and prompt and decided action, especially in hot weather; therefore every dairy should be supplied with good and practical implements for each and

13. John P. Corbin, *Practical Hints on Dairying, or, Manual for Butter Makers* (Whitney's Point, N.Y., 1891), 3, 10, 32. Corbin belonged to the American Dairymen's Association and attended its convention in Utica, N.Y., in 1871. This organization devoted to agri-cultural improvement was composed entirely of men; evidently Corbin adopted the masculine term from this group. That makes it all the more notable that Corbin bal-anced it by the term "dairywoman," which the organization did not use.

every operation in the manufacture of butter, for the use of them is one source of its profits, also of the health, comfort, and happiness of dairy women. In these days of scarcity of good help and high prices of butter, there is an unlimited demand for good Butter Workers, those that women or any person of judgment can use to advantage, by saving time and strength, also by improving the quality of butter, thereby making money by their use, besides saving broken down constitutions. All butter makers experience more or less aches and pains caused by working butter. . . .

Many good butter makers have been obliged to abandon dairying, for the lack of strength to work the butter, and all greatly feel the need of something to alleviate and facilitate this heavy and fatiguing labor. The health and lives of more women have been sacrificed by working butter than by all other duties of the dairy; therefore, a simple, practical Butter Worker has long been desired and much needed in every dairy. . . . the Eureka supplies the great desideratum (the universal want). . . . Every dairyman and dairywoman that we have yet heard from, who has tried one of these workers, testifies to its worth and appreciates its merits.

This passage assumes that while the task of butter making is done by both women and men and the advantages of the Eureka butter worker are universal, men whose wives and daughters work the butter need to be told how much time and energy the task involves and persuaded that it will be profitable to invest in improved tools.[14]

It was in this context that Corbin alluded directly to the article "The Hardships of Farmers' Wives" from the 1862 report of the U.S. commissioner of agriculture. In a direct echo of Dr. W. W. Hall's remarks, Corbin contended:

> It is perhaps safe to say, that on nine-tenths of our dairy farms, the WIFE works HARDER, and has more to endure, than even the hired help in the kitchen, or dairy room, or any other person on the premises. This is perhaps from want of reflection on the part of the husband, who ought to have more consideration how many steps she has to take, and how unremitting are her labors.
>
> Hundreds, and thousands of dollars are annually invested in farm machinery, but scarcely anything to facilitate the labors in the Dairy room; although liberality in dairy implements, is a source of its prof-

14. Corbin, *Dairying*, 3, 18, 8, 61–62.

its, and also of the health, comfort, and happiness of the Dairy-woman.

Corbin's appropriation of Hall's language transforms its meaning. Rather than bemoaning the burden of women's work and struggling to point out its moral significance and its indirect monetary value as Hall does, Corbin celebrates women's skills and their direct contribution to the farm family income. His exhortation to men to invest in improved tools to lighten women's labor is rooted in the rural tradition of women's work, not in urban middle-class notions of feminine domesticity. His final verses express the distinctive perspective of farm people on the organization of work:

> Every dairyman should consider,
> That many hours of toil,
> 'Tis woman's lot to bear,
> And should grant to her what'ere he canst,
> And all her labors share.[15]

Shared responsibility for the dairy was both a value that Corbin advocated and a custom that farm families practiced in the Nanticoke Valley.

The exchange of roles between women and men was more common in the manufacture of dairy products than it was in most other types of farm and household labor. The allocation of particular tasks changed from day to day, depending on what else had to be done; from season to season, depending on the amount of milk being produced; and from year to year, depending on the family's available labor supply. Husbands and wives took over each other's usual tasks in the dairy when either was ill, away, or too busy to perform them. This flexibility resulted in part from the many built-in temporal constraints the dairy process involved. As Corbin put it in *Practical Hints on Dairying*: "To make dairying a successful enterprise . . . there are a great many little items and points that are very essential. . . . Milk and cream should be properly cared for, properly churned and in due time; the butter salted and worked in a proper manner, also the proper time. . . . It often happens than only one hour of negligence or delay in taking care of milk or cream, churning or working the butter, will greatly deteriorate the quality of the butter."[16] Because of

15. Corbin, *Dairying*, 64, 66.
16. Corbin, *Dairying*, 8.

the distinctive rhythm of work in dairying, too, only family labor could be relied on.[17]

Women and men who lived and worked on farms that produced butter for the market engaged in a substantial amount of joint and closely coordinated labor. Because women participated in milking and churning, the division of labor by gender on local farms did not correspond with the difference between subsistence and market-oriented production. Women did not simply provide services and produce goods such as food and clothing while men performed income-producing work; women were also actively involved in the most highly valued form of farm labor. In the Nanticoke Valley, women's work was as integral to the earning of farm income as it was to the provision of family subsistence. Dairying was simultaneously the most flexible of farm tasks and the most crucially important to the farm economy; women and men were most equal in the very operation that was most important to the long-term welfare of family farming.

The gender division of labor in the Nanticoke Valley was common in other family farming regions, and American farm women often participated in income-producing labor. The article "The Industrial Education of Women" included in the 1871 report of the U.S. commissioner of agriculture took a more realistic view of women's work on farms than Dr. Hall had done nine years before. The article begins with the assertion:

As sensible beings, we must take facts as we find them. . . . It is idle to indulge in sentiment and deplore the necessity of rural work for

17. Dairy farmers have always relied more on family labor and used less hired labor than other types of farmers. Dairy farming is a prime example of the type of commodity production that is still conducted on family farms even in an advanced capitalist economy. Mann and Dickinson argue that family farming persists when production time exceeds labor time; in concrete terms, there is a lot of waiting between morning and evening milking and processing tasks must be performed at irregular hours. This problem depresses the rate of profit and creates inefficiencies in the use of capital such that there is no incentive for capitalist producers employing wage labor to enter the operation. Susan A. Mann and James M. Dickinson, "Obstacles to the Development of a Capitalist Agriculture," *Journal of Peasant Studies* 5 (1978): 466–81. Furthermore, family farmers engaged in simple commodity production evaluate their enterprises differently than do capitalist investors, focusing on the long-term accumulation and intergenerational transmission of property. Dairy farmers cannot afford to hire barn labor in the same way that they can the more intensive harvest labor. Nor can hired help with no stake in the family enterprise be counted on to work at the hours and with the care necessary for success. For discussion of these aspects of dairy farming in the twentieth century, see Sarah Elbert, "Women and Dairy Farms: A Century of Change," paper presented at the conference on American Farm Women in Historical Perspective, Madison, Wis., October 1986.

woman; the fact exists that millions of the human race, even in this country, must by the sweat of the face aid the transmutation of the soil into bread before it can be eaten, and of that class there are nearly as many women as men. It is true that the heavy work of the farm, the teaming, the "breaking up," and the drudgery, fitted only to sturdy strength, is done by men in this country, as it should be, and as it is not to such an extent in any other. . . . It is equally true that no meager share of food production and preparation for the supply of our countrymen, and the surplus for European consumption, is allotted to the (physically) weaker sex.

The author upheld the principle of gender distinctions in labor, for he believed in inherent differences between women and men. Yet he contended that

it is a necessity that women should have some knowledge of the principles and processes involved in rural arts. . . . Women who must necessarily have some share in the work of life, as all worthy of the name do have, will dignify and ennoble their own characters, instead of degrading them, in practicing these arts.

In his view, women's agricultural labor not only was appropriate but also made a valuable contribution to the survival of family farms and the wealth of the nation. He attempted to assess the worth of women's work on farms:

Of the six hundred millions of pounds of butter, worth $180,000,000, how much comes from the labor of women in milking and churning, and all the cares of dairy management? Of two hundred and forty millions of pounds of cheese, worth $36,000,000, how much is manufactured by the wives and daughters of farmers? The eggs and poultry, amounting to many millions more, are due to an industry in which the farmer's wife has by far the larger share of skill and labor. The sweets of the hive are largely collected under the directing care of women. Millions of dollars, many more than those appearing in the census of market-garden products, are produced in kitchen gardens by feminine labor. No inconsiderable amount of small fruits, both for home use and for village and city markets, is grown and picked by feminine hands; and the quantity and value of wild berries—strawberries, raspberries, whortleberries, blackberries, cranberries, and other kinds—would annually aggregate far more than the fortune of one millionaire. Then if the casual or regular labor of women, in assistance volunteered or required in planting, weeding, cultivating, haying, harvesting, and even the care of live stock, be computed at its true value, and its real percentage of our total farm production calculated, how would the figures swell the sum, and magnify the proportion of wealth wrung from the mine of the farm by the hand of woman![18]

This list, compiled from the state reports submitted to the U.S. commissioner of agriculture and compounded by the figures recorded on the agricultural census, includes the major forms of income-producing labor in which Nanticoke Valley women engaged. When the author worried that "few appear to be aware of the part actually taken by women in rural affairs," he was speaking to urban people. Women and men in the Nanticoke Valley were well aware of the substance and significance of women's work.

Placing the gender division of labor in this perspective highlights the importance of women's work in commodity production, but it explains neither why farm family labor was organized in this way nor what its consequences were for relations among women and men. To analyze the meaning of women's work, we must not only place it within the context of the farm family economy but also examine the way that work structured relations between women and men and how people interpreted the significance of their distinctive and shared labor. The next chapter considers work relationships between women and men, analyzing how particular husbands and wives related to each other through their labor.

18. "The Industrial Education of Women," in *The Report of the Commissioner of Agriculture for the Year 1871*, ed. J. R. Dodge (Washington, D.C.: U.S. Government Printing Office, 1872), 336–37. The author of this article is not named.

CHAPTER SEVEN

Work Relationships
between Women and Men

We had churning to do.

—Helen Davis Benton, Diary, 1889

Nanticoke Valley diarists provide a copious record of the work performed by individual women and men and by the other members of their households. Most daily entries begin with an observation on the weather and move immediately to a description of the things the diarist had accomplished that day. Men used their diaries as memorandum and account books, recording the amount of hay they harvested or when the cows freshened, the work they exchanged with neighboring farmers, and the bargains they made with artisans and storekeepers. Women noted which rooms they swept, how long it took to churn the butter, and when they finished a dress, as well as who helped them with their work or came to visit. Some of this information might help people conduct their business or plan their work, but much of it had no obvious utilitarian purpose; rather, it helped diarists feel that they had accomplished something significant. Diarists only occasionally expressed how they felt about their day's labor. Most often, satisfaction came as they looked back at their achievements.

Men's diaries illuminate their practices and beliefs about the allocation of labor by gender, while women's diaries and autobiographies highlight their experiences of work and perspectives on the gender division of labor. This chapter not only compares the viewpoints of women and men but also compares families that had a substantial degree of sharing and flexibility in the work of women and men with families that had a clearer division of labor. Many diarists noted what the other members of their household were doing, not only if they worked together but also if they were engaged in separate tasks. A strong sense of the family farm as a corporate enterprise permeates the diaries of both women and men. Women's diaries show a somewhat greater awareness of men's daily work than most men's diaries show of women's, but some men had sufficient contact with women's work, and regarded it as sufficiently important, that they recorded the labor of all the members of their household. The diaries of George Riley and Judson Riley, his son, which extend from 1865 through 1890 and from 1876 to 1897 respectively, provide a full and vivid account of the gender division of labor on the family farm from two men's perspectives.

The Riley Family

Both women and men had a set of routine daily tasks. Usually these chores were presumed rather than described in the diaries, although they might be indicated by such phrases as "chored around" or "done the work." Occasionally, however, George described his wife's workday in more detail. Typical entries read: "Lucy Ann has been washing and weaving carpet, churning, mopping & etc. as usual," or "Lucy Ann has been ironing, baking brown bread and cookies & etc., making chair cushions and doing chores" (7 May 1866; 13 December 1880). Even though these lists are incomplete, they contain a larger number of distinct tasks than George's descriptions of his own workdays. Usually he worked at one task all day, or spent the forenoon doing one thing and the afternoon doing another. Lucy Ann's days were much more complex. She had a number of processes to manage simultaneously, rather than a set of tasks that could be executed sequentially. Each made different demands on her time and attention. Some required continuous watching, while others could be tended to intermittently. Lucy Ann had to orchestrate them all, and also to respond to interruptions from her husband and children.

Women's work had a profoundly different temporal rhythm than men's work did. Their work was also inherently less susceptible to rationalization. Dr. Hall observed that "farmers . . . whose force of character is such that every thing on the farm, outside of the house, goes on like clockwork" ought not to expect their wives "to have similar management indoors." Slight disorders inevitably arose in even the best-managed households.[1] Catharine Beecher was also acutely aware of the impossibility of reducing women's work to an invariable system, as much as she tried to introduce order into household labor. In the chapter of *The American Woman's Home* (1869) titled "The Preservation of Good Temper in the Housekeeper," Beecher cautioned that "a housekeeper's business is not, like that of the other sex, limited to a particular department for which previous preparation is made. It consists of ten thousand little disconnected items, which can never be so systematically arranged that there is no daily jostling somewhere." Beecher advised women to expect to have their plans disrupted by the demands of family members, rather than become annoyed by the interference.[2]

If Lucy Ann Riley's work on any given day was more varied than her husband's, it varied less from day to day through the year. George did barn chores each morning and evening, but he spent the major portion of his day doing things that changed with the seasons. Routine household tasks took up a much larger portion of Lucy Ann's time. Moreover, seasonal tasks were superimposed on her daily schedule and created additional pressures, rather than bringing welcome relief. Although berry picking was a form of recreation, making jam and jelly certainly was not; the short respite that going outdoors afforded was followed by hours of bending over a hot stove. George occasionally remarked the effects of his own activities on his wife's work. The large crews of men who came to do the haying, thrash grain, or frame a building lightened his labor, but they intensified Lucy Ann's. When the neighbors came to help George move the woodhouse, for example, he noted: "Fifteen took dinner and supper here today—four to breakfast—makes thirty-four meals in all." Lucy Ann was solely responsible for the cooking (11 August 1882).

George Riley clearly distinguished in his diary between the work for which Lucy Ann was normally responsible and the times when she helped him with what were properly his tasks. By writing that she "helped" him, he both upheld the principle that this work was his responsibility and gave his wife credit for her assistance. The phrase reinforces the distinction between men's and women's work at the same time that it records the crossing of the boundary between the two. The number and variety of these instances demonstrates that even though George Riley believed in the conventional division of la-

1. Dr. W. W. Hall, "The Health of Farmers' Families," in *The Report of the Commissioner of Agriculture for the Year 1862* (Washington, D.C.: U.S. Government Printing Office, 1863), 464.
2. Catharine E. Beecher and Harriet Beecher Stowe, *The American Woman's Home* (New York: J. B. Ford, 1869; Hartford, Conn.: Stowe-Day Foundation, 1975), 213.

bor, he routinely relied on his wife's help for the completion of essential farm tasks for which men were assigned responsibility.

Detailed analysis of the nature of these tasks and the frequency with which Lucy Ann performed them reveals that she helped her husband most often with the most labor-intensive and physically demanding farmwork. This entry is typical: "Planted corn and finished planting potatoes today—worked hard to finish. Lucy Ann helped us and Juddie. Ida washed and done the work in the house" (24 May 1875). Women's help was most essential during haying season. "Saving the hay" was by definition an emergency on nineteenth-century farms, for the grass had to be cut, dried in the fields, and then carted into the barn before it got wet; if it were rained on, much of its nutritive value would be lost. On farms the size of the Rileys', it took about half a dozen people to do the haying by hand under normal circumstances. Neighboring farmers customarily did their haying cooperatively, working first on one farm and then on another. Although the women did not move from farm to farm with the men, they generally helped get in the hay on their own place. George Riley's diary indicates that Lucy Ann turned and raked the hay every year from 1865 through 1869, even when she was six months pregnant. George purchased a horse-drawn mowing machine and hay rake in 1871, after he was disabled by rheumatism. This investment lightened the labor, and Lucy Ann's help was no longer required on such a regular basis. She was still expected to help in the meadow whenever George was short-handed or the hay had to be got in quickly, however. Lucy Ann helped pile the hay onto the wagon and unload it in the barn almost every year through the 1880s. Sometimes she used the horse rake while her husband mowed, but more often she did the hand labor while the men used the machinery.

Lucy Ann was involved in the grain harvest much more irregularly than with the haying, but she did occasionally help out. At times the entire family worked in the fields. One fall day, for example, George wrote: "Drawed in over six hundred bushels of grain today. Lucy Ann helped me and Juddie helped like a little hero and Ida helped to mow away the oats. Got along first-rate" (3 September 1873. Ida was sixteen, and Judson was seven years old.) Later in the fall, Lucy Ann spent several days in the potato field. Sometimes she and George worked together, but often she dug potatoes while her husband was doing something else.

George Riley always regarded Lucy Ann's participation in these tasks as a temporary expedient, an adaptation to an unusual situation of labor shortage. Although he regularly counted on his wife's help with the haying and the potato crop and occasionally called upon her to assist him with a wide range of other tasks, he did not regard field work of any kind as her proper labor. This becomes clear when George was ill. When he was only temporarily unable to work, George reluctantly asked Lucy Ann to perform those tasks which could not be postponed until his recovery. When his disability continued for a week or so, he hired men to work on the farm rather than shift the burden of outdoor labor to his wife. During one bout of illness, George wrote: "Finished planting potatoes, Juddie and me. Lucy had to help after getting through washing" (25 May 1885). This entry contrasts sharply with Helen Davis's complaint that she had to help her father with his haying after she had done a large washing; George Riley understood his wife's burden of labor and regretted the necessity of asking for her assistance. If his allegiance to the principle of the gender division of labor was based in part on a recognition of the importance of his wife's responsibilities, however, his actual practice diverged significantly from the ideal he espoused. His wife's labor was essential to the completion of crucial farm tasks he regarded as his responsibility. Yet George never questioned the principle itself, writing that Lucy Ann "helped" him with his tasks when the two worked together in a fully cooperative manner. For George Riley to have recognized that Lucy Ann did more than "help" him would have required him to revise his ideas about the proper work roles of men and women.

The operation of the dairy was a joint responsibility in the Riley family. George and Lucy Ann worked together at some tasks; some were usually performed by one of them, but were frequently taken over by the other. George and Judson were responsible for watering and foddering the livestock, but Lucy Ann and Ida were able to do the chores. Lucy Ann often took the place of one of the men in the barn. When George and Judson were both sick, George noted: "Do not get out to do many chores today. Lucy Ann has most of them to do again" (24 March 1880). On other occasions, Lucy Ann did the chores as a matter of choice rather than necessity. For example, on Sundays she took her turn staying at home to do the chores while the others went to church. All the members of the family customarily participated in milking their eight or so heifers; however, when the men were occupied with the haying or the harvest Lucy Ann milked all the cows herself. To some degree, this choice was hers; in later years Lucy Ann often milked while the men hayed rather than help with the haying so the men could finish in time to do chores.

Butter making was Lucy Ann's responsibility, and George generally included it in his lists of his wife's regular chores. Often, however, he did the churning himself. One entry gives a detailed description of what prompted him to assist with this task:

> Helped Lucy Ann some, attended to the churning, took up and salted & etc., helped a little bit about making a cheese, washed dishes & etc. Lucy had washing, cheese making, churning together with all the rest of her housework to do and would have done it all if I had not helped her. (11 July 1881)

This entry is two-sided; George recognized that his wife was over-worked and voluntarily came to her assistance, but if he had been away from the house or fully occupied with his own work that day she would have been left to do it all by herself. Undoubtedly many days she did as much and more. Still, George often churned when Lucy Ann had other equally pressing and laborious work to do, such as washing, boiling sap, or making preserves.

George occasionally helped Lucy Ann with the household work. The task his diary mentions most often is washing. At times, George helped Lucy Ann with her work so she would be free to help him. One Monday in early summer, he "churned and helped Lucy a little about washing and done chores & etc. in the forenoon, and Lucy and me dropped one-half acre of sowed corn in the afternoon" (13 June 1887). Judson's diary records several instances in which he and his mother worked together indoors and out: "helped Mother wash and churned this forenoon, Ma went out and helped us plant potatoes this afternoon" (20 May 1880). There was, then, a certain reciprocity in the labor of women and men. George also helped with the washing so the family could go out visiting together in the afternoon. As long as Ida lived in the household, George did not help the two women with the laundry on a regular basis. After Ida moved to her own house in 1879, George routinely assisted his wife on washday by carrying large quantities of water, lifting heavy tubs, and helping pound and wring out the clothes. George made a special effort to lighten his wife's labor when she was feeling poorly. Judson commented: "Mother is not feeling well, and Father worked in the house" (11 April 1885). The men became more aware of the strenuous nature of washday as Lucy Ann grew older. On his wife's forty-ninth birthday, George noted that "she is not feeling well yet since Monday's washing" (31 January 1883). Judson made the connection explicit: "she worked too hard at washing I guess" (17 October 1882).

George was able to take over running the household when Lucy Ann was ill. In the winter of 1881–82, for example, he and Judson

Alice Johnson Loomis washing dishes, c. 1912. Photograph taken by Lee Loomis. Nanticoke Valley Historical Society, courtesy of Leigh and Dorothy Ames.

did the cooking, laundry, and housecleaning for two weeks with only occasional assistance from Ida and the neighbors. George took a certain pride in his ability to do housework. Shortly after Lucy Ann was taken sick, he wrote: "Juddie and me done the chores and the washing for the first time that we done the washing wholly" (9 January 1882). From one point of view, it is important that George was familiar with housework and was willing to perform it when necessary, rather than incur the expense of hiring a woman to help in the household temporarily. Yet from another point of view, it is equally significant that George did not often do housework. He assumed the tasks the conventional division of labor assigned to his wife only when she was unable to perform them; his skills did not mean that he and his wife ordinarily shared or exchanged this work. Sometimes George did stay home and get dinner started while the rest of the family went to church or paid a visit, thus ensuring that Lucy Ann was not always left behind when the others went out. He did not record the times she stayed home to prepare meals or tend children, however; these certainly outnumbered the times he remained at home to do household chores.

One unconventional area of shared responsibility and mutual helpfulness that George Riley's diary documents is the manufacture of clothing. George sewed many of his own garments, both with the sewing machine and by hand. Lucy Ann helped him with some of these tasks, just as he occasionally lent her a hand. George took pride in his ability to do most of the work himself, remarking that he "cut out and made a shirt with a little of Lucy's help" (9 July 1878). At the same time, George never made clothing for other members of his family, nor did he teach this skill to his son.[3]

What, then, was the meaning of the division of labor between George and Lucy Ann Riley? The Rileys followed the conventional allocation of tasks. While each was responsible for a certain set of tasks, their work often brought them into close contact and at times they assisted each other with the most laborious and time-consuming chores. The exchange between them was not always an equal one; Lucy Ann worked in the fields more often than George worked in the house. This asymmetry suggests that they saw field work as more crucial to their welfare than most household tasks. The crucialness of

3. George Riley may have learned to make and repair clothing in his youth, when he joined the Gold Rush. He and the other local young men who went to California spent several years in a milieu where women were scarce and men had to fend for themselves. Other Nanticoke Valley men learned sewing skills during the Civil War. Still others, such as Chauncey McIntyre, were taught to sew their own shirts by their mothers.

any task depends on both its importance to the farm-family economy and the urgency of its temporal demands.[4] Haying was the most crucial seasonal task, just as dairying was the most crucial daily one. The Riley diaries do not suggest that George controlled his wife's labor time. Lucy Ann seems to have put aside her household work voluntarily to join her husband in the fields; she shared his definition of what constituted an emergency and what the good of the farm required, and she was both willing and able to assist with pressing tasks at planting, haying, and harvest. At the same time, the regularity and extent to which George helped Lucy Ann with the washing is also remarkable. The connection between his washing while she churned and his churning while she washed suggests that the dairy process provided the primary basis for their mutuality. Not only did George and Lucy Ann share and exchange tasks more often in the dairy process than in any other aspect of the farm operation, but their joint responsibility for the work in barnyard and buttery also led to greater mutuality in other aspects of household labor.

After George Riley's death, Judson and Lucy Ann carried on the work in much the same way as before. Between 1890 and 1894, Judson noted that Lucy Ann regularly planted and dug potatoes and planted, hoed, and harvested corn. He often spoke of these as joint activities, noting that "Mother and me picked potatoes all day just as hard as we could work" or "Mother and me worked in our corn all day" (29 May 1893; 16 June 1893). Judson did not help his mother with the laundry as often as his father had done, perhaps because Lucy Ann shared that task with Ida. Judson took much of his mother's household labor for granted. Nevertheless, he understood its significance. One summer Sunday, after several weeks when both of them had been too exhausted to attend church, Judson wrote: "We staid at home all day. We have so many things to see about that we can hardly both leave. I do wish that Mother might have some things easier, she stays at home and works all the time. She has had a hard time through her life and always worked like a slave. If ever I can manage it she shall not work so hard anyhow" (11 June 1893).

Judson's marriage brought another woman into the family early in 1894. If Judson hoped that this might reduce his mother's workload, he was soon disappointed, for the two women could not work together comfortably. During the first summer after Judson and Lillie's

4. Corlann Bush has developed a precise definition of the "crucialness" of men's and women's work on farms and used it to analyze the impact of technological change on grain farms in the West. Bush, "The Barn Is His, the House Is Mine: Agricultural Technology and Sex Roles," in *Energy and Transport: Historical Perspectives,* ed. George H. Daniels and Mark H. Rose (Beverly Hills, Calif.: Sage Publications, 1982), 235–59.

marriage, Lillie did not work outdoors very often; perhaps, as a village resident and minister's daughter, she had not been accustomed to participating in such tasks as haying. Lucy Ann went to the fields more regularly and performed a wider range of tasks outdoors; when Judson needed help, his mother was more likely than his wife to join in the labor. By late fall, it was obvious that Lillie was physically unsuited to such work. Her pregnancy had not excused her from helping Judson thrash buckwheat and set up corn in the field, and the strain those tasks involved may have contributed to her miscarriage. From that time on, Lillie almost never particpated in field work. The next spring, after Lucy Ann had left the farm, Judson planted corn by himself and found it "slow work alone" (22 May 1895).

After Lucy Ann moved to Ida's house, Lillie took over her responsibility for making butter during the winter. But Judson helped his wife churn most Saturday mornings, when Lillie was cleaning and baking in preparation for Sunday, and on Mondays he churned while she was washing. Lillie and Judson both milked. Judson was primarily responsible for the barn chores, although Lillie helped out occasionally. When Lillie had a small baby and Judson was away, "Mother was down and done some chores for me" (6 January 1897). Judson Riley did not succeed in lightening his mother's burden of labor; rather, he made sure that his wife did not have to work as hard as his mother had done. Although there is a certain irony in the fact that Lucy Ann did the chores so that the younger woman would not have to, the situation made sense from Judson's perspective. He had grown up appreciating the importance and understanding the burden of women's work. When he married a woman who could not withstand arduous physical labor, he made sure that she did not have to perform it, either indoors or out, by assuming the heaviest tasks himself. Although Judson and Lillie Riley worked together outdoors less often than George and Lucy Ann Riley had done, they worked together indoors more often. Judson "helped" Lillie more often than she "helped" him. The fact that she could not "hay it as good as a man" did not mean that her husband did not value her work. Judson espoused the same ideas about the gender division of labor as his father had; he was simply more consistent in practice than his father had been. While the transition from one generation to another on the Riley farm involved some readjustment in the allocation of tasks between men and women, it did not involve any decline in the degree of reciprocity between them. In the Nanticoke Valley the gender division of labor did not rigidly segregate women and men into different work routines; it was, rather, a flexible pattern of organizing work that generated shared as well as separate activities.

The Benton Family

Helen Davis Benton's diary presents a woman's own perspective on her labor. Helen was a generation younger than Lucy Ann. The Benton and Riley farms were similar; both were medium sized and oriented toward commercial dairying. Like most women diarists, Helen recorded both her own work and that of her husband in great detail. More important, she expressed her feelings about her labor with a frankness and forcefulness that is unusual even among women diarists.[5]

Helen thought of her day as divided into three parts by the meals she had to cook and clean up after. In the forenoon, once she had done the "morning work" of building fires, making breakfast, getting her children up and dressed, and washing dishes, she began whatever task was supposed to be done that day according to the weekly rotation. In the afternoon, when the "dinner work" was completed, she hoped to finish the day's major tasks in time to sit down for a while before she had to start supper. In the evening, after she had washed up the supper dishes and settled the children down for the night, she did the mending while visiting with her family and friends, or she simply went to bed early because she was tired. These daily household chores were so routine that Helen rarely described them in detail. Occasionally she complained about how much time they took: "Do the best I can, it gets late before I can get my work done up in the morning" (8 December 1891).

Helen wrote more about the weekly cycle of housework. She dreaded Mondays, for washing was the most difficult and disruptive of household tasks. She had to get up especially early in order to heat the water, and unless she "set to work with a will" she could not possibly finish before it was time to put dinner on the table. The men usually helped Helen by carrying water from the well into the kitchen and emptying the heavy tubs. During the first year she was married, Helen remarked appreciatively one Monday that "Leroy did not go off to work in the forenoon but helped me" (8 April 1878). When all the men were too busy, however, Helen remarked with a mixture of resentment and resignation: "I had to draw my own water,

5. The volumes of Helen Davis Benton's diary that document her life on the Benton farm include 1878, the year she married, and a continuous series from 1888 through 1897. She left a more complete record of her household labor than most other Nanticoke Valley women who kept diaries, and she expressed her feelings about her work more eloquently as well. At the same time, neither her household routine nor her attitude toward housework was strikingly different from what other women recorded. Where Helen's account accurately represents the experiences of other local women diarists, I allow it to stand alone; where it does not, I discuss differences between Helen and other women.

got very tired" (18 March 1889). Helen attempted to lighten her labor by such shortcuts as soaking the clothes overnight and spreading the white ones on the grass to bleach in the sun. If she had any energy left after the clothes were hung out to dry, she might use the hot water to scrub the floors and windows; a general mopping-up was necessary in any case, for water had been splashed all over the kitchen. Washing dominated the day and took over the house, and Helen felt that she "looked like fury" when it was done (7 June 1878).

Helen approached washday with grim determination. Soon after she was married, Helen wrote: "Washing days will come. . . Plumah helped me wash so that dreaded operation is passed, performed, finished. I did not do but little this afternoon but clean up" (28 October 1878). The language of this entry emphasizes the completion of the process, as if laundry could be done once and for all instead of recurring week after week. At times Helen was able to take pride in getting her clothes done early: "I was quite smart, had my washing out before Mother was up" (6 May 1878). But when she was especially zealous she regretted it later: "Got to washing early, ironed a good many things after dinner, and was tired and cross" (13 July 1878). Generally Helen was happy when she "got through and changed my dress before dinner" (13 May 1878).

Helen usually began the ironing on Tuesday, but she seldom was able to finish it, for she was delayed by the daily work or distracted by other tasks. When she did complete the ironing on the prescribed day, she noted it as a special accomplishment: "I have for once got my washing done Monday and my ironing on Tuesday" (12 June 1894). Because heating irons and baking both required a hot fire, Helen often saved fuel by doing both tasks at once: "I baked pies and bread, and while I had a fire I ironed nearly all the clothes that were dry" (6 March 1888). In the middle of the week, she took up tasks in whatever order she chose. Like most women, Helen preferred cooking to cleaning house. One morning, for example, she "did not want to clean and so did some baking"; on another, she "made fried cakes [doughnuts] and left my sweeping and bed-making till after dinner" (29 April 1891; 4 May 1889).

"Saturdays always bring work," Helen observed (13 April 1878). The day was especially hectic because the entire house had to be cleaned, special foods had to be prepared, and whatever had been left undone during the week had to be finished before the Sabbath rest. On a typical Saturday, Helen "had all sorts of work to do, baking and washing dishes and churning and mopping and so on" (11

Alice Johnson Loomis ironing, c. 1912. Photograph taken by Lee Loomis.
Nanticoke Valley Historical Society, courtesy of Leigh and Dorothy Ames.

May 1878). Sometimes she felt overwhelmed. One Saturday in early summer:

> I had a busy time. Everything seems to be behind time. We got up late and the dishes were not washed and had potatoes to pear and milking to do. I had to step around. I made pies, churned, mopped the well room, and helped Aunt Jane with her carpet. (20 June 1891)

Helen felt a sense of accomplishment at having made it through the day in spite of its disorder.

Helen did not find much satisfaction in her regular housework.[6] No matter how many tasks she enumerated in her diary, she seldom felt that she had done anything significant. One fall Friday, for example, she wrote: "There were a good many things to do, nothing of much account, still must be done" (23 October 1893). "This is one of the days that I work hard and do not accomplish much," she noted on a typical Saturday (6 June 1878). Helen was often discouraged by the fragmentation of her time, remarking that she "did a little of everything and not much of anything" (17 January 1874). She was also oppressed by the repetitive nature of housework. "I did the same as every Saturday, the same things are to be done over and over again," she commented during the first year of her marriage (18 May 1878). On other occasions, Helen was distressed by the seemingly endless number of things to be done. "I was glad to get one job done, but others come so fast that I despair of ever getting caught up," she re-

6. Although recent feminist analyses of household labor have tended to neglect rural women, they have provided both historical perspectives on changes in domestic routines and insightful interpretations of how women feel about this work. As Ruth Schwartz Cowan and Susan Strasser have pointed out, neither changes in household technology nor the commodification of formerly domestic activities have lightened the burden or transformed the character of housework. Cowan, *More Work for Mother: The Ironies of Household Technology from the Open Hearth to the Microwave* (New York: Basic Books, 1983); and Strasser, *Never Done: A History of American Housework* (New York: Random House/Pantheon Books, 1982). Many of the qualities of housework which rural women noted in the nineteenth century, especially its repetitive nature, still shape women's experience of housework today. See Ann Oakley's *Woman's Work: The Housewife Past and Present* (New York: Random House/Pantheon Books, 1974), and *The Sociology of Housework* (New York: Random House/Pantheon Books, 1974). For innovative theoretical analyses of the meaning of household labor on family farms during the twentieth century, see Sarah Elbert, "The Farmer Takes a Wife: Women in American Farming Families," in *Women, Households and the Economy* (New Brunswick, N.J.: Rutgers University Press, 1987), 173–99; Gould Colman and Sarah Elbert, "Farming Families: The Farm Needs Everyone," *Research in Rural Sociology and Development* 1 (1984): 61–78; Carolyn Sachs, *The Invisible Farmers: Women in Agricultural Production* (Totawa, N.J.: Rowman & Allanheld, 1983).

marked later that year (3 December 1878). She often remembered her mother's saying that she "danced all day in half a bushel"; this colloquial phrase meant "always in a hurry, but getting nowhere."[7]

One of the primary ways Helen overcame the depression the routine of housework induced was by working especially hard. She was aware that slowing her pace did not lift her spirits; one Saturday: "Did not have very much that I was obliged to do, so it took a good while to do that little" (11 April 1891). Helen found physically demanding work more satisfying than less taxing work, for she could measure her efforts by her exhaustion. After a long day of housecleaning, for example, Helen remarked that "I feel as though I did something" (30 October 1894).

Although the weekly round of household chores provided some variation in Helen's routine, it could also become an impediment to her sense of accomplishment by setting a standard impossible to fulfill.[8] Helen accepted the conventional rotation of household tasks as an ideal, but she recognized that its demands were unrealistic and allowed herself a more flexible work schedule. One diary entry from the first year of her marriage succinctly expresses Helen's sense of herself as a housekeeper:

> We had churning to do, and ironing must be done of course. I did not have time to iron the startched clothes before dinner so let them go. I can find enough to keep me busy every day, but I lack a little ambition as well as everything else. (9 July 1878)

Saying that she lacked ambition was not merely a form of self-deprecation but also a declaration that she would not attempt to do what some other women did. Rather than feel guilty at her failure, Helen simply worked as hard as she could and then quit; more than that, she felt, could not reasonably be expected of any woman. Over

7. This translation was supplied by Nanticoke Valley native Lamont Montgomery Bowers in his Memoirs, 19.

8. Women established the conventional weekly household routine to give them a sense of order and accomplishment in their domestic labor. Weekly rotations provided some variation in daily activities and enabled women to feel that a given task was completed for the time being. For some women, however, these routines were as much a source of frustration as of satisfaction, since they set standards that seemed impossible to fulfill. These routines were promulgated by professional educators committed to the reform of domestic economy and published in household manuals distributed nationally, so they were often remote from the realities of farm women's lives. Joan M. Jensen, *Loosening the Bonds: Mid-Atlantic Farm Women, 1750–1850* (New Haven: Yale University Press, 1986), 114–28, analyzes manuals on domestic economy directed specifically at rural households during the early nineteenth century.

Jessie Dudley Allen and her mother, Alice Haskins Dudley, beating rugs, c. 1910. Nanticoke Valley Historical Society.

time, Helen became more resigned to and relaxed about her deviations from the prescribed household routine.

Sewing was very different from housework. It involved distinct projects rather than a never-ending cycle of chores. It did not have to be done at a certain time but could be fitted in around other activities. And, as it was done sitting down, it often represented a welcome relief from physically strenuous labor. Many women found sewing especially congenial. But Helen Davis Benton did not enjoy sewing and did no more than absolutely necessary. She was frustrated by how long it took to finish things. Often Helen remarked, not the progress she made on a project, but her failure to complete it; for example, she spoke of "that lingering dress of mine," "my skirt that I worked on so long ago," and "a pair of drawers that I have had around for some time" (23 October 1893; 20 August 1888; 17 September 1891).

When she did finish a project, Helen felt more relief that the task was over than pride in what she had accomplished.

Spring cleaning was in many respects the opposite of sewing. It demanded extraordinary physical effort and a direct frontal attack, rather than coordination, concentration, and patience. It disrupted the entire domestic routine, instead of fitting into it. It also produced less tangible results than sewing did. Yet for a woman like Helen the process might be more satisfying. Each spring, she threw herself into a fierce whirlwind of cleaning. After several weeks of intense activity, when she grew tired of cleaning or had to turn to other tasks, she declared the entire project done. "Decided that we will say tonight that we have finished housecleaning," Helen resolved one June first (1894). The once-and-for-all activity of spring cleaning was more satisfying than the weekly housecleaning.

Just as Helen Davis Benton preferred active physical labor to more sedentary tasks, so she often chose to work outdoors. Her participation in the work of the farm increased significantly over time. During the first year she was married, Helen neither worked in the garden nor helped with the haying; a decade later, she did both as a matter of course. By 1888, she regularly helped hoe and dig potatoes, rake and get in oats, cut and husk corn, and pull beans. Sometimes she even chopped her own wood. Helen's increased participation in farm labor was clearly a matter of personal choice as well as of family necessity.

It took time for Helen to become fully integrated into the work of the Benton farm. When she first joined the family, three adult Benton men and a young hired hand worked the two adjacent farms, so Helen was not needed outdoors. Yet Helen was interested in the men's work and she occasionally "went down to the barn a little while" and "helped a little about doing the chores" (23 October 1878; 18 September 1878). The departure of Leroy's father and brother for the West gave Helen the opportunity to expand her activities. By 1888, although Leroy still had primary responsibility for the milking, Helen generally took over this task during haying and harvest: "I milked several cows tonight, the men worked late at mowing" (9 July 1889). Helen's work in the barn was a matter of choice as well as necessity. When she "felt rather lonesome and a little blue," she "milked a couple of cows for Leroy"; joining her husband in the barn evidently lifted her spirits (14 April 1889). In 1897, the year that Helen and Leroy's older daughter enrolled in the Academy in Union, the Bentons quit employing a hired hand during the summer. They were able to save the hired hand's wages for their daughter's education because Helen assumed the extra burden of labor. By then, milking and doing chores was a responsibility that Helen, Leroy, and Ethel shared. When Leroy came home late after working on neighboring farms, Helen noted without complaining that she milked and did the chores herself. Conversely, when Helen was overwhelmed by other work, Leroy and Ethel did the chores alone. In the summer of 1897, for example, she noted: "I have not done much but work with cherries. Leroy got thirty quarts. I got them almost done and then gave out. They all milked but me" (15 July 1897). Helen felt the need to apologize when she was unable to go to the barn. In 1894, she wrote that "Leroy had to do chores alone with Ethel's help, I felt so bad" (15 October 1894). The language expresses both how ill Helen felt and her regret that she was unable to fulfill her regular responsibilities.

The most substantial change in Helen's work over these years was her increased participation in milking and barn chores. At the same time, Leroy's role in the processing of dairy products also expanded. In 1878, Helen was responsible for "seeing to the milk" and churning the butter. She was not particularly fond of this task. Sometimes she found it frustrating: "I churned all the forenoon, what time I could get, and quite a while in the afternoon, but gave it up as a bad job. I did not accomplish anything" (29 December 1897). Occasionally her impatience provoked her to more direct action: "Had butter to take care of, a nice large churning. I did not feel like doing much, I dumped considerable" (12 June 1891). After ten years of marriage, Leroy had largely taken over this task. In 1889, Helen recorded that "Leroy churned" three times as often as she stated that she churned; sometimes she noted simply that "we had churning to do." By 1891, Helen presumed that Leroy ordinarily did the churning and recorded only the times she made butter because he was away or involved with other farm tasks.

The opening of the creamery did not lead to any dramatic shifts in the allocation of tasks within the Benton household. The Bentons began taking their milk to the Maine village creamery in 1893. There were a variety of arrangements for hauling the milk; generally the Bentons took turns with the families on neighboring farms, and sometimes Leroy, Helen, and Ethel passed the task back and forth among them. In 1897, after Ethel left for school, her parents had to figure out which of them should haul the milk. At first they alternated days. Helen began going with the milk every day "so Leroy can work, but my work gets along slow" (6 September 1897). Then "Leroy went with the milk. . . I find my work gets along better when I am here" (17 September 1897). Finally Helen resumed taking the milk down herself "so to let Leroy get his work done" (6 October 1897). It is significant that Helen ultimately assumed this task; her workdays were deemed best able to bear interruption. Perhaps her household chores were regarded as less crucial than Leroy's field work; clearly her time was already more fragmented than his. But it is equally important that the Bentons engaged in a process of experimentation to see how to allocate this new task. Taking in the milk was not automatically typed as masculine simply because it was physically strenuous, involved traveling to a public place and conducting a market transaction, and required considerable record keeping.

This series of changes in the organization of work in the dairy operation is significant, first, because it shows that the allocation of tasks between women and men was flexible. In the Benton family, the division of labor by gender was almost entirely reversed over two decades. Leroy and Helen readjusted their allocation of tasks because of their personal preferences, the presence or absence of other workers, the resources available to the household, and the compatibility of particular tasks with the other work each person did. Even within the constraints of farm operations and of the conventional gender division of labor, women and men made choices about their work. Second, the changes the Bentons made between 1878 and 1897 moved in the direction of greater mutual responsibility for the dairy and more extensive sharing of particular tasks. Leroy and Helen spent more time working together in the barn and passed tasks back and forth between them more often in the later years of their marriage than they did at the beginning.

By the time they had been married twenty years, the Bentons had attained the same degree of joint activity in the barn and the fields that had characterized the Rileys at a similar stage in their lives two decades earlier. Dairying played a pivotal role in Leroy and Helen's flexible and shared work routine. Just as George and Lucy Ann Riley's joint responsibility for the dairy led them to help each other with other farm and household tasks as well, so Leroy and Helen's common interest in the dairy took precedence over their more distinct gender-specific tasks. The fact that the primary responsibility for churning butter was assigned to the opposite sex in the two families underlines the fact that the meaning of the gender division of labor did not lie in the particular tasks women and men performed but rather in the place their work occupied in the family economy and the way in which their labor structured their relationships with each other. Both Lucy Ann Riley and Helen Davis Benton participated in income-producing labor with their husbands, and for both couples the dairy was central to the development of a joint and flexible work routine. In this respect, they exemplify the experiences of the vast majority of women and men who lived on Nanticoke Valley farms during the late nineteenth century.[9]

The Marean and Gates Families

A few local families divided farm and household tasks quite clearly along gender lines and did not share the work of the dairy. William and Deborah Allen Marean were one such couple. Married in 1855, they were almost the same age as the Rileys; their only child died in infancy. The Mareans' farm in Allentown was slightly larger and considerably more valuable than the Rileys' farm up the hill, and its dairy operation was larger in scale. The Mareans' relative prosperity and their lack of children meant that they hired help; William had the year-round assistance of a young man, while Deborah had the help of a young woman during the summer. With these two young people, the Mareans had exactly the same labor supply as the Rileys. According to William's diaries for 1878 and 1879, he and his hired hand were responsible for both milking and butter making; William did all the chores and churning whenever the youth was away. Neither Deborah nor the hired girl participated in the dairy process. Deborah kept poultry and gathered eggs, and William killed and dressed the chickens before he took them to Maine village along with the butter and eggs, but this was their only coordinated labor. William was solely responsible for the garden. While the hired hand worked in the fields, William devoted himself to horticulture, starting plants early in hot and cold frames; his tomatoes, small fruits, and flowers regularly won prizes at the fair. William did not call upon his wife to help him outdoors, nor did he assist her indoors. Indeed, William almost never mentioned his wife's work in his diary. He refers to "women's work" only when Deborah left the household to help nurse their niece and they had no hired girl: William "got breakfast and done up the work" (29 January 1879). On the Marean farm,

9. The patterns of labor in the Riley and Benton families are typical of those in most of the farm families for whom diaries have survived in the community. The gender division of labor was not appreciably different on farms that were smaller than those of the Rileys and the Bentons, nor in families that had different numbers of sons, daughters, and other relatives in the household or nearby.

then, there was a marked separation between men's and women's work, and the men performed tasks such as gardening and butter making that were usually part of women's responsibilities. This distinctive allocation of tasks between husband and wife was based on their own preferences, but it was possible only because they could afford to hire both male and female help. Few Nanticoke Valley farm families were in that position. The value of the Marean farm put them in the top tenth of landowners; their dairy was among the largest fifth; only a handful of local farmers hired so much labor. By these criteria, it was the Mareans rather than the Rileys and the Bentons who were exceptional.

While the case of the Mareans suggests that wealthier farm families sometimes observed a stricter gender division between indoor and outdoor labor than ordinary farm families did, the example of the Gateses demonstrates that such a gender division of labor was not necessarily based on economic position. The Gates family was not better off than the Rileys and the Bentons; their farms were slightly smaller and less valuable, and their dairy operations were on precisely the same scale. Yet the gender division of labor in the Gates family was almost as clear and inflexible as that in the Marean family. For the Gateses, the strict division of labor between women and men was a matter of personal preference and intergenerational tradition.

Over three generations, the men rather than the women in the Gates family held primary responsibility for the dairy operation. In the late 1870s, Livingston Theodore, his wife, Agnes Brockett, and their five children lived on the farm that had once belonged to Theodore's uncle. Theodore and the older boys did all the milking and barn chores. Agnes skimmed the cream, but Theodore usually did the churning. Just as Agnes and her twelve-year-old daughter Grace did not go to the barn, so they did not work in the fields during haying or harvest. Nor did they cultivate the garden, although they preserved vegetables and fruits. The language of the diary reflects the salience of this gender division. Theodore and Agnes both spoke of "the men" collectively when discussing outdoor labor. For example, Theodore wrote: "The men worked at oats   Ag and Lyd went to Sewing Circle to Mrs. Brown's" (16, 17 August 1876); and Agnes wrote: "The men worked in the flat cutting brush" (23, 24 August 1876). The ample supply of male labor in the Gates family ensured that Agnes and Grace were never called upon to help in the fields, meadows, orchard, or potato patch. In addition to the men in the household, who included Agnes's father, Theodore relied on his brother Byron and their father, Cyrus, who lived on the adjacent farm.

The strict division between women's indoor and men's outdoor labor in the Gates family did not mean that Agnes abstained from income-producing work or was excluded from marketing and decision making. Not only did Agnes share in the labor of the buttery, but she kept a flock of chickens and sold poultry and eggs. In contrast to Deborah Allen Marean, Agnes Brockett Gates marketed her own produce. She sold her eggs to the "egg man" who came by the farm each week; she killed the chickens herself and took them to Taylor Brothers in the fall. These sales were recorded under Agnes's name in the accounts Theodore and Agnes jointly kept.

The Gateses' sharing of the task of writing in their 1876 diary is even more remarkable than the segregation of their labor. Theodore and Agnes took turns keeping the diary.[10] Not only was each responsible for recording the other's activities, but each had access to the information recorded by the other. Although they performed distinct tasks, Theodore and Agnes thought of themselves as partners in a common enterprise and shared their most important economic responsibilities with each other. The substance of the diary confirms what its form suggests. Husband and wife jointly conducted financial transactions with village merchants. For example, Agnes wrote that they went to Maine and "Looked over account at Taylors owe them $52" (2 October 1876). Sometimes Agnes dealt with village merchants independently of her husband. For example, Theodore wrote: "Ag goes to Maine has talk with Sherwood Sold Shoulder and eggs" (29 January 1876). Both her husband and local merchants regarded Agnes as competent to be the family's economic agent.

In the next generation, Russell Buck and Velma Leadbetter Gates established an equally distinct if somewhat different division between men's and women's work. In 1892, Russell and Velma rented a farm adjacent to that of his parents; he and Byron worked together on a daily basis. Russell's diaries for 1892 and 1893 document the work routine he and his wife established; Velma's entries in the diary during the last third of 1893 record her perspective on their working relationship.[11]

10. It is possible to identify the author of a particular diary entry only by the nouns and pronouns used. Theodore and Agnes's hurried scrawls are very similar, and they used the same colloquial phrases. They also recorded the same kinds of information in the diary; most entries note the weather, the work of all family members, their social activities, and the state of the children's health.

11. Although Velma probably kept a diary throughout her married life, only those volumes her husband or his father began have survived. In 1893, Velma wrote in her husband's diary from mid-August through the end of the year. Russell and Velma did not pass the diary back and forth between them as his uncle Theodore and aunt Agnes

Russell and Velma divided the farm and household work more than they shared it. According to Russell's diary, Velma joined him in the forest, fields, meadows, and orchard only rarely. Some entries suggest that her participation was a matter of companionship, while others indicate that Velma's assistance was necessary: "Plant potatoes all day   Finish up potatoe piece   Vell helps" (11 June 1892). Once Velma helped rake and get in a load of hay at Byron's place (20 July 1892). But Russell made sure that Velma did not ordinarily have to help with the haying; instead, he arranged for the haying to be done by the men of the Gates family, the neighbors with whom they customarily worked, and, if necessary, hired hands. Picking up and culling apples was the only farm task in which Velma regularly engaged. Compared to the women of the Riley and Benton families, Velma rarely worked with her husband out of doors.

Russell Gates took responsibility for the dairy process. Velma did not participate in the milking, much less do chores. Her diary mentions only two times when she joined her husband in the barn. Once she wrote: "I go down to the barn to keep him company while he milks" (11 October 1893). That was evidently pleasant enough. But having to deal with the animals did not suit Velma at all. The other entry reads: "I go down to the barn and help get the cattle into the stall (terrible)" (20 November 1893). This was not an experience that Velma would repeat. Nor did she participate substantially in the other stages of the dairy process, even though they were conducted in the house. Velma may have set the milk to rise, skimmed the cream, and washed up the dairy utensils, but she rarely took responsibility for the churning. Sometimes she shared this task with her husband, but on the few occasions when she had to do it by herself she complained: "Russ goes up home and picks apples   I mop and bake pumpkin pies   put a band on his fine shirt   had to do the churning all alone   it makes me very tired" (28 October 1893).

Like Deborah Allen Marean and Agnes Brockett Gates, Velma Leadbetter Gates kept chickens. Velma established her own poultry flock as soon as they moved to the rented farm. After Russell built a chicken coop, Velma took responsibility for setting the hens, gathering the eggs, and killing and picking the chickens. Velma traded the eggs both with Maine village storekeepers and with the itinerant mer-

---

did; once Velma took up the task of diary keeping, she performed it consistently. Russell did not keep his diary private from Velma, however, even while he, rather than she, was responsible for writing in it.

chants who traveled through the rural area buying eggs and butter
and selling groceries and notions. The egg accounts in the back of the
diary indicate that this money was regarded as Velma's own.

Just as Velma rarely assisted her husband with the farmwork, so
Russell rarely helped his wife with the domestic labor. In his diary,
Russell did not describe Velma's regular work in any detail, although
he did praise her cooking and sewing skills. When his wife was ill, he
did not attempt to do the housework; instead, they hired a woman to
help. (Velma paid for her services out of the egg money.) Russell was
not totally devoid of domestic skills. Occasionally he stayed home
from church to get dinner started while his parents and his wife attended services. Once he wrote: "Father, Mother and Vell go to
Maine to church   I stay at home and get their dinner   only the
potatoes" (3 April 1892). Russell underlined the final phrase in his
diary, perhaps to emphasize his helpfulness, but perhaps to emphasize his inability to prepare an entire meal. Remarkably, Russell knew
how to weave and spent several snowy days helping Velma make car-
peting during the months before the couple moved into their own
home. He took an active interest in furnishing the house and participated in the spring cleaning as well. Russell's involvement with the
house did not extend to the routine domestic labor. He noted that he
"helped Vell wash" by bringing her water only six times during the
nineteen months he kept the diary in 1892 and 1893, and Velma never
recorded his assisting her with the laundry. Indeed, her entries about
washday document the couple's failure to coordinate their separate
tasks. On 23 October 1893, Velma wrote: "I washed but had to leave
my white clothes in the tub   washed six pair of old pants   awful
tired   Russ dug 12 bu. potatoes." The next day: "Hang out my white
clothes   then Russ starts his old swill kettle and I have to take them
down again."

Russell and Velma Leadbetter Gates maintained a strict division of
labor, but they shared financial information and transactions much as
Theodore and Agnes Brockett Gates had. It was evidently Russell's
choice to "take the farm to work by the halves," and he conducted all
the family's transactions with their landlord. On the other hand,
Velma was fully informed about their financial affairs and actively involved in their dealings with local merchants. Velma had some cash
and credit of her own; usually she used it to purchase necessary supplies for the household. In the same way, Russell bought things for
Velma out of the money he obtained from marketing farm produce.

Russell and Velma Leadbetter Gates's daughter, Louise Gates Gunsalus, explained the division of labor and sharing of authority be-

tween her parents during the time she was growing up. Louise was aware that her mother's pattern of work distinguished her from other farm women:

> My mother never went to the barn, which was contrary to all the other farm women around here. She said the woman's place was not in the cattle-barn. She loved horses, but not cows. But she made the butter and she skimmed the milk.

Louise explained that her mother carefully delimited the work she would perform. Velma's ideas about "the woman's place" were based on family tradition:

> It wasn't peculiar in my mother alone, but I think most of my father's family and my mother's family had very definite ideas about what they would do and what they wouldn't do, and what other people did didn't trouble them very much. And my mother and her mother never were working around the barn. And there were enough men in the family to do it and they didn't expect them to, and it wouldn't have done them any good if they had.[12]

In Louise's mind, both the general determination to act on personal convictions and the specific idea that women should not work in the barn were passed down from one generation to the next. The Gates and Leadbetter families had compatible traditions in the matter of women's work.[13] Equally important, women in the Gates and Leadbetter families claimed the right to decide what they would and would not do; women asserted control over their own labor and the men recognized their autonomy.

12. Louise Gates Gunsalus (1894–1983), interview by author, 20 March 1981. Louise's recollections of her mother's doing the churning come from a period much later than that covered by this diary. Louise dated her memory of her mother's churning around 1912 or 1913. Velma's diaries for 1913 and 1914 confirm that both she and Louise regularly participated in the separating and churning. Although Velma never milked or helped with chores, she did increase her involvement with the dairy process over time.

13. It is not clear how many generations of Leadbetter women had not worked in the barn. Rosella Leadbetter Benton, whose brother William was Velma Leadbetter Gates's father, stated explicitly that she had learned to do barn chores in her youth and willingly performed them during the Civil War. On the other hand, Velma said that her mother, Catherine Barnum, did not go to the barn. Although Catherine's mother had been born a Leadbetter, Catherine had lived with her aunt and uncle Arabella Leadbetter and Cyrus Gates in her youth and may have absorbed their attitudes toward women's and men's proper work. The facts are less important than Velma's belief that her preferences were validated by family tradition.

Velma Leadbetter Gates's limited participation in the dairy operation did not mean that she played a subordinate role in the family's
decision-making process. Instead, the situation seems to have been
quite the opposite: Velma was able to refuse to go to the barn in part
because of her strong position in the family. Louise explained that
her parents had come to an understanding about their working and
financial relationship at the time they married. Louise's mother had
insisted on such an agreement because of her previous experience as
a self-supporting businesswoman. "When she was married, she felt
just terrible to think that her income was gone, she'd be dependent
upon my father." Velma's familiarity with relationships between husband and wives in other farm families also made her cautious about
becoming a "dependent" wife; she knew that some husbands could
not be depended on to provide their wives with adequate spending
money, yet they expected their wives to work hard both indoors and
out. According to Louise, Velma believed that a clear understanding
between husband and wife protected the woman from exploitation as
well as ensuring her self-respect. So, like other Gates women before
her, Velma took responsibility for certain farm operations and insisted that her husband be responsible for others; some were shared
between them, but the terms of their sharing were explicit. This allocation of tasks gave Velma control over her own work and made her
contribution to the family economy very clear.[14]

Louise Gates Gunsalus contrasted her parents with Leroy and
Helen Davis Benton, whom she had known well when she was growing up. She recalled Leroy as neither physically strong nor of an active temperament: "He was poorly and not overly ambitious." To
illustrate this aspect of his character, Louise repeated a story her
mother had told her. Once when Velma went to visit the Bentons during the day, she found them all resting; Helen lay on the sitting-room
lounge, while Leroy was in bed. When she inquired how he was feeling, he replied that he was "comfortably sick." The phrase struck
Velma as a quintessential statement of Leroy's usual attitude toward
physical labor: he was just sick enough to avoid having to work but
not so sick as to be actually suffering. Louise was convinced that
Helen did a lot of the farm work and was the one who kept everything going. "She recognized that her husband was a little slow in
getting things done," Louise recalled, "but of course he was not

14. Louise Gates Gunsalus, interview by author, 12 July 1981. Louise acknowledged
that she shared her mother's views about relations between husbands and wives. Her
account is thus an accurate rendition, if not necessarily of what motivated Velma at the
time these events occurred, then of what Velma believed to be true of her own life and
taught to her daughter.

well."[15] Helen Davis Benton stood in sharp contrast to Louise's mother, and Louise's impression that Helen did "a man's work" on the Benton farm says as much about the Gateses as it does about the Bentons. Louise understood that Helen was personally inclined toward strenuous physical labor and did not complain about her husband's less active temperament. At the same time, Louise could not really believe that Helen would have chosen to do so much work outdoors unless her husband failed to fulfill the role the Gates women regarded as normative for men. Louise's recollections of the Benton family simultaneously acknowledge variations in the gender division of labor between families and illustrate the tenacity with which different people might hold to their own views of what was proper. Even more striking, however, is the fact that the Gateses did not feel that Helen Davis Benton was oppressed or exploited by the reversal of what they regarded as the proper gender division of labor. Instead, they seemed to regard Helen as the dominant one in family decision making as well as in work, and they heartily approved of her ambition and authority.

The working relationship between Russell and Velma Leadbetter Gates underlines the dialectical connection between the division of labor and relations of authority among husbands and wives. While Russell and Velma performed relatively few tasks together, they cooperated in the production of the farm's most important cash crops and each contributed independently to the farm income as well. This kind of coordination was one consequence of a mutual respect that most other couples attained through the experience of shared labor.

The organization of work on Nanticoke Valley farms involved both relationships among women and relationships between women and men. During the late nineteenth century, the conventional gender division of labor did not segregate women and men into separate work routines. Husbands and wives shared responsibility for the dairy, the most valuable of farm operations. They cooperated in doing chores, milking cows, and making butter in various ways; the barnyard and buttery was often their common domain. The mutuality and flexibility that characterized the dairy process extended to other farm and household tasks as well, not simply as a necessary adaptation to the demands of the dairy operation but also as a voluntary application of the habits of cooperation developed in dairying to other, more gender-marked tasks.

15. Louise Gates Gunsalus, interview by author, November 1981.

There were definite asymmetries in the degree to which women and men helped each other with the tasks for which each was distinctly responsible. Typically, women assisted men in the fields and meadows more often than men assisted women in the house. Men and women alike regarded planting crops for food and feed, saving the hay, and getting in the harvest as more crucial to their welfare than routine household tasks. These farm tasks were both labor intensive and tightly time constrained; mobilizing a large enough labor force to complete them quickly was essential to the success of the farm. (Among the tasks for which women were responsible, only planting and harvesting vegetables and preserving vegetables and fruits were as demanding; ordinarily men assisted women in the garden, while women worked collectively at canning and food preservation.) Women recognized the crucial importance of these farm tasks, and they put aside their routine work to assist the men with them when it seemed necessary. Although their work was heavy, these women were not "laboring drudges" exploited by their husbands; they were, rather, integral members of farm families who controlled their own labor and chose to join men in the performance of what all regarded as vital and valuable work.

Men also assisted their wives and mothers with household tasks so that the women would be free to help them outdoors. Some men recognized that doing the laundry required more sheer muscular strength than most of their own farm labor, and they helped the women in their households by carrying water even when the women did not join them in the fields or meadows. More often, however, women shared the task of washing with one another. Generally men helped with housework as an expedient so that women could help with farmwork. And for every instance in which men assisted with women's household work so that their wives could work outdoors, there were many more in which women simply put aside their dull round of domestic chores to join their husbands in the hayfield or the potato patch. The repetitious and confining quality of household routine made participation in farm tasks especially attractive for many women. If George Riley took pride in his wife's ability to "hay it as good as a man," Helen Davis Benton did not perceive her work in the meadows in such gendered terms. She enjoyed being released into the open spaces out of doors, expending physical energy in tasks that were completed once and for all, and working in association with her husband.

CHAPTER EIGHT

Work Relationships
among Women

We worked and talked and the time went right away.
—Helen Davis Benton, Diary, 1894

The organization of work on Nanticoke Valley farms structured relationships among women as well as between women and men. Women shared their most gender-marked tasks with other women both within and beyond their households more often than they did with the men who lived in their households. This chapter examines women's distinctive tasks and the relationships among women that were based on cooperative labor. The analysis moves back and forth between one household and another, and between paid and unpaid work, because the social and economic relationships among women that arose through work were characterized by a similar fluidity. If a woman did not have enough help within her household to perform a given task, she would seek assistance from relatives and neighbors; if female kin and friends were unavailable, she might engage hired help. These tasks ranged from an afternoon's canning to a month's care in sickness. Customarily women friends and neighbors worked cooperatively on a variety of tasks on an intermittent basis over extended periods of time, although they might seek the help of specialists with particular projects. Sharing work linked women in flexible, multidimensional networks of mutual aid.[1]

1. For a fascinating account of women's work sharing in an earlier period, see Laurel Thatcher Ulrich, "'A Friendly Neighbor': Social Dimensions of Daily Work in Northern Colonial New England," *Feminist Studies* 6 (1980): 392–405.

"We work some and talk a little more"

Sewing was a nearly universal part of women's work in the Nanti-coke Valley. Before the turn of the twentieth century, women did not buy their clothing ready-made. When they wrote in their diaries that they purchased a dress at a village store or in a large Binghamton shop, they meant that they had bought the fabric; they had to ex-pend considerable time and effort to make it up before they had the satisfaction of appearing in their new attire. Toward the end of the century, many women bought knitted underwear; those who could afford to would purchase winter coats. A much larger proportion of men's clothing was bought ready-made, but women still sewed their husbands' shirts. They made all of their children's garments, and they made over and mended articles that had become the worse for wear.

Dressmaking was the most absorbing task. Women's levels of skill varied markedly. Some had to call upon others for help in cutting out even the simplest waist, while others could copy intricate designs from fashion plates in popular magazines. During the late nineteenth century, women's dresses were elaborately made. Although rural women wore simple dresses and cotton aprons when they did their daily work, they wanted to be more formally and fashionably attired when they had company or went to church. Most were aware of changing styles and sought to follow them, though the amount of cash and time they had at their disposal was strictly limited. Assem-bling dresses was both complicated and time-consuming, so women usually shared some of labor it involved.

Women did not work on dresses intermittently, but rather made them in short bursts of sustained activity. Eighteen-year-old Jennie Carley, for example, made a dress in five days after the school term, purchasing the cloth and trimmings with money she had earned by teaching. She began to cut out the bodice herself, but soon sought help with it from her older sister Joanna. Her mother assumed some of Jennie's regular household chores so she could spend most of her time on her sewing. After four days of intense labor, Jennie wrote: "my head ached so I had to stop. Ma told me to go to bed. I laid there till most noon." In the afternoon, Jennie and her mother worked together; by the end of the day they had "finished dress!" (10 November 1864). When women were working hard to get a dress done, the task might interfere with their other activities and even im-pinge on their hours of sleep.

Women exchanged information and shared labor more exten-sively in sewing than they did in any other kind of work. Sometimes kinswomen worked cooperatively; sometimes one woman employed another. This was a continuum rather than a dichotomy, however, and in practice the two were often almost indistinguishable. Women sometimes paid their relatives for assistance, while neighbors sometimes helped one another freely with the expectation that eventually the favor would be returned. The same woman who was employed on one project might herself hire help for another.

For Velma Leadbetter Gates, dressmaking was a profession. The women in the Leadbetter family had taken pride in their sewing for generations, and when necessary they relied on their skills to earn a living. Velma Leadbetter had learned to sew, embroider, and even make lace from her grandmother. Her aptitude earned her an apprenticeship with a French dressmaker in Binghamton, and she eventually opened a shop in Wilkes-Barre, Pennsylvania. After Velma married Russell Buck Gates and returned to the Nanticoke Valley, she used her sewing skills within the neighborhood network of mutual aid among female relatives and friends. Local women frequently sought her expert assistance in dressmaking, asking her advice about what would look well and be economical, commissioning her to purchase material and design patterns for them, and relying on her to cut out, fit, and sometimes sew the garments. She was generally recompensed in some way: with produce from their gardens and orchards or prize chicks from their poultry flocks, with their labor in heavy housecleaning, or with payment in cash. Since Velma was a professional dressmaker, even her relatives paid for her services. At the same time, her work for her friends and neighbors had a cooperative character.[2]

Velma recorded a week she spent sewing for Helen Davis Benton in 1893:

> Monday 9 October   I get up early   do my chores   Leroy comes up after me to sew   Russ come down horseback   stay all night   we sing in the evening and don't go to bed until about 12 o'clock baste Helen's black dress and commence her gray dress
> Tuesday 10 October   Get up with bad head-ache but go to sewing   fit Helen's dress then lie down an hour before dinner . . . Em & Carrie & Gene come up there and bring Aunt Rozella home   they go home early   I sew until night   then give out

2. Louise Gates Gunsalus (1894–1983), interviews by author, 20 March and 12 July 1981; Paul and Louise Gunsalus, *A Record of the Descendants of Thomas and Anna Rowley Leadbetter* (Maine, N.Y.: privately printed, 1980).

Wednesday 11 October   Russ digs potatoes churns & boils up a kettle of swill. . . I baste and finish Helen's dress
Thursday 12 October   Get up and bake bread   Leroy comes up after me with Ethel   sew all day   Mrs Corbin & Miss Prince and children come there   Leroy brought Milton and I home   Russ was abed   Paid me $1.85
Friday 13 October   I work around all day. Russ & Milt goes hunting and chestnutting all day.

Helen recorded those same days in her diary:

Monday 9 October   When Vell came she worked on my dress. We had one day to ourselves. Russ came down and staid all night.
Tuesday 10 October   Mother Benton came home from East Maine. Vell here.
Wednesday 11 October   Leroy went down with the milk this morning. . . I sewed all the time I could get.
Thursday 12 October   Roena, Lydia, Marcia and Fannie came over. I had my chicken. It was a pleasant day. Vell and Milt here.
Friday 13 October   I did my ironing and left all that I could and sewed. I think that if I get through with that I will be very glad.

The similarities and differences in the ways the two women recorded those days are as interesting as how they shared and divided the labor. Velma did the skilled work of cutting, basting, and fitting, while Helen did the simpler and more tedious seaming. Velma spent three days in Helen's household, so she was free to devote herself to sewing; Helen carried on her normal activities and sewed when she could. Helen noted Velma's presence in much the same way she did that of other members of the Leadbetter family who came to visit; indeed, Velma's presence is described more in social terms than as paid employment in Helen's diary. "We work some and talk a little more," Helen wrote after one long winter afternoon of sewing (12 January 1894). In Velma's diary, on the other hand, the work predominates; visiting with Helen and their mutual relatives provided only temporary relief. Velma enjoyed the time she spent with Helen, but she regarded the sewing she did for her friend as work.

Many rural women were paid in kind or cash for helping others with dressmaking. This was not a regular occupation in the same way the dressmaking might be in the city; country dressmakers did not keep shops. For rural women, dressmaking was a more casualized occupation. Dressmakers went to the houses of their customers or received them at home, and few could support themselves on the money they earned. At the same time, dressmaking was one way that rural women could contribute toward their own support or supplement the family income, precisely because it could be done on a flexible schedule at home and in the neighborhood. Grace Howard, who grew up on a farm in West Chenango, studied with a professional dressmaker in Binghamton so she could earn money in the rural community. She had found employment as a servant in an urban boardinghouse exhausting and confining; her diary is filled with complaints of isolation and loneliness while she was working in the city. Being a dressmaker in the country, on the other hand, enabled her to combine gainful labor with sociability.

Women like Velma Leadbetter Gates thought of their sewing as an art, not just as a necessity. The most eloquent testimony to women's desire to use their skills to beautify their surroundings as well as to adorn their persons is not in their diaries but rather in the pieces of fine needlework that have been handed down in Nanticoke Valley families. Ranging from young girls' samplers through brides' embroidered linens to old women's crocheted doilies, these pieces employ techniques not found in contemporary popular pattern books; local women passed on their mothers' skills and developed new forms of their own. These artifacts exemplify women's willingness to devote many of their precious leisure hours to work that was creative and expressive rather than merely functional. Not all women chose this mode of enhancing their daily lives; some read and wrote poetry, while others played the piano and sang. There was a common impulse behind all these activities, but women's love of beauty and their desire to bring it into their world received its most lasting embodiment in their needlework.

Nanticoke Valley families count quilts among the most precious of the artifacts that have been passed down to them. The evidence of the diaries, however, suggests that in this community during the late nineteenth century quilting was neither as universal nor as sociable an activity as it was later thought to have been.[3] Historically, women

3. During the twentieth century, quilting has received attention first as American "folk art" and more recently as a women's art form. While recent scholarship has correctly criticized the distinction between "high art" and "craft" which has excluded much of women's artistic production from art history, it has tended to celebrate the art of quilting and divorce it from both its functional purpose and other forms of women's work. In the 1930s and 1940s, art historians emphasized the abstract designs that accorded with their modernist aesthetic; in the 1960s and 1970s, women's historians stressed the narrative elements that express women's life histories. Both distort the varied meanings quilts had to their makers. I have documented the matter-of-fact way in which local women approached quilting during the late nineteenth century in part to counteract this romanticization.

began to make quilts when they stopped weaving sheets, blankets, and coverlids. Quilts utilized materials women had on hand and turned old cloth to new purposes. The preparatory work of piecing blocks could be done at intervals of relative leisure and spread out over a period of months or years. The process of quilting, however, involved the same kind of intense labor that making dresses did. Most women who grew up in the valley knew how to quilt, just as they all learned how to sew. Some took a special interest in the art and became quite adept, while others quilted no more often than absolutely necessary and preferred to tie "comfortables" (comforters) when they had to make bedclothes.

The accounts of quilting contained in women's diaries are mostly matter-of-fact records of tasks undertaken and completed; they treat quilting like any other sewing project. Women often worked alone, not only when they pieced blocks but also when they did the final stitching. Louisa Carley McIntyre Dence, for example, made two quilts without any help at all during a two-week period in 1875. Ordinarily women who lived together would share the labor, but they often worked on the quilt at different times. Helen Davis Benton's diary contains a number of accounts of quilt making that suggest the variety of circumstances under which such projects were carried on. In January of 1877, just a year before her marriage, Helen made a quilt while she was staying with a female friend her own age. The task preoccupied Helen for a week. Help from her friend, two female relatives, and an expert neighbor was essential in getting it done, but Helen's description of the process makes it sound more like a bout of intense labor than like a social activity. Helen helped make a quilt just after her stepbrother, Sam Andrews, was married. She and her new sister, Mary Pope Andrews, put the quilt on a frame, and a number of women—both single and married, both relatives and neighbors—came to the Davises' house to help (28 February 1877). This instance most closely resembles what people have come to think of as typical of women's quilting. But other instances were quite different. Helen made a quilt for herself a year after her marriage; she did the quilting all alone in an upstairs back chamber, so it took her a month to finish. A decade later, Helen, Aunt Jane, and Mother Benton made a quilt; the three women worked together every afternoon for over a week. Two years later, Helen began a quilt by herself; on the days that she "did not do much housework" she "got along quite a little," but she needed Jane's help in the end (28 January 1891). Helen Davis Benton, then, seemed to regard quilting primarily as a utilitarian activity. She was no more patient with it than with sewing, and she enlisted what help she could get to finish each project as quickly as possible. Even so, Helen often worked alone, and she seldom had the assistance of anyone outside the house. The way Helen did her quilting was not unusual. Of the three dozen instances of quilting mentioned in the Nanticoke Valley diaries, only three—including Helen Davis and Mary Pope Andrews's quilting—involved a gathering of women who did not usually live and work together. This does not mean that there were no "quilting parties" in the Nanticoke Valley. But quilting as a social event was clearly separated from quilting as a household work activity.

Mutual Aid in Sickness

Women called upon one another for assistance with sewing projects that required an extra pair of hands or skills they did not possess. The aid women provided to one another in sickness was quite different; women shared the whole range of their responsibilities. The ways in which this happened illuminate both the nature of women's work and the ties among women that joined one household to another. The help ranged from baking bread to taking full charge of the household; it might occupy an afternoon or continue for months. Some aid was offered freely and some was recompensed in cash, but no matter what the arrangement, most assistance took place within the context of long-term relationships among women. The expectation that aid would be given and returned when the need arose was central to women's relations with one another. Mutual aid joined women to their mothers, sisters, and daughters when they lived in separate households. It formed much of the substance of kinship among aunts, nieces, and cousins, between mothers and their sons' wives, and among women who married into the same family. It also created bonds among neighbors resembling those among kin in their intimacy, scope, and duration. It was this sharing of ordinary burdens, this experience of taking up one another's yokes and working for a while in one another's households, that created and expressed a sense of commonality among women.

In 1875, Louisa Carley McIntyre Dence kept a diary during a six-month period when both she and her son, Chauncey McIntyre, were ill. Her account records how neighbors and kin cooperated to maintain the household when the wife and mother was unable to fulfill her normal responsibilities and there was no daughter to carry on the work. The thirty-four-year-old Louisa and her twelve-year-old son were living with her second husband, Samuel, and their eight-year-old son, Alfred, on the small farm north of Glen Aubrey which Louisa had taken over from her parents. Her married sisters, Polly Barnes and Elizabeth Slack, lived on adjacent farms just two miles farther north along the creek; another sister, Jennie Carley Graves, lived on the outskirts of Binghamton.

Throughout Louisa's and Chauncey's illnesses, women from the neighborhood came over almost every day. Some brought provisions, some helped out with the housework, and some took care of Chauncey; occasionally they nursed Louisa herself. Louisa's female relatives came to stay with the family when her condition was most serious. Eventually they decided that Louisa simply had to have regular help in the household. Emma Barnes, Polly's sixteen-year-old daughter, stayed for six weeks.

Mutual aid and employment were not distinct forms of work relationships among Nanticoke Valley women; rather, they flowed into one another within the milieu of kinship and friendship that linked women in the community. The employment status of many women who lived and worked in households other than their own remains ambiguous in the available records. Although in the absence of specific information about payment the question cannot finally be resolved, it seems that a female relative would be paid for helping out in the household if she had given up other paid employment in order to do so. Nonkin were almost always paid something for their labor. On the other hand, some mothers sent their daughters into other households as a form of reciprocation for services their families had previously received; no money changed hands in most of these instances. Women shared their labor in multifarious ways. The flexibility of the system of mutual aid was one of its crucial virtues, for it enabled women to share their resources in emergencies as well as respond to the predictable changes of family life.[4]

Hired Help

What was it like to work as hired help in Nanticoke Valley households? There was no radical discontinuity between kinship, friend-

4. The role of young women in networks of mutual aid in London working-class neighborhoods is described in Anna Davin, "Working or Helping? London Working-Class Children in the Domestic Economy," in *Households and the World-Economy*, ed. Joan Smith, Immanuel Wallerstein, and Hans-Dieter Evers (Beverly Hills, Calif.: Sage Publications, 1984), 215–32. There are substantial parallels between close-knit urban working-class neighborhoods and the Nanticoke Valley in this regard.

ship, and employment; even when there was no actual kinship tie between a woman and her "hired girl," the relationship between them was in part modeled on kin relations. Employment did not, in itself, create social distance, although it might reproduce existing inequalities between people. In the countryside, hired help and their employers not only had similar occupational and ethnic backgrounds, but often shared a common religious affiliation or lived in the same neighborhood. Class and ethnic differences were more obvious in the villages, where young Irish immigrant women worked as domestic servants in the households of Protestant merchants. On farms, service brought people into close cooperative relationships, for hired help were integrated into the household whether or not they belonged to the family. People sought to hire help whom they knew would easily fit into domestic life as well as diligently perform their assigned tasks. This does not mean, of course, that the relationship between employer and employee was not a hierarchical one. But questions of authority were handled as much in generational as in contractual terms.

Some young women who worked as servants in farm households felt like daughters. The seventeen-year-old Martha Warner, who grew up in Glen Aubrey, "hired out" to the Fuller family, who farmed in the town of Barker just east of Nanticoke, for three dollars a week from April to October of 1872. The family consisted of Mr. and Mrs. Fuller, "the boys" (sons whom Martha always treated as a group in her diary), and three daughters, Jennie, Sophia, and DeEtte. DeEtte was just Martha's age, and the two girls worked together every day; occasionally their activities intersected with those of Mrs. Fuller and the other girls. Martha did not do a larger share of the more difficult or disagreeable work than DeEtte did, nor did she work longer hours. She took a certain pride in their accomplishments, noting that she and DeEtte had baked a dozen pies one day and that "Mrs. Fuller, Sophie and I have canned 117 quarts of plums and made 44 pounds of preserves" over a two-week period in late summer (2 September 1872). Martha and DeEtte were jointly responsible for "taking care of the butter," from skimming the milk through churning to packing the finished product. During haying and harvest season, they also took over the milking: "DeEtte and I milked 24 cows . . . the boys worked at haying all day" (25 July 1872). They did not help in the fields, however, except to draw in oats. The work Martha did at the Fullers' was strikingly similar to the work she did at home. The major difference between the time she spent at home and the time she worked at the Fullers' was that she earned almost fifty dollars through her employment. Her day-to-day interactions with the family were not shaped by the financial arrangement between them but rather by friendship and shared labor.

Helen Davis was employed as a servant at least twice during her youth. In the late summer of 1874, just before Helen entered the Whitney's Point Academy at the age of nineteen, she went to live with and work for the Clark family in the village in order to contribute toward the cost of her education. Her diary entry for the first day eloquently expresses her feelings about her new situation: "I ate breakfast at Roena's and then Bridget departed for her new place of abode" (17 August 1874). Calling herself "Bridget" was Helen's way of saying that she had become a domestic servant in a village household, a position usually occupied by young women from a lower class and minority ethnic group. Helen needed a job to continue her education, and Mrs. Clark, whose husband was a minister, took an interest in young women attending the academy. At the same time, Helen was not paid more than an Irish servant would have been, nor was she treated like a member of the family. Helen was aware of the ambiguities of her position, writing after she had been there a month that "Mrs. Clark and my humble self have worked quite hard all day" (24 October 1874). Although Mrs. Clark worked along with Helen, she left the heavy and dirty tasks for the younger woman to do. She also expected Helen to keep on working while she herself went out. Helen's working days had no fixed limits; she was on call whenever she was not at school or church, although occasionally she noted that she "worked for myself" in the evening on some sewing. Sometimes Helen escaped to visit her sister, but she was called back when Mrs. Clark needed her.

Helen's experience at the Ketchums' three years later followed much the same pattern. She recorded her agreement to work there with unconcealed distaste: "Mrs. Ketchum was here to see me, I am going to work there. What a word—work! work!" (12 January 1877). She "started for my new home" on the first of March. Although Ketchumville was just over the Tioga County line about five miles northwest of Maine village, Helen felt "so far away from home and everyone that I know" that she was quite lonely (4 March 1877). It was not so much the distance as the demands of her work that kept her from seeing her friends more often. The establishment in Ketchumville was not only a farm but also a hotel that catered to travelers and regular boarders. Helen was the only hired help, so she had to be ready to serve guests at any hour of the day or night seven days a week. The job seemed endless: "About eight I thought I would go to bed but two gentlemen came in and wanted supper" (24 April 1877).

Helen's relationship with Mrs. Ketchum was somewhat more equal than it had been with Mrs. Clark. Mrs. Ketchum herself worked as hard as any farm woman; she and Helen cooperated on some tasks and divided others fairly flexibly between them. But there were still inequalities in their division of labor. Sometimes Helen resented her employer's comparative freedom:

> I got breakfast and Mrs. Ketchum made some pies and a tin of gingerbread and soon after breakfast went down to her Mother's and drove her new pony and Bridget had the rest of the work to do. (1 September 1877)

When Mrs. Ketchum was unwell she took to her bed, while Helen had to keep on working no matter how ill she felt. Occasionally the situation upset Helen so much that she could or would not carry on:

> I got up and got breakfast. Mrs. K. was sick. I did nearly all the work that was done in the forenoon. I got the dinner work done and sat down to make button holes when four men come and wanted supper. Mr. K. got it. I felt pretty bad and had a cry a little. I guess it did me good, I have felt better since. (3 August 1877)

Such moments of rebellion followed by tears improved Helen's state of mind temporarily, but they did not alter her situation.

These two accounts represent the extremes of possible relationships between Nanticoke Valley families and the young women they employed. Most young women who worked as hired help occupied a position somewhere in between that of a daughter and that of "Bridget." Although native-born women working in the rural community did not experience the exploitation and exclusion that marked the situations of Irish immigrant women in villages or of most domestic servants in cities, some were not treated like daughters.[5] What mattered was not merely the servants' burden of labor but also the degree of inequality in the division of labor between themselves and family members. The social distance between servants and their employers and the effective distance between their family and friends and their place of work were equally important. The women

5. This exploitation occurred more often in nonfarm than in farm households. In the country as well as the city, servants' conditions were most difficult in commercial boarding establishments. Faye Dudden, *Serving Women: Household Service in Nineteenth-Century America* (Middletown, Conn.: Wesleyan University Press, 1983), examines rural as well as urban households.

who had the most positive experience belonged to the same social network as the families for whom they worked; not only could they continue many of their former relationships and activities, but they already were friends with the daughters in the household. These young women were integrated into the social lives as well as work routines of their employers.

In the Nanticoke Valley, treating hired help "like one of the family" was regarded as the ideal. People were uncomfortable with the class and cultural differences in their community and preferred to avoid dealing with them. Modeling employment on kinship was one way to negotiate across such differences. Relying on mutual aid among friends and neighbors was even more effective; the assumption that everyone was equal and over the long run would have similar needs was fundamental to reciprocal relationships among households. This assumption was, perhaps, easier for women to act on than it was for men. Rural women whose family fortunes differed nonetheless had similar work to do. Young women circulated among households of their kin and nonkin working with or without wages depending on the needs and resources of everyone involved.

Sharing Labor

Women's work sharing was important not only for what it enabled them to accomplish but also for its impact on the quality of their working lives. Women could complete some tasks more quickly by cooperating with one another than by working alone, and they might not undertake some projects at all unless they could rely on the expertise of other women. But women worked together more often than considerations of efficiency and proficiency would have required them to do. Sharing work was a way of breaking the monotony of their daily routine and of escaping the isolation of household work. Women valued the sociability of sharing labor, and they created opportunities to do so.

Few women in the Nanticoke Valley worked alone. If a woman was the only female in her household, she relied on her family and friends for assistance and companionship. Lucretia Ketchum Vandemark lived with her husband, Wilson, on a small farm near Union Center; all three of their children had married and left home. Still, Lucretia and her daughters assisted one another as much as possible. When Sylvia Vandemark DuBois had a baby, Lucretia went to stay with her for a week: "taken care of Sylvia and the baby. It cries a good deal" (5 March 1893). A month later, Sylvia and her children came to stay with her parents. "Sylvia and I done a large washen, in the afternoon worked on her dress," Lucretia noted the day after her daughter arrived (3 April 1893). Lucretia and her neighbors relied on one another for assistance on a regular basis. Mrs. Gibbs, who lived on an adjacent farm, came over to help Lucretia paper her sitting room; Lucretia "went up and white washed" at her neighbor Ann's house (26, 27 April 1893; 10 May 1893).

Most women in the Nanticoke Valley shared their households or their houses with other women on a permanent basis, as well as receiving and paying visits that might last an afternoon, a week, or a month. The regular presence of other women in the household lightened each woman's burden of labor. In the summer of 1888, Helen Davis Benton remarked: "Taking it all together there are five women of us and we all manage to keep busy" (8 July 1888). Three of the women were staying on the other side of the house; Rosella Benton was ill, so her sister Jane Leadbetter and her niece Saville Leadbetter Jackson were tending to her. Helen's widowed friend Lavantia Briggs Lewis was staying on her side of the house; Lavantia had come the previous spring when Helen was ill but stayed on for a year and a half. These women were also kept busy by the added duties of haying season; at least six male members of the Leadbetter family had come to help Leroy with the haying that week, so there were seven men to feed and all the chores to do as well. Having other women in the household helped women to get through such busy times without becoming exhausted.

Sharing labor enabled each woman to perform the tasks she preferred. The work relationship established by Nellie Paisley and her new sister, Grace Howard Paisley, shows how two women might share and divide the labor for which they were responsible. Nellie did not enjoy housework; she did the laundry irregularly and often lamented that her bread turned out poorly. On the other hand, Nellie took a lively interest in the poultry and willingly helped with barn chores: "Johnnie started for Binghamton . . . I milked and watered the horses and got down the Hay. After Johnnie came home I took up the carpet, moped and put it down again. Felt as if I had done a good turn. Johnnie and Pa helped me a good deal" (30 January 1891). Nellie preferred active physical labor to more sedentary pursuits. She was able to follow her inclinations without feeling that she was neglecting her domestic duties after Grace joined the household. Grace did the washing and ironing every week, took over the regular cooking, and made household linens and clothing for the entire family. She and

Nellie worked in the garden and preserved fruits and vegetables together. Nellie was free to work outdoors gathering and boiling sap, hiving bees, and tending her poultry flock; she did the chores with her brother and churned and packed the butter herself. The two women, with different but complementary skills and preferences, worked together harmoniously.

Women shared their most distinctly gender-marked labor with other women within and beyond their households more often than they did with their husbands, fathers, and sons. Still, work relationships among women interacted with work relationships between women and men. Within the household, the reciprocity and flexibility that characterized same-gender and cross-gender relationships enhanced each other. Helen Davis Benton was able to spend so much of her time in the barn with her husband because other women shared the work of the house with her. She was not solely responsible for preserving and preparing food, making and mending clothing, or cleaning the house; often she was outside helping Leroy in the fields and meadows while her female relatives were getting meals, sewing, or sweeping. Similarly, in the Paisley family the arrival of Grace Howard Paisley, who assumed responsibility for routine household tasks, allowed Nellie Paisley to spend more time working outdoors with her brother John.

Women who had no other women in their households with whom to share their gender-specific tasks turned to their female relatives and neighbors for assistance. Similarly, men who could not expect their wives, daughters, and mothers to assist them in planting, haying, and harvesting shared those tasks with men on other farms. Yet in families like the Gateses, who observed a fairly strict division of labor by gender, the work women and men performed cooperatively with members of their own sex in other households was carried on within social relationships that were not segregated by gender. Velma Leadbetter Gates shared her work most often with women in the households with whom her husband exchanged work. Often they coordinated their work sharing in order to be together. When Velma did her cooking up at Lydia's, Russell was haying with Byron on his parents' farm; husband and wife were able to spend the day in close proximity and eat dinner together. Velma sewed for their neighbor Mrs. Dillenbeck while Leroy and Mr. Dillenbeck worked on repairing the Gates's back stoop. Lucretia and Wilson Vandemark, like Velma and Russell Gates, did not help each other very often in the fields or in the household; they turned to neighbors of their own sex when they needed assistance. At the same time, Lucretia and Wilson shared their work with other couples in their neighborhood and kin group. Often Wilson worked with the husband while Lucretia worked with the wife; thus "Wilson sowed oats for Luke" while Lucretia whitewashed for Luke's wife Ann (10 May 1893). Women's and men's work relationships with other women and men in their kin groups and neighborhoods not only overlapped but actually coincided. Thus gender divisions within the household might be counteracted by the sharing of work between one household and another.

CHAPTER NINE

Valuing Women's Work

How much comes from the labor of women?
　　　—Report of U.S. Commissioner of Agriculture, 1871

How did Nanticoke Valley residents think about the value of the labor that women performed? Did women and men have a common understanding of the value of the labor each performed, or did the differences in their work experiences give rise to different perspectives, divergent ways of valuing the distinctive work they did? The question is complex, for it involves both rural residents' conceptions of the value of labor and their notions about gender. Women and men did not necessarily agree about these things; they may have held different beliefs even though in practice they coordinated their activities. This chapter examines not what women contributed to the farm family economy but what women and men thought about the labor women performed in an expanding market economy.

The valuation of work is an ideological matter. The term "valuation" indicates that value is an ascribed rather than inherent quality; it is attributed to things by people rather than intrinsic to the things themselves. Value is socially defined, and the amount of value assigned to different things is socially determined. In any society, the value of various types of labor arises from the social relationships into which people enter through their work.[1] Gender relations, like class

1. This definition is informed by Marx's discussion of value, but differs from it in crucial respects. Although Marx believed that the value of commodities is socially determined, he contended that the value of any product is the amount of socially necessary labor expended in its production; the value of labor thus determines the value of

relations and relations of domination and subordination based on race, affect the way labor is valued. In gender-divided societies, women's and men's work are usually seen as having different kinds of value. In male-dominated societies, men's work is generally regarded as more valuable than women's work, even though women often question and occasionally contest the devaluation of their labor.[2] The way work is valued is shaped by struggles among different

---

commodities. The value of labor itself is determined by the same law: the amount of labor necessary to reproduce the laborer, both directly through the services he requires and indirectly through the commodities he consumes in order to be fit to labor again, determines the value of his labor time. As the pronouns suggest, Marx's account is gender biased as well as focused on wage labor under capitalism. Although Marx recognized the importance of reproductive labor in a way that bourgeois political economists did not, he failed to explore how labor power is reproduced and how reproductive and productive labor are articulated in the family and society. Marx thus replicated within his own theory the assumptions about gender relations which underlay classical political economy. My analysis, which focuses on the process by which capitalist relations of production and concepts of value became established, must necessarily take as problematic the very features Marx assumed: the responsibility of women for reproductive labor within the family and the devaluation of that labor. My definition of value, then, is less absolute and more relational than Marx's. The distinction between use value and exchange value, while helpful as a way of characterizing two types of value any one object may possess, is less helpful as a way of characterizing different types of labor. When applied to women's and men's work, it tends to reify the differences between their products rather than describe the relationships into which women and men enter through their labor. Accordingly, I have avoided those categories and focused instead on processes and relationships.

2. This conceptualization of gender and work has been influenced by feminist analyses of both capitalist and noncapitalist societies; the distinction between gender-divided and male-dominated societies is based on comparative studies done by anthropologists, while the statement about the devaluation of women's work is based on historical studies of England and the United States. Relevant books and collections of articles include (in chronological order of publication): Sheila Rowbotham, *Women's Consciousness, Man's World* (London: Penguin Books, 1973); Michele Zimbalist Rosaldo and Louise Lamphere, eds., *Woman, Culture and Society* (Stanford, Calif.: Stanford University Press, 1974); Rayna R. Reiter, ed., *Toward an Anthropology of Women* (New York: Monthly Review Press, 1975); Diane Leonard Barker and Sheila Allen, eds., *Dependence and Exploitation in Work and Marriage* (London: Longman, 1976), and Diane Leonard Barker and Sheila Allen, eds., *Sexual Divisions and Society: Process and Change* (London: Tavistock Publications, 1976); Zillah R. Eisenstein, ed., *Capitalist Patriarchy and the Case for Socialist Feminism* (New York: Monthly Review Press, 1979); Anne Phillips and Barbara Taylor, "Sex and Skill: Notes toward a Feminist Economics," *Feminist Review* 6 (1980): 79–88; Eleanor Burke Leacock, *Myths of Male Dominance: Collected Articles on Women Cross-Culturally* (New York: Monthly Review Press, 1981); Alice Kessler-Harris, *Out to Work: A History of Wage-Earning Women in the United States* (New York: Oxford University Press, 1982); Bettina Berch, *The Endless Day: The Political Economy of Women and Work* (New York: Harcourt Brace Jovanovich, 1982); Patricia Caplan and Janet M. Burja, eds., *Women United, Women Divided: Comparative Studies of Ten Contemporary Cultures* (Bloomington: Indiana University Press, 1982); Eleanor Burke Leacock, Helen I. Safa et al., *Women's Work: Development and the Division of Labor by Gender* (South Hadley, Mass.: Bergin and Garvey, 1986).

groups about the nature and amount of value attributed to their labor as well as by the way those groups relate to one another in the
work process.

The Expanding Market Economy

Since the valuation of labor is socially determined, it also changes
historically. Fundamental changes in the organization of production
which restructure the social relationships into which people enter
through their work also transform conceptions of value. The transition to capitalism in the United States from the mid-eighteenth
through the late nineteenth centuries involved structural shifts in the
orientation, organization, and evaluation of work; new notions of
value were part and parcel of the process of capitalist expansion.
American farmers were gradually drawn into national and international markets. As they devoted an increasing proportion of their land
and labor to the production of marketable commodities, so they came
to regard their cash crops as more valuable than their subsistence-
oriented production.[3]

At the same time, farming was not restructured entirely on a capitalist basis. Unlike the urban artisans whom they closely resembled at
the beginning of the process of capitalist transformation, farmers did
not become divided into employers and wage laborers; property and
labor remained unified in most farm families. The fusion of the
family with the enterprise meant that farmers had distinctive goals;
the long-range accumulation of property and the intergenerational
transmission of the farm remained more important than short-term
profits. The organization of work was shaped not solely by the labor
requirements of farm operations but also by gender and generational relations among husbands and wives, parents and children.
Farm families continued to produce much of their own subsistence
and to organize their work in ways not dictated by the market.
So, too, they did not entirely accept capitalist conceptions of value;
their concrete activities, gender and generational relationships, and
long-range goals provided a basis for alternative ways of evaluating work.

While the unity of family and farm gave rural residents a distinc-

3. The standard histories of agriculture by Bidwell and Falconer, Gates, and Danhof emphasize the market orientation of American farmers before the Civil War.
Robert A. Gross, "Culture and Cultivation: Agriculture and Society in Thoreau's
Concord," *Journal of American History* 69 (1982): 42–61, is an excellent local study of
commercialization.

tive position within and perspective on the capitalist system, the social relations among people in the local community were equally important in providing a basis for resistance to capitalist conceptions of value. Rural communities were characterized by customary modes of exchange which were not capitalist in character; farmers, artisans, and laborers were bound together by long-term, reciprocal relations of interdependence.[4] The notion of "independence" that republican farmers espoused during the late eighteenth and early nineteenth centuries did not refer to the independence of one farm household from another but rather to the independence of each property-owning family from landlords and employers and to the collective independence of the rural community from speculators and merchants. A "yeoman" farmer owned the land and livestock necessary for agricultural production and could, with the labor of his wife and children, produce enough to support and reproduce his household without having to mortgage his land or borrow his working capital. As the pronouns suggest, this notion of "independence" was profoundly gender marked; the "yeoman" farmer was, according to republican ideology, the adult male head of a household, the legal owner of its property and its representative in civil society. This conception was as much a political ideal as an economic one. In fact, it was realized in the political domain more completely than it was in the economic realm, for from the early nineteenth century on most adult white males in rural communities were enfranchised, but by the Civil War many farm families were working mortgaged or rented land.

4. This analysis of the social relations of rural communities during the early nineteenth century is based on a variety of community studies for New England, the mid-Atlantic, the upland South, and the upper Midwest. Community studies that directly address the question of relations among farmers, artisans, and laborers include Susan Geib, " 'Changing Works': Agriculture and Society in Brookfield, Massachusetts, 1785–1820" (Ph.D. diss., Boston University, 1981); Jack Larkin's "The World of the Account Book: Some Perspectives on Economic Life in Rural New England in the Early 19th Century" (paper presented to the Society for Historians of the Early American Republic, Sturbridge, Mass., July 1988), and "The Merriams of Brookfield: Printing in the Economy and Culture of Rural Massachusetts in the Early Nineteenth Century," *Proceedings of the American Antiquarian Society* 96 (1986): 39–72; Hal S. Barron's *Those Who Stayed Behind: Rural Society in Nineteenth-Century New England* (Cambridge: Cambridge University Press, 1984), and "Staying Down on the Farm: Social Processes of Settled Rural Life in the Nineteenth-Century North," in *The Countryside in the Age of Capitalist Transformation*, ed. Steven Hahn and Jonathan Prude (Chapel Hill: University of North Carolina Press, 1985), 327–43; John Mack Faragher's *Sugar Creek: Life on the Illinois Prairie* (New Haven, Conn.: Yale University Press, 1986), and "Open-Country Community: Sugar Creek, Illinois, 1820–1850," in *The Countryside in the Age of Capitalist Transformation*, ed. Hahn and Prude, 233–58; Steven Hahn, *The Roots of Southern Populism: Yeoman Farmers and the Transformation of the Georgia Upcountry, 1850–1890* (New York: Oxford University Press, 1983).

The "independence" of the rural community as a whole from speculators and merchants was founded on the exchange of goods and
services among local households. Because this exchange took place
primarily among households that owned and worked their own
property, it was regarded as occurring among equals. Prices for both
goods and services traded among rural households were not dictated by supply and demand or even by the prices of such goods
in the market beyond the local community; rather, they were set
by custom and maintained by consensus. This agreement does not
mean that relations among rural households were indeed equal:
some people had to work for others because they did not have
enough property to work for themselves, and some farmers had to
depend on others for such essentials as teams and plows. But these
inequalities were based on generation and gender as much as on
class; relations between well-off and poor families were marked by
reciprocal and continuing obligations rather than mediated by the
market.5

The transition to capitalism in the countryside undermined the
collective independence of farm households. Historically, American
farmers successfully resisted proletarianization. Concerted action to
defend and extend freehold land tenure began during the Revolution and culminated in the Civil War; white farmers established
the principle of freehold tenure in the West despite the power of
slaveholders and the profits reaped by land speculators. Resisting
the impact of capitalist enterprises on rural communities was more
difficult. After the Civil War, farmers organized to control the prices
they received for the commodities they sold, seeking to regulate
the market so that they, rather than shippers and processors, reaped
the returns from the crops they sowed. Rural artisans were unable
to avoid absorption into the urban industrial order, and the deindustrialization of the countryside made farmers more dependent on
capitalist firms for equipment and supplies. Nevertheless, farmers
continued to rely on one another for many goods and services necessary for agricultural production. They sought to substitute labor
for cash, to borrow rather than to buy, and to depend as much as
possible on their own and their neighbors' resources. These strategies
of saving, they believed, would help them remain independent of the
market and enable them to accumulate property. The social relations
of interdependence which these strategies involved provided the basis

5. Geib discusses the way in which relations between wealthier and poorer households sustained the fiction of equality at the same time that they allowed, or even required, wealthier households to support poorer ones.

for resistance both to the capitalist market and to capitalist notions of value.[6]

This historical perspective on the transition to capitalism in the countryside suggests that farm families who participated in the

6. The recent discussion of the transition to capitalism in rural America has been marked by continuing controversy over the degree to which farmers were oriented toward the market. These differences reflect not only differences in the economic histories of various regions, especially between New England and the mid-Atlantic and between coastal and inland communities, but also theoretical differences among historians. Classical economists have applied the model of "homo economicus" to the evidence and asserted that since farmers produced crops for the market they must have internalized its values. This line of argument began with the discovery that most farmers were not "self-sufficient" but rather engaged in extensive exchange relationships within and beyond the local community: Rodney C. Loehr, "Self-Sufficiency on the Farm," *Agricultural History* 26 (1952): 37–41; James T. Lemon, "Household Consumption in Eighteenth-Century America and Its Relationship to Production and Trade: The Situation among Farmers in Southeastern Pennsylvania," *Agricultural History* 41 (1967): 59–70; and Carole Shammas, "How Self-Sufficient Was Early America?" *Journal of Interdisciplinary History* 13 (1982): 247–72. Historians have recently attempted to show that prices in local markets varied with prices in regional, national, and international ones: Winifred Rothenberg, "The Market and Massachusetts Farmers, 1750–1855," *Journal of Economic History* 41 (1981): 283–314; and Bettye Hobbs Pruitt, "Self-Sufficiency and the Agricultural Economy of Eighteenth-Century Massachusetts," *William and Mary Quarterly* 41 (1984): 333–64.

Radical political economists, following Marx in assigning primacy to modes of production rather than to circulation, have distinguished simple commodity production, the sale of crops in the market, from capitalist agriculture, the production of crops for profit. The initial statement of this perspective is Michael Merrill, "Cash Is Good to Eat: Self-Sufficiency and Exchange in the Rural Economy of the United States," *Radical History Review* 4 (1977): 42–71, with comments in *Radical History Review* 18 (1978): 166–71, and 22 (1979–80): 129–46. A more general theoretical treatment is Kevin D. Kelly, "The Independent Mode of Production," *Review of Radical Political Economics* 11 (1979): 38–48. The controversy between radical and classical economists has been carried on in a dialogue about Winifred Rothenberg's article, "The Market and Massachusetts Farmers, 1750–1855," between Rona S. Weiss and Rothenberg, *Journal of Economic History* 43 (1983): 475–80, and by Michael A. Bernstein and Sean Wilentz, "Marketing, Commerce, and Capitalism in Rural Massachusetts," *Journal of Economic History* 44 (1984): 171–73. Allan Kulikoff, "The Transition to Capitalism in Rural America," *William and Mary Quarterly* 46 (1989): 120–44, offers a tentative synthesis of this question; Kulikoff explores the political dimensions of "yeoman" society and raises the problem of gender.

Most theoretical discussions of this question remain quite abstract, positing a "household mode of production" without tying it closely to the concrete activities of farm people or elucidating how that mode of production became transformed during the nineteenth century. The most complete analysis, which traces the emergence of capitalist relations from precapitalist ones in a single region, is Christopher Clark, "The Household Economy, Market Exchange, and the Rise of Capitalism in the Connecticut Valley, 1800–1860," *Journal of Social History* 13 (1979): 168–89, and *The Roots of Rural Capitalism: Western Massachusetts, 1780–1860* (Ithaca: Cornell University Press, 1990). Richard L. Bushman describes the goals, strategies, and perspectives of ordinary families in "Family Security in the Transition from Farm to City, 1750–1850," *Journal of Family History* 6 (1981): 238–56. In "Families and Farms: *Mentalité* in Pre-Industrial America," *William and Mary Quarterly* 35 (1978): 3–32, James Henretta considers how farmers thought about their economic activities as well as what they did.

market did not conduct all their economic relationships with people in the local community on the same basis that they did their transactions with the regional commodity market. Nor did they apply capitalist criteria for evaluating labor to all of the different kinds of work they did. Different ways of evaluating labor coexist in society, not simply because the replacement of one conception of value by another is a gradual and uneven process, but also because different work processes occupy different positions in relation to capitalist modes of production. The application of a capitalist calculus of value to all forms of labor is not complete until all types of work are commodified—a condition that twentieth-century society is approaching but has not yet reached. Similarly, different ways of conducting economic relationships coexist; the social relationships into which people enter through their work can vary significantly, depending not only on the work processes involved but also on the gender and generational positions of the parties to those relationships. Advanced capitalism has not yet reduced all working people to abstract, universal labor power and turned all human relationships into relations among things. In the nineteenth century, especially in rural communities, commodity fetishism did not prevail; farmers were still aware of the concrete qualities of labor and of the human dimensions of the relationships into which they entered through their work.

The degree to which farmers valued marketable commodities and devalued other forms of production can be investigated empirically. Although the elucidation of farmers' thinking on this matter is a more complex task than the computation of what proportion of their resources they devoted to commodity production, account books and diaries yield insight into the mental world of family farmers. The character of work relationships can be examined directly and the degree to which they were conducted on a market basis assessed. Finally, the articulation between different conceptions of value and different kinds of work relationships can be examined at the level of the household and community. The analysis that follows examines the various types of labor in the Nanticoke Valley during the late nineteenth century, focusing on the ways men and women evaluated work and conducted their economic dealings with one another. It explores people's conceptions of value primarily though the social relations of work, for it is only through the ways people recorded their economic interactions with others that their notions of value can be perceived. This method ensures that the analysis deals, not with individual and perhaps idiosyncratic definitions of value, but rather with the socially defined and generally accepted conceptions of economic relations which prevailed in the community.

Gender is a primary category in this analysis because men and women occupied different positions in civil society and stood, in principle, in different relations to the capitalist economy. As the heads of farm households, men owned productive property and represented their households in the market. Women gained access to property only through their relationships with men; legally and economically, their identity was subsumed by that of their fathers and husbands. In the process of capitalist expansion, an increasing proportion of economic and social life became controlled by a system in which women were fundamentally disadvantaged. Other modes of social and economic organization in which women occupied a more equal and/or independent position declined in importance; although they persisted in some aspects of social life, they were increasingly peripheral to the centers of money and power.

Furthermore, the gender division of labor intersected with capitalist expansion to produce substantial asymmetries in men's and women's relationship to the market. In most family farming regions of the northern United States, commercialization penetrated those farm operations for which men were responsible more rapidly and deeply than it did those for which women were responsible. Grain was the first great cash crop sold on the international market; from the late eighteenth through the mid-nineteenth centuries, the grain trade stimulated the commercialization of the rural economy and financed the purchase and development of western lands. Women on arable farms continued to engage in subsistence production in the garden, barnyard, and kitchen, but their work had a different meaning than it had had before. Formerly both women and men engaged primarily in production for use rather than for sale. Only the "surplus" that was left over once household needs were met was sold; small amounts of a great variety of products formed the stuff of economic exchange in local communities. Now men's cash crops, grown on a larger scale for more distant markets, were quite distinct from women's subsistence production. Even if women continued to sell small quantities of such products as eggs, poultry, and feathers, this operation was often regarded as a sideline to the primary farm operation, yielding "petty cash" for the household rather than making a significant contribution to the farm income. In arable farming regions, the gender division of labor corresponded to a significant degree with the distinction between commodity and subsistence production. By capitalist criteria, women's work was less valuable than men's work.

In some regions, however, the commodities farms began producing in larger quantities for sale were traditionally the responsibility of women. Dairying is the prime example, but market gardening and poultry raising were also important in the immediate vicinity of coastal cities and industrial villages. These involved women's work directly in the market economy.[7] The participation of women in commodity production had significant consequences for their position in farm families and rural communities. At the same time, women's active involvement in commercial dairying cannot be assumed to flow automatically from the traditional gender ascription of this operation. The gender division of labor was not a fixed normative structure that remained unchanged through the transition to capitalism. Men increasingly participated in dairying as the scale of production expanded. In some regions, they seem to have taken over the process entirely as it became commercialized. This shift is not surprising; in many regions of the world men's monopoly of market transactions, coupled with their ownership of land and control of credit, leads to their assertion of control over commodity production in agriculture.[8] In the transition to capitalism, women can become relegated to subsistence production even if they have previously engaged in production for local exchange. Gender relations in the evaluation of work change historically as the labor process and economic context of production are transformed.

Commodity Production

Dairying was the predominant market-oriented farm operation in the Nanticoke Valley; more farms sold dairy products than any other commodity, and the dairy was their primary source of income. Farm families regarded dairying as their most valuable form of work, and they devoted a substantial proportion of their land and labor to that operation, giving its demands priority in their work routines and arranging the rest of their activities around it. Dairying was also the most gender-integrated work process on Nanticoke Valley farms; men, women, and children all participated in the dairy operation in

7. Joan M. Jensen, "Cloth, Butter and Boarders: Women's Household Production for the Market," *Review of Radical Political Economics* 12 (1980): 14–24.

8. The classic analysis is Ester Boserup, *Women's Role in Economic Development* (New York: St. Martin's Press, 1970), and Ester Boserup, ed., *Women and National Development: The Complexities of Change* (Chicago: University of Chicago Press, 1977). Lourdes Beneria and Gita Sen, "Accumulation, Reproduction, and Women's Role in Economic Development: Boserup Revisited," in *Women's Work: Development and the Division of Labor by Gender*, ed. Eleanor Burke Leacock, Helen I. Safa et al. (South Hadley, Mass.: Bergin & Garvey, 1986), 141–57, critique Boserup's original formulation and summarize current feminist approaches to women in development.

flexible and varied ways. Because of the integration of family members' labor in simple commodity production, the contributions of men and women, parents and children were not evaluated separately. Individuals' contributions to the final product varied, depending on their commitment and skill, but these qualitative differences were not related in any systematic way to gender, nor could they be quantified and cast in monetary terms. The butter receipts or milk checks were credited to the family's account by the village merchants who shipped butter on commission to distant urban markets, or they were paid in cash by the wholesalers or customers in nearby cities to whom farmers sold their butter. Although family accounts were kept under men's names at village stores, women charged their own purchases against their family's account and credited their own produce to it. In the most important form of commodity production, then, women's and men's work was evaluated in the same integrated way that it was performed.

Other commodities sold in substantial amounts by a significant number of Nanticoke Valley farms included potatoes, apples, and poultry and eggs. Some farms sold only the surplus beyond what they required for their own use, but others produced much larger quantities for the market. The potato crop was in principle men's responsibility, but in practice women performed a considerable proportion of the labor. Men often wrote that their wives "helped" them with this task, while women generally recorded that they worked in the potato patch. Men sold potatoes along with other farm products in urban markets, and the receipts were part of the farm income. Although the sale of potatoes was more subject to masculine control than was the sale of dairy products, men recognized the labor women contributed to this operation. Other forms of commodity production were more clearly gender divided. Apples, maple sugar, and field crops were regarded as the product of masculine labor; if women occasionally helped with the work, their contribution was entirely subsumed by the men. Men marketed these commodities themselves, both within and beyond the local community.

On the other hand, women almost always controlled the poultry operation. Women sold eggs to village merchants or urban wholesalers, and the receipts were universally regarded as their own. Women generally traded their eggs more or less directly for supplies they needed for the household; sometimes they applied the balance to their family's account, but sometimes they kept separate egg accounts in their own names. Men did participate in the work that poultry keeping involved, especially by building and whitewashing chicken

coops, but this work was regarded as part of their general responsibility for farm maintenance rather than as a distinct contribution to
the poultry operation. Even more important, men grew the grain
used for chicken feed, yet this work was not regarded as entitling
them to a share of the income from eggs and chickens; only when
farmers purchased commercial feed would its cost be deducted from
the returns in computing the income the poultry flock yielded. Wom-
en's responsibility for the poultry thus subsumed their husbands'
contributions.

Women valued their poultry operations highly, for they knew that
the "egg money" was a crucial source of cash or credit to meet household needs. The money came in regularly from spring through late
fall; although the amounts received at any one time were small, they
added up to a considerable sum. Equally important, "egg money" enabled women to meet the demands of necessary but unexpected ex-
penditures and to get through periods when little cash was coming in
from other sources. When women marketed their own eggs and kept
separate accounts of how they spent the money, however, men were
not necessarily aware of the total value of the poultry operation and
the contribution it made to family income. The fact that at any one
time eggs brought in comparatively small sums of money relative to
the farm products men sold in large batches once or twice a year may
also have predisposed men to regard poultry as a petty form of commodity production. Women's control over the poultry operation gave
them a certain autonomy, but it did not guarantee that men would
recognize the value of their labor.

Subsistence Production

Nanticoke Valley farm families devoted a substantial proportion of
their resources to commodity production, but they also engaged in
subsistence production. During the late nineteenth century, as they
expanded the scale of their dairy operations, they did not dis-
continue many subsistence-oriented activities. Instead, they withdrew
land and labor from other, less lucrative market-oriented operations
and devoted those resources to dairying. They also scaled down some
operations, tailoring them to farm and household needs and elimi-
nating the surpluses that had formerly been sold. Farm families continued to produce their own meat, vegetables, and fruits as well as
most of the feed required by their livestock. Nanticoke Valley farmers,
like American farmers more generally, did not evaluate their subsis-

tence production in terms of the market; rather, they thought of their "living" as qualitatively different from the commodities they produced for sale.

Francis A. Walker, the superintendent of the census, remarked this fact in the introduction to the *Report on the Productions of Agriculture as returned at the Tenth Census, 1880.* The 1870 U.S. census had asked farmers to estimate the aggregate value of all farm products, but the results had not been satisfactory. Walker explained:

> It is undoubtedly true that . . . the returns of the aggregate value of farm products is likely to be inadequate by reason of the utter indisposition of the average agriculturist to reckon whatever is consumed upon the farm for the support of himself and his family among the products he is called upon to appraise. The spirit of the command, "thou shalt not muzzle the ox that treadeth out the corn," has a wider application in the mind of the farmer than to the dumb animals he employs. It would be altogether alien and repugnant to his sentiments to give a value, for the purposes of a statistical return, to the garden truck that is carried into the house; the fuel picked out of his woods; the fruit that his children eat; the corn that is sent to the mill for home use; or even the pig that is killed at Christmas. It stands, in his mind, like the corn which the unmuzzled ox, in the olden days, caught up as he made his round among the grain on the thrashing-floor. The statistician may just as well accept this limitation of the returns of the value of farm products first as last.[9]

Walker regarded farmers' refusal to appraise the value of what they consumed as irrational; such "sentiments" inhibited rational calculation of the total value of their farm products and the increase in their capital. Agricultural reformers also lamented the failure of farmers to calculate the costs and profits of their subsistence-oriented operations and weigh them against the returns they would receive from investing their resources in commodity production. Agricultural reformers judged many common subsistence-oriented farm operations as uneconomic, for they evaluated them according to a capitalist calculus. This "the average agriculturist" steadfastly refused to do, for it was "alien and repugnant to his sentiments."

In their own minds, farm families' "living" was entirely different from the commodities they sold and purchased. Farmers did not cal-

9. Francis A. Walker, "Introduction," *Report on the Productions of Agriculture as Returned at the Tenth Census, 1880,* xxvi.

culate the cost of the things they produced for their own use and
compare it to the cost of buying those same things in the marketplace. Subsistence and commodity production were not regarded as
equivalent or interchangeable modes of supplying family needs and
accumulating farm property. The family's "living" was the foundation
of its security and the guarantee of a modicum of independence from
the fluctuations of the market; subsistence production was closely allied in people's minds to land ownership. Finally, the farm family's
"living" was not a means, but rather an end in itself; as the gerund
form of the word itself suggests, it encompassed an entire way of life.

Both men and women engaged in subsistence production. Often
they did so in gender-segregated ways, as men took responsibility for
providing meat and women for supplying vegetables. But men and
women often cooperated in the processing of these products; for example, when men slaughtered animals women helped preserve the
meat and rendered the fat. Indeed, in the realm of subsistence production the produce of men's labor passed through women's hands
more often than the produce of women's labor passed through men's
hands, for women did the final preparation of most farm produce for
family consumption. Women were also involved in recycling farm
produce from one operation into another; for example, they commonly fed skimmed milk and scraps to the pigs. Although
subsistence-oriented operations were often divided by gender, men's
and women's subsistence-oriented work was integrated in the annual
cycle of the family farm.

As long as subsistence production was regarded as different in kind
from commodity production, women's and men's subsistence-oriented work was regarded as having the same kind of value. Furthermore, as long as the value of the things farm families produced for
their own use rather than for sale was not regarded as quantifiable
but rather was conceived in more concrete and particular ways, the
value of women's and men's subsistence production could not be
compared. Women and men both produced tangible things. Baskets
of beans, piles of pumpkins, and stacks of stovewood were simply different from one another. So long as they were not given monetary
equivalents, they remained distinct in quality and incommensurable
in quantity. The labor that produced them was not interchangeable
any more than the products were. Indeed, in subsistence production
people's relationships were not mediated through things the way they
were in the market; people related to one another directly through
their work activities rather than through an abstract evaluation of
their labor. Women and men interacted as producers and processors

of family subsistence. Because their work was not interchangeable and was perceived in qualitative terms, it could be regarded as characterized by gender difference. At the same time, because their work was integrated in practice and was not evaluated quantitatively, invidious comparisons between women's and men's work could not be made.

Wage Labor

Both women and men were paid wages for the work they did for people who did not belong to their families. Men had many more opportunities for employment than women did, and they were paid at least twice as much for their labor. On farms, men were hired both on an annual basis to do daily chores and on a seasonal basis to do field work; in the community, men also found casual or regular employment in transportation and construction. Women were hired only on a seasonal or short-term basis by farms; a few found steady jobs as domestic servants in villages. Since people assumed that everyone who grew up in a rural area learned agricultural skills in the course of daily life, they did not regard farm or household labor as deserving special compensation. Wages for this ordinary labor differed markedly by gender. According to the statistics reported for the Nanticoke Valley on the 1875 New York State census, "female domestics and women hired for common household work" were paid $2.00 a week, while men who worked as common laborers and farmhands earned $1.00 a day during the off season and $2.00 a day during haying and harvest.[10]

Employment opportunities and wages were just as unequal in the skilled trades. These occupations were absolutely segregated; while men practiced a wide variety of trades, women were confined to dressmaking, millinery, and weaving. Women's trades were more casualized than men's. Only the Maine village milliner kept a stock of goods and was regarded as a businesswoman. In 1875, women employed at "dressmaking, sewing, and other women's hand labor" were paid $1.00 a day; skilled male artisans earned from $2.25 to $2.50 a day.

10. These wage rates were recorded under "Miscellaneous Statistics" on the manuscript enumeration forms for the towns of Maine and Nanticoke in 1875. The fact that each of the three enumerators gave the same rates indicates that these wages were standardized throughout the community. Those for unskilled labor include the cost of board; those for skilled labor do not.

Schoolteaching was the only profession open to women as well as
men, and it was seasonal and ill paid. At mid-century, the young men
who taught during the winter term were paid more than the young
women who taught during the summer. In the minds of school trustees, parents, and pupils, this wage differential was presumed to reflect differences in men's and women's qualifications. Although men
did enjoy greater educational opportunities than women did, the sex-
linked wage differential was not based on individuals' education and
experience; rather, it reflected men's relative advantage in the labor
market and the belief that young female teachers could not maintain
their authority over the older male pupils who attended school during the winter session. The lower wages paid to female teachers reinforced the popular presumption that their work was inferior. For
example, Lala Ketchum lamented the departure of the man who had
taught in Maine village and feared that the district would hire "some
cheap woman teacher" to take his place (1 November 1863). By the
end of the century, few men taught in the country districts; they simply could not be hired for such low wages. Educated women, on the
other hand, had few other opportunities for employment.

The devaluation of women's work was firmly established in the rural labor market. The gender segregation of the labor market and
gender differentials in wages reinforced each other. Women's employment opportunities were so restricted and women's wages so low that
it was almost impossible for women to support themselves outside of
a family economy. Although most women did not share the belief
that their own labor was inferior in quality to that of men, they were
well aware that they were paid only a fraction of what men earned.
The contrast between commodity production, in which women's work
was integrated with that of men and accorded an equal value, and
wage labor, in which women's work was segregated and devalued, was
quite visible to women in the Nanticoke Valley. Although women
were subordinated to men in the ownership of property, women who
did not have access to farm property through the men in their families or households were in an even more disadvantaged economic position relative to men.

Sharing and Exchanging Work

Commodity production, subsistence production, and wage labor all
took place within rural households, involving husbands and wives,
parents and children, kin, and coresident workers. Other types of
work relationships involved members of different households. As men

on adjacent farms cooperated in such tasks as logging, plowing, and haying, lent one another teams, tools, or feed, or performed the myriad of small services that neighbors were supposed to do for one another, they were not engaged in either market exchange or direct employment. Similarly, as women gathered to sew, borrowed household supplies from one another, and watched out for the needs of one another's families, they were not buying and selling either commodities or labor. Most of the work relationships among people in different households within the rural community took this form. Women and men were involved in sharing and exchanging work more often than they were in wage labor; both borrowed and lent supplies more often than they bought and sold commodities.

Cooperation among neighbors and friends was crucial to the security of farm families. Like the subsistence production that it so often supported, sharing resources gave people a certain independence of the market. Households bound together in networks of mutual aid could rely on one another for resources they were unable to command in the marketplace. They could get through lean periods without becoming indebted to merchants or compromising their tenure of the land. Although in many instances the quantity of labor or supplies involved was small, amounting to no more than assistance with the morning milking or a cup of sugar to make preserves, these instances occurred so frequently that they constituted a crucial strategy for "getting by." Similarly, although people generally needed only short-term help, the system as a whole was based on and generated long-term reciprocal relationships among families and households.

Sharing and exchanging work was also built into commodity production. The increase in the scale of dairying on Nanticoke Valley farms was founded on farmers' customary cooperation in haying and harvesting. Although the introduction of horse-drawn mowing machines and side-delivery rakes reduced the amount of labor that haying and harvesting required, this increase in efficiency no more than kept pace with the increase in the quantity of feed that growing herds of cattle required. Indeed, some forms of mechanization, such as the horse- or steam-powered thrashing machine, actually required farmers to cooperate in a task they had performed independently before. The interdependence of farm families facilitated the simultaneous expansion of commercial operations and continuation of subsistence operations that took place in the Nanticoke Valley during the late nineteenth century.

While both women and men shared and exchanged their resources with friends and neighbors, women and men generally participated in these networks in gender-specific ways. The work they shared with people in other households was the most gender-marked work they did. The social dimension of this labor is closely connected to its gender segregation. Men sought help from men, and women from women, for tasks allotted exclusively to them by the gender division of labor but needing more hands than their household provided. Thus a woman might turn to a neighbor for help in cutting and fitting a dress, for she could not expect her husband to assist her. In practice, the gender definition of tasks was more flexible within households than it was between them. For example, a woman might "help" her husband with the haying on their own farm, but she would never join the haying crew that went round from farm to farm. Cooperative work groups that included people from different kin groups were seldom gender-integrated. However much a family might deviate from local conventions in their performance of tasks within the household, they would participate in cooperative labor in accordance within the roles deemed appropriate in the community. This work, then, represented the public gender division of labor.

Different Perceptions of Work Relationships

Comparison of the work relationships among women with those among men, as they were recorded in diaries and account books, reveals that women and men thought about their most gender-marked labor in fundamentally different ways and conceived of the social relationships into which they entered through their work in radically different terms. Within the agricultural community, indeed, there were two distinct types of economic relationships defined primarily by the gender of their participants. Women thought of their sharing of work in terms of mutual aid, while men thought of their exchange of work in terms of the market. Neither women's nor men's model was dominant within families and in the local community. These two models were balanced and integrated in rural culture, just as women's and men's gender-marked labor were balanced and integrated within the farm family economy.

It is clear, from both diaries and account books, that men saw their cooperative labor in terms based on the market. When George Riley came home after helping his neighbor plant corn, for example, he wrote in the back of his diary, "one day's labor for James Emerson, $1.00." When Emerson came to help him cultivate corn, Riley recorded: "one day's labor by James Emerson and team, $1.50." Riley and Emerson kept such running accounts for an entire year, noting as many as a hundred occasions when they worked together. Then they balanced the books. In 1870, for example, Riley wrote: "Settled with James Emerson today—tried to settle last night, did not succeed very well—finally we settled today with a good deal of talking, finally got all things arranged with pretty good feeling" (15 October 1870). No cash actually changed hands at this annual reckoning; the small balance was simply carried over to the next year's account. The value of this labor was set as a matter of custom rather than determined by supply and demand, but it was given a cash equivalent and duly recorded. Shared labor was treated as though it were a form of employment. Men also treated their borrowing and lending of supplies as though it were an exchange of commodities. The loads of hay, bushels of grain, and sides of beef that Riley and Emerson passed back and forth were all given cash equivalents in their accounts. Goods and services were treated as interchangeable.

When men worked in cooperative groups on such seasonal tasks as haying and thrashing, they carefully organized the work so that each farm benefited equally from their common labor. Some cooperative work groups made sure that each farmer contributed an equal number of man-days; others arranged that each farmer contribute the same proportion of the total labor that the group spent working on his farm. Men were also careful that no farmer was consistently favored by the order in which the work was done. When the task was completed, no reckoning was necessary.

This preoccupation with equity suggests that perceived inequities caused conflict among men who worked cooperatively. Some men were quite generous in their judgment of what constituted a man-day. Thus after his first day of labor with the youth who had just moved onto the adjacent farm, George Riley wrote: "Sowed 2 acres grass seed for Elviron Frost and he worked enough to Pay it or we will call it so" (30 April 1870). Other men firmly upheld commonly accepted standards for the length of a working day, especially in situations of short-term cooperation. The market form that men gave to their labor, however, did not ensure that they always agreed. Even short-term labor exchanges might result in disputes over the value of the work involved, and men's long-term relationships might become complicated by discrepancies in the accounts kept by the two parties. Men refused to work with those they believed had taken advantage of them. Since men cast their transactions in the form of contracts, they sometimes resorted to litigation to achieve what they regarded as an equitable settlement. Most of these lawsuits involved very small amounts of money, indicating that men's honor was at stake.

Even when men's work relationships were fully reciprocal and extended over many years, they were recorded as if they were composed of a series of discrete transactions. This accounting system was applied to the cooperative labor of male relatives as well as to work relationships among neighbors. Relatives often had first claim on one another's time, teams, and tools, but they still conducted their economic relations within a framework defined by the market. When George Riley's daughter and her husband, Bert Davey, lived on the adjacent farm, the two men worked together on a daily basis and alternated responsibility for the barn chores. At the same time, each man's work on each family's farm was meticulously recorded. George and Bert "settled up" periodically just as Riley and Emerson did. No matter how strong the ties of kinship and friendship that bound men together, they thought of themselves as independent producers who associated with one another through a myriad of face-to-face bargains in the marketplace.

Women did not keep such accounts of the ways they worked together. Because men rather than women were regarded as their families' representatives in the market, men rather than women kept the family account books. The commercially printed diary books used by most residents of the Nanticoke Valley contain a section at the back for "cash accounts" and "memoranda." Men used these pages to keep running records of their dealings with other farmers, laborers, and artisans and to compile ledgerlike accounts of their transactions with village merchants. Sometimes they inventoried their land and livestock or added up their major debts as well. Women rarely kept accounts of their dealings with members of other households in the back of their diary books. If they kept accounts at all, they recorded the money they received from the sale of eggs and chickens to local merchants and what they bought with the credit they earned. Many women listed simply the number of eggs they gathered from their hens each day, or noted the dates the cows were bred or freshened. Such records were usually scattered through women's daily entries rather than systematized in the back of the book. Women did note some of their economic dealings with other women in their daily entries. But they did so only when actual wage labor or commodity exchange was involved, as when they paid a dressmaker for her services, employed a hired girl, or sold butter, eggs, or lard to another woman. Women paid one another for the things they exchanged only when these dealings involved commodities usually sold on the market; however, they did not always pay one another for such items.

Women's diaries reveal that they participated in extensive networks of cooperative labor and mutual aid. When women recorded their sharing of labor, they did not do so in the same way that men did. They neither assigned monetary values to the work each performed nor specified who benefited from their joint effort. All they wrote down were the names of the women who worked together. When any single diary entry is taken out of context, in fact, it is difficult to distinguish a social visit from an occasion of cooperative labor. Women recorded their work sharing in terms that were direct and personal, unmediated by forms of exchange derived from the market.

Women conceived of their cooperative labor differently than men did; they thought of their shared and distinctly gender-marked labor in terms of mutual aid, while men thought of their own social and gender-specific labor in terms of the market. While men translated even their work relationships with kin into employment or exchange, women modeled all of their work relationships on kinship. Velma Leadbetter Gates and her husband's mother, Lydia Buck Gates, worked together without keeping track of the days the way Russell and Byron did; they freely shared foodstuffs and textiles rather than assign prices to them as their husbands did for hay and firewood. Equally important, women who were neighbors rather than kin interacted in much the same ways that female relatives did. Thus Helen Davis Benton relied on her friend Lavantia Briggs Lewis to care for her in sickness, run her household, and take her place in the dairy and hayfield; Lavantia needed a home during her widowhood, but she did not exchange her labor for room, board, and a wage. Helen called upon her neighbor Mrs. Gray for help with sewing, spring cleaning, and making preserves, yet just as often Helen walked up the hill to Mrs. Gray's because she was blue or bored. Female neighbors, like kinswomen, were bound together in intricate networks of mutual assistance; they did not count the cost of the help they rendered one another, but were more conscious of how the entire system benefited them all.

Women's social networks were based on and sustained by the reciprocation of long-term, normatively defined obligations. Women had their own ways of regulating their work relationships. These were designed to ensure, not so much equity, as those governing the market did, but rather reciprocation. How much help any woman was expected to give another depended on her available resources as well as on the other's needs. Women monitored one another's needs and resources as carefully as men computed their own credits and debits. Women judged to be able but unresponsive to others' needs would be subjected to informal pressures, not from a needy woman but from other women who were also involved in the mutual-aid network. Women who repeatedly ignored others' needs would find themselves ostracized by the network and unable to call upon others for assistance—except in cases of life-threatening illness, when women demonstrated the virtues of neighborliness to the insufficiently generous. These forms of social regulation, like the norms they enforced, were modeled on kinship and extended to the neighborhood.

Gender and the Market

The social meaning of this divergence in women's and men's ways of conceiving of their work relationships is complex, for it involves each gender's understanding of the other's mode of economic life as well as of their own. Did women and men apply their own gender-specific models to the work done by the other gender, or were they aware of the differences in their ways of conceiving of their economic relationships with others? How did women and men accommodate their divergent conceptions within the farm family economy and in the conduct of social relationships in the local community? Gender is, after all, a relational system. Even though women and men occupy different positions and see the world in terms of their own experience, women and men may also understand the situation and point of view of the other to some degree. Inequalities of power and differences in meaning systems create miscommunication and conflict, but these difficulties are mediated by forms of interrelatedness which allow women and men to sustain family ties and reproduce their ordered differences from one generation to the next. Women and men in rural communities understood their distinctive ways of evaluating labor and thinking about work relationships as part of the system of gender relations through which they conducted their lives. Yet women had a more comprehensive perspective than men did. Because women did not have power within the dominant system of property relations and were subordinated to men in their families, they needed to understand the dominant system and the views of men; for most subordinated groups, understanding the system as a whole and the perspective of the dominant group is a survival necessity. Men did not need to understand the perspectives of women in the same way.

If women and men had used their own models of work relationships to judge each other's gender-specific cooperative labor beyond the household, they would have agreed about men's work and disagreed about women's work. Because women did not apply market models to the labor they shared with other women, much of the work they did was invisible within the terms men accepted. Women's work sharing rarely appears in men's diaries and account books. Only, but not always, when one woman paid another cash for her labor or for some farm product would the transaction figure in the accounts their husbands kept. The rest of their cooperative labor was "of no account" in men's eyes. If men had judged women's work by the standards they applied to their own, much of the work women did would have appeared to be without value.

On the other hand, if women had judged men's work within the terms of their own model of mutual aid, they would have readily recognized its importance. Much of the work men did with other men made sense within the kinship-based conceptual framework that women accepted. Women often recorded men's cooperative labor in the same terms they did their own; women wrote that men worked "with" rather than "for" one another and that men "lent" one another things rather than bought and sold them. The fact that men did not think of these interactions in the same way did not affect women's judgment of their significance. Women's shared work did not have value within men's market model of economic relations, but men's cooperative labor had an integral place in women's model of relationships among families and households in the community.

Still, women and men did not generally apply their own model of work relationships to the other gender. Women were well aware that men did not think of their work relationships in the same way that women themselves did. While women recorded men's cooperative labor as if it were mutual aid, they expressed some concern that their husbands did not treat other men according to the norms that governed such relationships among women. Women worried that their husbands might pursue short-term financial self-interest to the detriment of long-term reciprocal ties with relatives and neighbors. Usually they confided this concern only to their diaries, although on rare occasions they spoke directly to their husbands. Women tried to control the tensions that men's business dealings generated among their friends by engaging in compensatory socializing or performing unsolicited favors, communicating their awareness of the reciprocal and continuing nature of obligations.

It is more difficult to ascertain what men thought about women's work relationships. Men paid so little attention to women's nonmarket cooperative work that there is no positive evidence to interpret. The very silence of men's account books and the absence of women's work sharing from men's diaries are powerfully suggestive. Men did not pay attention to work relationships among women in the way that women paid attention to those among men. Men did not extend their own understanding of exchanging work to cooperative work among women. Rather, men seemed to treat women's gender-specific shared labor as if it neither concerned them nor directly impinged on their activities. Perhaps, from their perspective, that was true.

Women's gender-marked shared labor was both clearly distinct and qualitatively different from men's cooperative work. It was characterized by a different kind of value as well. Women's shared labor had the same kind of value that subsistence production did. It was concrete and irreducible, multifarious and intricate; its meaning lay in its direct responsiveness to human needs and in the social relationships through which it was carried on. The work men exchanged had, at least in men's minds, the same kind of value that commodity production did; labor time and products were transformed into their quantitative equivalents, and human relationships were expressed as if they were relations among things. The two types of work had such different kinds of value that they could not be compared. At the same time, they also seemed, at least to men, to be quite separate; the distinction between them was fundamentally a matter of gender.

In the Nanticoke Valley, women had a bifocal perspective on the different kinds of work women and men did and the different forms of work relationships into which women and men entered. They were able to comprehend men's work relationships through their own kinship-based model, but they were also aware of the fact that men understood these relationships differently. On the other hand, men were unable to comprehend women's work relationships through their own conceptual framework. If they judged women's work in terms of the market, it appeared to be without value or became entirely invisible. If they refrained from such judgments, women's work appeared to be a distinct mode of activity which was fundamentally defined by gender. At best, men had a bifurcated vision, regarding women's work as qualitatively different from their own.

Women were responsible for integrating the distinct ways in which women and men cooperated along gender lines beyond the household. Women took care that the relationships into which they entered through their gender-specific work overlapped and intersected with those of their husbands so that their family had coherent and stable social relations with other families and households. Men took little responsibility for the way their work relationships fit together with those of the women in their families and local households; men were able to get along on the assumption that they need not concern themselves with the other dimension of social relations.

So, too, women rather than men were primarily responsible for integrating the gender-specific subsistence labor that women and men undertook within the family and household and for accommodating their own gender-defined subsistence labor to the commodity production in which women and men jointly participated. In both forms of production, women participated in the work for which men were responsible more often than men participated in the work for which women were responsible. In subsistence production, women often performed the final processing, transforming the raw materials that were the result of men's labor into things their families could consume. Women often set aside the subsistence-oriented labor they alone performed in order to assist men in commodity production. While they did so because they, like men, regarded this as the most valuable form of labor, they were also concerned with the integration of women's and men's working lives.

Women were acutely aware that their own sense of the meaning of cooperative labor was not shared by the larger society. However much the patterns of mutual aid that women maintained were fundamental to work relations among men as well as women in the local community during the late nineteenth century, women knew not only that men saw their interactions in terms of bargains and carefully assigned a cash value to each component of their exchange, but also that the regional economy within which they were enmeshed validated men's model of the market rather than their own model of neighborly reciprocity. Women in the Nanticoke Valley were careful to ensure that they were not excluded from commodity production. Even after centralized creameries had superseded women's traditional role in the dairy process, they continued to milk and do barn chores to make a visible contribution to the family income and maintain their legitimacy as partners in farm decision making. But farm women did not subscribe uncritically to the model of social relations based on the marketplace. Rather, they espoused an alternative vision based on cooperation, and practiced mutuality and flexibility in their sharing of labor with their husbands as well as with their women friends. Indeed, women created a set of work routines which exemplified reciprocity within the most important form of commodity production. The income-producing nature of dairying validated women's mode of cooperative work across as well as along gender lines. As long as mutual aid remained a primary resource for farm families and women remained important participants in commodity production, women's views of work and the value of their labor could not be disregarded.

Men's adoption of market models to conceptualize their work relationships with other men was not the result solely of their involvement in commodity production, nor did it signify their wholehearted espousal of capitalist social relations. Men applied market models to work that was not part of commodity production. They chose to commit a substantial proportion of their resources to subsistence production, which they thought of as a secure base to counter the risks commodity production entailed. Men's adoption of market models was, at least at first, primarily a matter of gender. Men's position as the representatives of their families and households in civil society defined their perspective. Their allegiance to the ideal of "yeoman" independence was political as well as economic; it was as much about masculinity as about capitalism. Yet it rendered men vulnerable to the definitions of value created by market exchange. While men resisted those dictates of the market which seemed inequitable and threatened their status as independent producers, they did not wholeheartedly espouse the alternative model of reciprocity and interconnectedness which women created and maintained in their practice of mutual aid.

In the late nineteenth century, just as subsistence and commodity production existed in a state of balance and integration within the farm family economy, so gender-divided and gender-integrated forms of labor coexisted as well. Subsistence production was largely gender-divided, but women's and men's products were integrated in the work women did to process these goods for family use. Commodity production was both gender divided and gender integrated; some operations were carried on by men and women separately, but women worked together with men in the most important income-producing farm operation. The system was characterized by a dynamic balance. As long as men participated in subsistence production, remaining loyal to their "living" as well as their cash crops and recognizing the utility of tangible things that could not be sold for cash, they would not devalue the subsistence production in which women engaged. As long as women continued to participate in commodity production, sustaining gender-integrated modes of work within the most valuable form of farm labor, men had to recognize the value of women's work and its interchangeability with their own. So, too, women's and men's distinct modes of sharing and exchanging labor were integrated in practice within the local community.

This gender system was riddled with contradictions. Women participated in income-producing work and performed much of the subsistence production that made capital accumulation possible, yet their names did not appear on the family's accounts with local merchants or the deed to the family farm. It was women who integrated men's and women's distinct economic relations with others of their own gender into the multidimensional and flexible networks of mutual aid which constituted social relations among families and households, yet women were not the official representatives of their families and had no legitimate power within the formal structures of civil society. These contradictions placed women at risk; they had grave difficulties supporting themselves outside farm family economies. These contradictions also placed at risk the entire system of production and set of social relations on which late-nineteenth-century rural life was conducted. Men's model of social relations was legitimated by the dominant ideology and reinforced by the power of the market. To the extent that it became hegemonic in the local community, not only would women suffer from the devaluation of their gender-marked labor, but the collective interdependence of the local community would be jeopardized as well. That did not happen in the Nanticoke Valley during the late nineteenth century. Women simultaneously participated in the form of work which was valued most highly by the market and sustained reciprocal relations among households in the local community which provided a bulwark against the market. In the process, they not only ensured that their labor would be valued in terms men respected but maintained viable alternatives to capitalist social relations.

PART IV

PATTERNS OF
SOCIABILITY

Visiting with Folks and Friends

All went to a quiltin.
—George W. Riley, Diary, 1880

An entry in George Riley's diary typifies the pattern of sociability in the Nanticoke Valley during the late nineteenth century: "Bert and Ida and Lucy and Juddie all went to G. W. Davey's to a quiltin" (6 February 1880). Riley's daughter and her husband, his wife and their son attended the party held at Bert's parents' home on a Friday evening. (George stayed behind to do the chores and care for Ida and Bert's ailing three-year-old son.) When "folks and friends" gathered, women and men, adults and children were all included. Husbands and wives, courting couples, and unattached youths mingled with widowed elders and young children in a gender-mixed, multi-generational milieu. While George Riley recorded this occasion as a "quiltin," the thirteen-year-old Judson described the event a bit differently: "Bert's folks had a spree over to their house but it did not amount to much" (6 February 1880). To Judson a "quiltin" was simply one kind of party; it was not gender marked. George and Judson Riley, William Marean, Chauncey McIntyre, and Leroy Benton all recorded that they went to quilting parties. Women's diaries also document that men as well as women attended quiltings; indeed, it was the presence of men that made a "quiltin" into a social event rather than an occasion of shared labor.

Most preindustrial societies have been characterized by a close connection between work and sociability. In the Nanticoke Valley, many traditional forms of work sharing had been converted into social gatherings by the late nineteenth century.[1] Quiltings might feature either cooperative labor or conviviality. The difference between these two types of quiltings is indicated by another entry in Judson Riley's diary: "Mrs. Davey and Mrs. Yarns and Mrs. Leonard com and helped Ma quilt" (3 April 1880). These women gathered in the afternoon to work; neither George nor Judson participated. Leroy Benton's diary shows how men might be drawn into the women's activities. In the fall of 1876, Leroy's mother spent several days working on a quilt with assistance from her women friends. "Miss Helen Davis came over to help on the quilt. They set me to work on the quilt. I pricked my fingers and then they laughed at me and I quit" (9 November 1876). Evidently the women teased Leroy to try the needle, and when he proved as clumsy as they expected they let him go. The fact that Leroy and Helen were courting explains this playful crossing of gender boundaries. While Leroy's incompetence underlined his masculinity and reinforced the feminine character of quilting, his participation in the gathering gave it a festive quality. Women often made the completion of a quilt into an occasion for celebration. Louise Gates Gunsalus recalled that in her mother's day women would come over in the afternoon to put the finishing touches on a quilt and prepare a special supper, and their husbands would join them for an evening of conversation and dancing.[2] While work sharing beyond the household flowed along distinct gender lines, social activities were not segregated by gender—at least when they were organized by women.

In the Nanticoke Valley, the gender-integrated character of social life resulted in part from its basis in kinship and locality. Women and men associated fairly freely because they were related as members of solidary kin groups, not solely as members of one or the other gender. In neighborhoods that grew up around kin, patterns of sociability developed along the same flexible and gender-integrated lines. Within the locality, too, the differences in the temporal rhythms and spatial dimensions of women's and men's working lives did not exert as marked an influence on social contacts as they did at the community level. Women could simultaneously manage their households,

1. The cooperative work parties that had been customary in the seventeenth and eighteenth centuries were no longer common. Local men continued to use the word "bee" to refer to occasions when large numbers of men gathered to perform some task for which they would not be paid and labor accounts would not be kept. For example, they had a "wood bee" for a man who was unable to supply his household with fuel after an injury and a "barn-raising" for a family whose barn had burned. These were regarded as special acts of charity rather than as normal ways of getting work done. Occasionally the churches sponsored "bees" to clean up the property or to make clothing and textiles for needy families.

2. Louise Gates Gunsalus (1894–1982), interview with author, 12 July 1981.

supervise their children, and get together with neighbors, even when their responsibilities restricted travel over greater distances. Social activities based in the neighborhood always included both women and men.

Yet gender integration was not simply a consequence of the kin-based and locally oriented character of social life, for many community-wide activities also involved both women and men. The more discrete character of men's tasks, coupled with the greater mobility inherent in their work, gave them relatively more freedom to interact with others beyond the locality. Combined with the formal exclusion of women from the public domain, this disparity might have led to sharp gender differences in social life. Men might have monopolized community-wide organizations while women were confined to more informal and less frequent contacts with relatives and neighbors, and husbands and wives might have had distinct social networks.

This did not happen in the Nanticoke Valley. During the late nineteenth century, both informal and formal social activities tended to counteract and overcome, rather than extend and reinforce, the separation between women and men that arose from their gender-specific labor and from male domination of the public domain. Husbands and wives had joint social networks in large part as a result of women's active efforts to create a common social life. Community-wide organizations were not always gender-integrated, for men rarely included women in gatherings based on their concerns as citizens, taxpayers, and economic agents. But women generally included men in the activities they organized, even when they planned social events through such formally all-female groups as the church women's auxiliaries. Women preferred family-based to single-sex patterns of sociability. From this perspective, the kin-based and locally oriented quality of social life must be seen as in part the result of women's deliberate and collective choice. Kinship and neighborhood were crucial resources for women in their efforts to nurture a gender-integrated mode of sociability, and women helped to sustain those forms of social relations over against social forms that organized people in other ways.

The Dimensions of Social Life

During the late nineteenth century, social activities were both numerous and varied. Leroy Benton described one evening in his parents' household: "Pa and I played music, he on the violin and I on the organ. Carrie and Charlie are playing Dominoes while I write. Plumah is knitting on my scarf, Jane is reading an Indian story. Mother is knitting. Father lays on the lounge" (11 January 1876. Carrie Leadbetter was Rosella, Plumah, and Jane's thirty-three-year-old niece). If neighbors dropped in, they might eat supper with the family, join in the music and games, or just make conversation. Some neighborhood gatherings were spontaneous; others were planned in advance and featured dancing and a late supper. The participants were the same friends and neighbors who shared work and informal visiting, but for a special event they all assembled at once, wore their best coats and dresses, brought rich cakes and sweet cookies, and—at least if they were young—didn't worry about getting a full night's sleep before it was time to do chores the next morning.

Other formal events engaged the whole community. The socials, exhibitions, and festivals sponsored by the churches were the most popular. These entertainments required a great deal of work. The organizers made and sold ice cream, cooked and served meals, and decorated and cleaned up the hall; participants spent many hours preparing recitations, musical recitals, and theatrical pieces. Church members and their children planned these events, but occasional churchgoers and members of other congregations attended them. Church-sponsored gatherings were too important a part of community social life to be passed up by any but the most determinedly antisocial or unanimously outcast of Nanticoke Valley residents. Like the outdoor concerts of the Maine Philharmonic Society and Community Band, they were open to all comers. Families and neighbors went together and socialized with their relatives and friends from other parts of the valley.

The temporal rhythms of social life corresponded with their spatial patterns. Daily visiting was quite local, unless guests stayed overnight. Parties, socials, and entertainments were held toward the end of the week—never on Sunday, but often on Saturday, when the imminence of the Sabbath offered the prospect of rest after recreation. Sunday was consecrated not only to attending church but also to family visiting. Married children customarily had dinner with their parents; those who lived nearby came every week, while those who had to travel some distance came once a month or so. The ritual of Sunday dinner was as well established and widely observed as the custom of Sunday courting. The seasonal cycle of rural life affected both the form and the frequency of social activities. Socializing was most frequent in mid-winter, when there was little farmwork to do. The

Three sisters. Nanticoke Valley Historical Society.

annual calendar was punctuated by holidays, ranging from the traditional agricultural rituals of May Day and Harvest Home through such civic observances as closing exercises in the district schools and election days in the towns.

Most social activities remained based in the neighborhoods and rural community throughout the nineteenth century. That localism did not mean that people were out of touch with broader cultural trends. Speakers appeared before local organizations to point out the dangers of Roman Catholicism, advocate the Greenback party platform, and show magic lantern slides of their travels in China. Buffalo Bill's Wild West show drew country people to Union and Binghamton. Nanticoke Valley residents were not dependent solely on secondhand reports for information about distant places, however, for many farmers journeyed west to visit relatives and investigate the prospects migration offered. Railroad workers, merchants, and even an occasional milliner went to New York on business and stayed to see the sights. Some people traveled simply for their own edification; for example, Leroy Benton went to the Centennial Exposition in Philadelphia in 1876 and to the Chicago World's Fair in 1893.

Nanticoke Valley residents constructed their social and cultural life out of the things they had in common with their relatives and neighbors. Voluntary organizations were a pervasive feature of local life. Each ostensibly served a distinct purpose, but all generated solidarity among their members and sponsored a variety of social activities. These groups often linked the locality with broader regional and national organizations. Rural residents adopted new organizational forms, such as mutual insurance clubs and cemetery associations, when such innovations served their purposes. If they sometimes did so much later than urban residents, this was not because they were "backward" and "out of touch with modern life," as early-twentieth-century urban critics of rural life suggested, but rather because they did not need those institutions; for example, kinship continued to provide adequate safeguards from catastrophe and public graveyards served as a common burying place. Furthermore, community residents often adapted national organizational forms to local conditions. The mutual insurance clubs they founded were permeated by ties of kinship and propinquity and represented more a formalization of than a departure from previous practice. Similarly, when Nanticoke Valley people decided to beautify their graveyard in accordance with popular "garden cemetery" designs, they adopted a cooperative rather than a proprietary structure. Leaders derived their power from their position in rural society rather than from their access to outside resources, and they acted primarily as community representatives rather than as agents of metropolitan culture. In a system that was as conservative as it was democratic, power flowed up from the local level rather than down from some extralocal center. In all these ways, the activities and perspectives of voluntary organizations were deeply rooted in the culture of the rural community.

During the late nineteenth century, Nanticoke Valley residents adopted new fashions in recreation, but they assimilated these activities to the structure of their social relationships. Croquet became a game for idle youths, bicycles a swifter way to go visiting, and baseball a controlled form of competition among different villages and age groups. When commercial entertainment became more available, the entertainments created locally became more elaborate. Church socials, once simple box suppers, were given themes: some incorporated traditional customs, others were taken from books of party games, and still others were invented to generate interest among people growing weary of the routine. In 1876, the year of the Centennial, one church held a "New England supper" where everyone "dressed old-fashioned" and ate a boiled dinner. Local residents projected themselves on a national stage, fusing memory, history, and fantasy into a compelling piece of mythic theater.

The Riley and Benton Families

Married couples in the Nanticoke Valley engaged primarily in joint rather than separate social activities. Couples who shared their working lives shared their leisure time as well, and those who divided tasks more sharply did not have distinct social lives. Instead of creating friendships with their own gender, they had joint social networks and engaged in common activities. Patterns of sociability tended to counteract, rather than reinforce, the differences between women's and men's routines which were created by their labor.[3]

George and Lucy Ann Riley exemplify couples whose work and social lives were both characterized by a high degree of joint activity. Their most frequent associates were neighbors. The same family names—Emerson, Frost, Wilson, and Allen—recur continually in the

3. The classic study of couples' social networks, which defines the dimensions of jointness and segregation in both the work and social lives of husbands and wives, is Elizabeth Bott, *Family and Social Network: Roles, Norms, and External Relationships in Ordinary Urban Families* (New York: Free Press, 1957). Later studies of the social networks of middle-class and working-class couples have refined the concepts Bott originally developed. This chapter draws on recent feminist theory, which emphasizes the economic and political dimensions of women's networks. For exemplary anthropological and historical analyses, see Carol B. Stack, "Sex Roles and Survival Strategies in an Urban Black Community," in *Woman, Culture and Society*, ed. Michelle Zimbalist Rosaldo and Louise Lamphere (Stanford, Calif.: Stanford University Press, 1974), 113–28; Carol B. Stack, *All Our Kin: Strategies for Survival in a Black Community* (New York: Harper and Row, 1974); and Ellen Ross, "Survival Networks: Women's Neighborhood Sharing in London before World War I," *History Workshop Journal* 15 (1983): 4–27.

diaries as coworkers in haying and sewing, guests at a maple-sugar party, and mourners at a funeral. The Rileys also participated in broader community activities as a family group. They went to church services, socials, and the annual camp meeting together. Lucy Ann and the children accompanied George to the local and Broome County agricultural fairs each year.

The joint character of the Rileys' social life is also indicated by the bilateral orientation of their relationships with kin. George and Lucy Ann maintained ties with both sets of relatives even though George's kin were available in a way that Lucy Ann's were not. George's family had settled in Allentown, and he had established a farm on the cheaper, relatively undeveloped land just up the hill on East Maine Road. Most of George's siblings had also moved to other neighborhoods in the Nanticoke Valley. George's widowed father lived with George and Lucy Ann for the last five years of his life. After that, George and Lucy Ann had only formal contacts with most of his siblings. They kept in touch with one brother through the Methodist Sunday-school class in Allentown, but George and Lucy Ann did not socialize with his family.

Lucy Ann Bicknell Riley's relatives lived in Tioga County, New York, and Susquehanna Depot, Pennsylvania. Lucy Ann was born in Tioga County, but by 1865 her mother had died and her father and youngest brother were living in Susquehanna. Her father came to visit every summer, and when he was no longer well enough to travel the Rileys went to visit him. Lucy Ann's brother Hiram Judson Bicknell once purchased the farm next door to George and Lucy Ann's, although he soon returned to work as a locomotive fireman rather than settle into farming. Most of Lucy Ann's married sisters and brothers continued to live in Tioga County. They paid only occasional visits to Maine, but the Rileys went to Tioga County every year, spending a week visiting around from house to house. Scott Bicknell, Lucy Ann's nephew, boarded with the Rileys in Maine one winter while he attended school. As Ida and Judson grew up, they formed independent relationships with their cousins, making long visits and exchanging letters.

The Rileys had at least as much contact with Lucy Ann's relatives as they did with George's, even though her relatives lived much farther away. This was, at least in part, a matter of choice. Obligations between parents and children were in principle involuntary, but relationships among siblings were much more variable. What they meant in practice was up to individual brothers and sisters, who might maintain their ties after they left their parents' household or—especially after their parents died—might loosen those ties. George and Lucy Ann Riley went out of their way to sustain their relationships with Lucy Ann's siblings, but they had less frequent contact with George's siblings than the geographical distance between them would have allowed.

The relationship that George and Lucy Ann had with "Aunt Lucy" is especially interesting. The term "aunt" was an honorific, a title of respect for an older woman. Young people also used it for their step-mothers. Lucy was Matthew Allen's second wife, and George Riley may have adopted the usage of his friend, Matthew Allen, Jr. The term signified a voluntary relationship between George Riley and Lucy Allen which was as strong as any relationship based on descent or marriage might have been.[4] Lucy Allen lived with Matthew, Jr., after her husband died in 1856. George Riley and Matthew Allen, Jr., worked together frequently and were both staunch members of the Methodist church.[5] Their families visited back and forth in the flexible combinations typical of kin. Lucy Allen acted as Lucy Ann's nearest older kinswoman, and when she died in 1876 Ida Riley Davey inherited some of her furniture. The relationship between the Riley and Allen families exemplifies the way that people became absorbed

4. I have not used the common anthropological term "fictive kinship" to describe the relationship between George Riley and Lucy Allen because it implies that "real" kinship necessarily involves biological reproduction and/or marital affiliation. For a critique of the reductionist assumptions of this approach and an argument that kinship is always an ideological matter, see David M. Schneider, *American Kinship: A Cultural Account* (Englewood Cliffs, N.J.: Prentice-Hall, 1980), and Sylvia Junko Yanagisako and Jane Fishburne Collier, "Toward a Unified Analysis of Gender and Kinship," in *Gender and Kinship: Essays toward a Unified Analysis*, ed. Jane Fishburne Collier and Sylvia Junko Yanagisako (Stanford, Calif.: Stanford University Press, 1987), 14–50.

5. The closeness of George Riley's relationship with Matthew Allen, Jr., comes clear at Allen's death. When Matthew died of an apoplectic stroke in 1879, just three years after Lucy Allen's death, George "staid over to Allen's last night—helped lay Matthew out after he died. Closed his eyes and mouth and dressed him for his coffin and grave." George also helped arrange for the funeral, reflecting that Matthew had "ben a Christian for more than 33 years that I have knowed him" (17, 18 November 1879). George's ties with the Allens did not end with the deaths of Lucy and Matthew. George served as trustee of Matthew's estate and held half of the property in trust for Matthew's son Charles. In the spring of 1880, Charles Allen came to board with the Rileys for a dollar a week plus help with chores. He had been living in the same house as his step-mother, Ann Barr Allen, and her son, George Barr. Evidently Charles feared that his stepmother's family would deprive him of his rightful inheritance, and he called upon his father's friend to provide him with a home removed from the center of the fray as well as to defend his financial interests. George shared Charles's apprehensions, remarking in his diary that Matthew "was run by George Barr and the whole Barr tribe to the extent that he didn't dare to say his soul was his own unless it was in accordance with their feelings" (17 February 1881). Charles stayed with the Rileys off and on for more than five years. Eventually he went to live with his cousin Belden Allen, who continued to live in Allentown.

into the social relations of a kin-based neighborhood and sustained those ties even after one family moved out of the immediate vicinity. The relationship between Lucy Ann Riley and Lucy Allen, too, illustrates the special meaning women might find in the social networks they entered through marriage. Lucy Ann Riley looked to her husband's friendship network for an older woman from whom she might receive the kind of support that another woman might have received from her own or her husband's mother. That this relationship was a voluntary one on all sides underscores the flexibility of kinship as a basis for social relations; people creatively adapted the kinship system to express their affections and meet their needs.

Leroy and Helen Davis Benton also engaged in joint social activities. There was a clear difference, however, between their informal local visiting on the one hand and their participation in community-wide gatherings on the other. Like the Rileys, the Bentons socialized jointly with relatives and neighbors, and they attended many church functions together. In contrast to George and Lucy Ann Riley, who participated in community-wide groups as a couple as well, Leroy Benton was much more active than Helen in organizations that met in Maine village.

Helen was more comfortable with her family and friends than she was with large groups in public settings. Louise Gates Gunsalus remembers Helen as rather shy, "very quiet, not a lively person at all."[6] As a young woman, Helen only reluctantly attended "sociables," writing after one evening that "Jennie and I went to the festival and had as good a time as I expected. I am not fond of any such thing" (2 July 1874). Helen was happiest at home with her relatives. She often remarked that her sisters' houses were always full of company; there she was drawn into social activities without any troubling self-consciousness. After she married, Helen's social life continued to center on her household, kin group, and neighborhood. She included the Bentons and the Leadbetters among her circle of intimates; Rosella Leadbetter Benton's relatives, especially her sisters and nieces, became Helen's closest friends as well. Helen and Leroy frequently socialized with their neighbors. Generally the neighbors came to the Bentons' house to visit, although sometimes Helen walked over to see Mrs. Gray by herself. Women came to work and visit with Helen during the day while their husbands and sons worked with Leroy. "We worked some and talked and the time went right away," Helen remarked after one such afternoon (3 February 1894). But when the gathering was a social one, women came with their husbands in the evening.

6. Louise Gates Gunsalus, interview by author, November 1981.

Leroy went out much more often than Helen did. He was a leader of the Maine Philharmonic Society and Community Band, sang in the church choir, frequented singing schools, and performed at concerts and funerals. When Leroy went off to practice, Helen often remained at home. Sometimes she accompanied him down to the village, but she visited with one of her sisters while he was at rehearsal. Helen did not seem to mind Leroy's absences—although she did note them in her diary—because she was seldom left alone. Nor did Leroy always go out to play and sing; Helen welcomed groups of musicians to the Benton home. She noted the spontaneous gatherings of neighbors with special pleasure. As Helen described one occasion: "A busy day. We washed and churned and had three men to dinner and four to supper. Leroy cut all of the grass in the lower meadow and got it all in but it was late though. Linnie and I did the chores. Mother's night blooming serus blossomed and we sent word around and we had quite a company on short notice" (3 August 1891). Even during haying season, the family found time for sociability.

Helen Davis Benton created some continuity in her life by marrying into a neighboring family; familiarity was important to her sense of self. Still, her siblings scattered throughout the community, while her residence was the focus for her husband's mother's extensive kin network. Helen relied for social contacts on both her married sisters and brothers and her husband's mother's kinswomen, but she placed primary emphasis on her relationship with her husband. This choice was supported by her kin, who incorporated Leroy into their social network, as well as by Rosella Leadbetter Benton, who allowed the couple some autonomy at the same time that she kept Helen company. Helen and Leroy had most in common within the neighborhood, where neither occupied a privileged position and where same-gender and cross-gender ties intersected and flowed into one another.

The Marean and Gates Families

The social lives of William and Deborah Allen Marean were characterized by mutuality even though their working lives were not, for they engaged in a wide range of joint activities with a common set of relatives and friends. Spontaneous visiting in the neighborhood involved both husbands and wives: "Deborah and I went to George Smith's avisiting. Got home and found Mr. Luce and wife at our house" (19 February 1878). Deborah sometimes went out without her husband, and groups of women sometimes came to see her by themselves. More commonly, though, the women got together in the afternoon and the men joined them in the evening: "Deborah went up to Mr. Atwaters avisiting in the afternoon, I went up in the evening" (9 January 1878); "Mrs. Vantuyle here avisiting in the afternoon, Mr. Vantuyle and Etta here in eve" (13 February 1878).

The Mareans both attended religious services at the Methodist Church in Maine village and Sunday-school classes in Allentown. Unlike Deborah, William was not a church member, but he accompanied his wife to most religious activities, and many church-sponsored gatherings were held at their house. The only religious activities Deborah attended alone were evening prayer meetings, which were restricted to church members.

Many of the Mareans' social contacts were with their relatives, for they lived in a kin-based neighborhood. Deborah visited her widowed mother Oladyne Spencer Allen and her aged uncle Matthew Allen regularly. William helped "Uncle Matthew" with his garden and took "Mother Allen" with him as he traveled around the community; Deborah and her older relatives visited other members of the Marean family. Most often, however, William's and Deborah's paths intersected in the homes of their kin.

William and Deborah visited with their relatives who lived elsewhere in the community about as often as they did with their neighbors who were not kin. Relationships were closest where kinship and propinquity reinforced each other; where they did not, each seems to have had roughly equal weight. Propinquity itself did not necessarily create sociability, however. The Mareans had very little contact with one group of their neighbors, for those families were oriented toward their own relatives living further north toward Glen Aubrey and did not mix with the residents of Allentown. On the other hand, the Mareans' relationships with friends in the neighborhood were as intense and multifaceted as those among kin. Most often, relatives and neighbors were mixed together in the groups of men who shared work in thrashing, the women who gathered to sew, and the women and men who exchanged visits and assembled for parties. Two groups that got together to eat warm sugar are representative. In 1878, "Uncle Matthew's folks," John Councilman, and the Vincent Mareans joined William and Deborah. The next spring, the party included "Mr. Vantuyle and wife, Etta and Aunt Ann, Charley Allen, Ervin Barr, Charley Burgess and Lettie" (1 April 1879). These people included both neighbors and kin, but they did not sort out neatly into family units. The Vantuyles and their daughter Etta were kin by marriage as well as neighbors, for another of the Vantuyles' daughters had married Matthew Allen's son Caleb a few years before he was killed in the

Civil War. Matthew did not accompany Ann Barr Allen, his second wife, but his son Charles Allen was there. So was Ervin Barr, Ann's nephew, and Charles Burgess, her brother's wife's brother. Lettie Smith Allen, the wife of Deborah's brother John, came over from an adjacent farm by herself. These gatherings were not segregated along lines of gender or generation. Rather, members of related families socialized freely with one another and drew in their other kindred and their neighbors.

Russell and Velma Leadbetter Gates resembled William and Deborah Allen Marean both in the strict segregation of their work and in their shared sociability. Their active social life brought Russell and Velma together; they socialized frequently, and almost always jointly, with relatives, friends, and fellow church members. Their closest friends, Leroy and Helen Davis Benton, were both relatives and neighbors. Russell and Velma were also friendly with the Loomises, who lived near their rented farm. Russell recorded a typical round of visits: "go to Maine with buggy. Vell goes down to Benton's with me, comes back and stops at Loomis's, I go home and do chores and go down in the evening" (26 February 1892). The Gateses did not socialize much with their other neighbors, although they did attend occasional "surprize" parties on neighbors' birthdays. Nor did they participate very often in community-wide gatherings, except for church-sponsored functions.

The vast majority of Velma and Russell's social contacts were with their Gates and Leadbetter relatives. Just as Russell's parents were their nearest neighbors and closest coworkers, so Byron and Lydia were their most constant companions at social events. The older couple drew the younger one into the visits they exchanged with their kin throughout Broome and Tioga counties. The Gateses kept in contact with family members who had left the region as well. When Livingston Theodore and Agnes Brockett Gates's son Samuel Brockett Gates came back to introduce the family to his sister's new husband James Harlan Wells and to marry his former neighbor Ida May Rozelle, he also brought belated wedding gifts for Russell and Velma from "Aunt Agnes" (28 January 1892). In the diary, Velma referred to her husband's relatives in the same terms that he used.

Most of Velma's Leadbetter relatives lived in East Maine. They came to visit the Gateses more often than Velma went to visit them, for the tension between Velma's father and her husband made it difficult for her to go home. As Velma and Russell's daughter and her husband explained it, William Leadbetter resented Russell for marrying Velma and depriving him of his youngest daughter's care in his old age, while Russell resented William's presumption that he had a right to Velma's time and attention regardless of her other family obligations.[7] Russell and Velma's diaries document that Velma tried to behave properly toward her father and still maintain the integrity of her own family life. Even after her marriage, she cared for her father when he was ill and went to visit him periodically. One of Russell's diary entries succinctly expresses his feelings about the situation: "Vell goes over home, father sick or supposed to be, Jim Welch takes her" (1 April 1893). Sometimes Russell accompanied Velma to East Maine and stayed with her siblings while she went to see her father. But Velma was reluctant to allow her father to separate her from her husband, so she usually invited her siblings and their children to the Gateses'. Her siblings were equally unwilling to have their relationship with their sister disrupted by their father, so they took the time and went to the trouble that travel involved to visit her.

In comparison to William and Deborah Allen Marean, Russell and Velma Leadbetter Gates had fewer kindred in their neighborhood and they interacted less often with neighbors who were not their kin. Instead, they sustained close relationships with a wider circle of relatives, visiting with their East Maine kin more often than they did with anyone except the Bentons. Velma and Russell went to considerable lengths to nurture close ties with the Leadbetters in spite of the tension with her father. The integration of Velma and Russell's kinship network was an achievement requiring considerable care, not an accident of geography or an automatic result of intermarriage. The joint character of their social life was a conscious choice, an expression of their understanding of the meaning of marriage. The primacy of kinship in their social life meant that they interacted with others not on the basis of their distinct work responsibilities but rather through ties that crisscrossed divisions of gender and generation.

Kinship, Neighborhood, and Sociability

Kinship and neighborhood were crucially important to women's efforts to nurture mutuality among women and men. These ties tended to overcome the disjunctions between husbands and wives which arose from the gender division of labor. For Velma Leadbetter and Russell Gates, kinship was a shared network within which they acted

7. Louise Gates Gunsalus and Paul Gunsalus, interview by Ian Mylchreest and Janet Bowers Bothwell, summer 1982; Paul Gunsalus, interview by author, winter 1982.

Children and grandparents in the Dudley family, c. 1890. (Left to right) Myra Dudley, Emaline Chloe Marean Dudley, Jessie Dudley, Jedediah Dudley. Nanticoke Valley Historical Society.

and interacted as a couple. For Deborah Allen and William Marean, the reinforcing ties of kinship and locality created a milieu within which their paths constantly intersected and conjoined. Social activities not only cemented friendships based on the sharing of work among women and among men; they also created commonality between husbands and wives. If households had been more isolated from one another, or if patterns of sociability had been as segregated along gender lines as patterns of work sharing were, then at least some husbands and wives might have lived in "separate spheres." But the form of social life that was based on kinship and neighborhood supported those elements in the lives of farm families which emphasized mutuality among women and men. For Helen Davis and Leroy Benton, the kin-centered and locally focused character of their common social life counterbalanced Leroy's greater interest in community-wide, formally organized activities. For Lucy Ann and George Riley, shared social networks and joint participation in both local visiting and community-wide gatherings fused and synchronized the otherwise somewhat different spatial structures and temporal rhythms of their working lives.

Kinship was a valuable resource for women in sustaining integrated modes of sociability in large part because it legitimated informal and flexible interactions across gender lines. When women and men interacted on the basis of kin relationships, they were defined not as women and men but in more particular and varied ways, as daughters and fathers, sisters and brothers, nieces and uncles, cousins, and so on. Those relationships involved specific expectations based on generation; although they were shaped by gender as well, they were closely conjoined with relations between daughters and mothers, sisters, nieces and aunts, female cousins, and so forth. In the kinship system of the Nanticoke Valley, women's relationships with men were not separate from their relationships with other women. Rarely did women and men meet on the basis of their gender identity alone.

Informality and flexibility in cross-gender interactions was also facilitated by the close connection between kinship and neighborhood which developed during the settlement process and was reinforced by the demographic decline of the late nineteenth century.[8] Contradictions within the kinship system, as well as the fact of propinquity, shaped how that connection was formed. Sibling solidarity was undermined by inequalities in inheritance, but it was also sustained by interdependence in the daily round of work and family life. Just as sibling relationships were, at least in principle, equal in a way that intergenerational relationships were not, so they were in principle voluntary rather than compulsory. Conflicts among siblings were avoided or defused by the diminution of contact rather than by confrontation; relationships were dissolved more often than conflicts within them were resolved. Beyond the sibling set, expectations of mutual aid were quite generalized; neither the nature of obligations nor the persons on whom they were incumbent was specified in any detail. This ambiguity helped to avoid the conflicts that might follow from people's perceived failure to fulfill specific obligations, as well

8. For the insight that the voluntary and generalized character of kinship facilitates its integration with friendship and neighboring, I am indebted to David Ross Jenkins, *The Agricultural Community in South-West Wales at the Turn of the Twentieth Century* (Cardiff: University of Wales Press, 1971), 170–74.

as to ensure that only those who were in a position to respond to others' needs would feel called upon to do so. Beyond an irreducible minimum, mutual aid among kin was always open to negotiation.

The flexibility and variability of relationships among siblings made them, in practice, largely indistinguishable from relationships among neighbors. When siblings and cousins were neighbors and people who grew up on neighboring farms intermarried, the distinction between kinship and proximity became blurred. The normative code governing relations among neighbors, like that among relatives, specified a set of mutual obligations regarded as absolutely necessary; beyond that minimum, everything was discretionary. Neighbors, like siblings, might share a great deal. "Friendship" was the term Nanticoke Valley people used for relationships formed by choice, on the basis of descent, affiliation, and/or association, which involved long-term, substantial, and reciprocal ties of mutual aid and intimacy. Friendship and kinship often coincided, but not all kin were friends, nor were all friends kin in the genealogical sense of the word. Friendship was, finally, a relationship between families, not a private affair between individuals of the same gender. Husbands and wives joined together in their friendships with other families, and ties of friendship allowed women and men to interact on a familiar and intimate basis without regard for the constraints of gender which might exist among strangers.

Together, kinship and neighborhood constituted a terrain that women and men had in common and upon which they met in flexible and varied ways. The social life they conducted on that basis helped to mitigate some of the divisions and inequalities that arose from gendered relations of work and property. Patterns of visiting linked women who shared work with men who exchanged it; they created a common interest for husbands and wives who did not often work together. Similarly, the integration of husbands' and wives' social networks helped to counterbalance the masculine bias in proximity to kin that resulted from inequalities in the inheritance of land. Women were central to the mutual aid and daily interchange that sustained continuing bonds among kin and generated them among neighbors.[9] Conversely, the way kinship shaped social interaction helped to relieve women of the burdens of caregiving. Among their kin, men took

9. While women were peripheral to property relations, they were also outside the conflicts that sometimes disrupted relations among kinsmen. Indeed, women who married into a family might help to keep the peace among brothers who lived in the neighborhood, in part by creating a pattern of daily interchange among households. This was true in spite of the fact that masculine popular opinion often blamed conflicts

responsibility for nursing the sick, keeping watch with the dying, and consoling the bereaved. In contrast to the kinship system that prevails in the contemporary United States, women were not the sole "keepers of kinship" for their and their husband's families.[10] The integrative character of kinship practices made them a valuable source of mutuality among women and men. Women who married within their own neighborhood occupied a special position, for they had continuing access to their parents' as well as to their husband's parents' kin; their ties of descent and affiliation became fused and reinforced each other in the regular round of local sociability. Still, women who moved into their husbands' neighborhoods were not without resources; if they were not independent, they were not isolated either. Many balanced and integrated their kin in other neighborhoods with their kin in the immediate vicinity. In the Nanticoke Valley, sociability partook both of intimacy and inclusiveness; on this terrain, women were more equal to men than they would have been either in isolated marriages or in the public domain.

---

between brothers on their wives; people had difficulty admitting that kin might come into conflict, and they held "outsiders" responsible instead. The prevalence of this belief probably underlined women's awareness of the importance of their peacekeeping role.

10. For a discussion of this feature of contemporary kinship, see Sylvia Junko Yanagisako, "Women-Centered Kin Networks in Urban Bilateral Kinship," *American Ethnologist* 4 (1977): 207–26. In the Nanticoke Valley during the late nineteenth century, men remembered family anniversaries, kept in touch with absent relatives, and passed on kinship information to their children. At least within the circle of "folks and friends," women were not solely responsible for sustaining interpersonal relations, nor was the work of caregiving clearly distinguished from other responsibilities such as settling estates and mediating conflict.

Community Organizations

Was the influence of women greater than that of men?
—Debate topic, Farmers' Jubilee, Mt. Ettrick, 1868

The people of the Nanticoke Valley joined together in community-wide groups through their network of neighbors and kin. Individuals did not shed their familial and local identities when they ventured into other sections of the community. People placed one another in terms of their family status, kin-group membership, and neighborhood, as well as in terms of their economic position. While formal organizations included people from various families and neighborhoods, they built on and extended rather than contradicted ties of kinship and acquaintance; community-wide groups incorporated the gender and generational relations that structured families and neighborhoods.

Many of the formal organizations that existed or became established during the late nineteenth century restricted their membership to a single sex. Those concerned with politics and business were predominantly men's groups, since public life was traditionally a masculine preserve. Women heard plenty of political speeches, for oratory of a more or less partisan cast was a prominent feature of most community gatherings, but women were not present in settings where active participation might take place. When particular interest groups constituted themselves as official bodies they did not question the exclusion of women. Political clubs and fraternal groups were by definition male; only the Good Templars' Lodge, a moral reform group, admitted women to equal membership. The early farmers' organizations also restricted their membership to men; only the Grange, the most radical and democratic of farm organizations, welcomed women as members. Most of the groups established within the churches, on the other hand, were women's organizations. Rather than autonomous bodies analogous to the men's groups that legitimately exercised institutional power, these were "ladies' auxiliaries" that provided a delimited field of activity for women within formal organizations controlled entirely by men. Women were excluded from the exercise of power, not only in the public world of politics and business but also within the formal structures of most social and religious organizations.

The masculine monopoly of formal power was legitimated by the notion that men acted as the representatives of their families in the public domain. In communities like the Nanticoke Valley, however, the public domain was not so removed from the social relations of kinship and neighborhood that men could shed their familial identities and local affiliations when they acted politically. Nor could the public activities in which men's groups engaged disregard the conventions that governed informal associations within the community.[1] When organizations whose membership was restricted to men sought to become established in the community or to expand in size, they generally conducted social activities for the families of members and potential members; men attended these events in the company of their wives and children. Men's organizations cemented the bonds among their members, not by treating men as isolated individuals who came together on the basis of gender and self-interest, but rather by incorporating men's identities as heads of families, members of kin groups, and residents of neighborhoods. This extension did not necessarily undermine male domination but it did diminish the distinction between formal power and informal association, and it meant that a substantial portion of organizational life was conducted on a territory within which women had a legitimate place. Only those

1. The hypothesis that women's subordination is systematically related to the disjunction between public and private domains was first developed by Michelle Zimbalist Rosaldo, "Woman, Culture and Society: A Theoretical Overview," in *Woman, Culture and Society*, ed. Rosaldo and Louise Lamphere (Stanford, Calif.: Stanford University Press, 1974), 17–42. Although Rosaldo initially posited a "universal, structural opposition between domestic and public spheres," she later came to understand that opposition as itself a cultural construction of modern Western capitalist society. Rosaldo also suggested that such categorical oppositions pay insufficient attention to how gender works in practice, neglecting both the interplay of women's and men's activities across the domestic/public divide and the sources of inequality in gender relations. Rosaldo, "The Use and Abuse of Anthropology: Reflections on Feminism and Cross-Cultural Understanding," *Signs* 5 (1980): 389–417.

groups which, like the Masons, sought to establish the position and advance the interests of a certain group of men by excluding others on the basis of class did not sponsor gender-mixed social activities; class and gender exclusiveness were closely associated. The more inclusive men's organizations sought to become, the more of their organizational life they conducted through family-based modes of sociability.

This practice provided Nanticoke Valley women with significant opportunities for participation in the organizational life of the community. Women were included as wives and daughters, mothers and sisters, when they would have been excluded as unattached individuals of the feminine gender. In organizational culture, as in family life, women sought to reshape the ties that bound them to men so that, instead of enforcing women's subordination and segregation, those ties provided a basis for gender integration and more equal participation in decision making. Women took the initiative, becoming the organizers of informal social events for all-male organizations; it was women's own efforts that ensured that gender-mixed activities comprised such a substantial part of organizational life. Within male-dominated but gender-mixed organizations, such as the churches, women used the formally subordinate female auxiliaries as bases from which they could enlarge their power. Instead of accepting the limited autonomy that auxiliary status allowed them and creating a separate "women's culture" within the churches, Nanticoke Valley women organized gender-mixed activities through their own organizations. Gradually women's groups became the vital centers of church life, generating egalitarian and integrated forms of association which redressed the imbalance between female membership and male leadership in the churches. Equally important, women used those activities to secure a strong position in the financial affairs of the churches. In the early twentieth century they gained equality in the formal governance structure of religious institutions as well.

The strategy women adopted to enlarge their participation in public life was consistent with the dominant ideology of "woman's place" as well as with the habits of sociability in the local community. The notion of "separate spheres" that prevailed in white middle-class urban culture rationalized women's exclusion from public life in part through the theory that women exercised moral "influence" on men in the domestic domain. Some middle-class women sought to use their acknowledged influence to change society and ameliorate their own situation, but "separate spheres" proved to be a problematic foundation for such efforts. Not only did the ideology underline

Georgia and Norman Wright. Nanticoke Valley Historical Society.

gender differences, but it also accepted in principle the distinction between the domestic and public domains; in practice, women's collective action was constantly undermined by the gendered boundary between the private household and the public world of politics. As the scale of urban life increased, the local neighborhoods and informal associations within which women could legitimately act became eroded and the social networks in which women were vital participants became marginal to the centers of power. Women's influence was by definition distinct from masculine power, and over time it became increasingly so in fact.[2]

In the Nanticoke Valley, not only were the notions of gender difference assumed by the ideology of separate spheres largely irrelevant to men and women alike, but the connection between public and private domains remained substantial. Women's influence was not circumscribed by gendered boundaries any more than their work and their sociability were; kin-based, locally rooted, and informal forms of community organization were hospitable to women. Nanticoke Valley men, like American men generally, could accept the notion of women's influence without feeling a threat to their masculine power, but in the rural community women's influence was at least potentially more significant than the dominant ideology acknowledged. In seeking to enlarge their influence through active participation in social life, Nanticoke Valley women adopted an effective strategy to work toward equality and gender integration.

On 7 January 1868, George Riley recorded the topic of a debate held by the Farmers' Jubilee in the Mt. Ettrick schoolhouse: "Was the influence of women greater than that of men?" The debate was sponsored by the Farmers' Club. Although the group's membership was formally restricted to men, the club's educational activities, according to Child's *Gazetteer,* were open to "the families of the members."[3] Like most grass-roots organizations, the group strove to be inclusive, so it discussed subjects of general interest to rural residents and encouraged entire families to participate. In a jubilee, farmers got together on a neighborhood basis to discuss some topic of political or social

2. Mary P. Ryan demonstrates that white middle-class urban women were able to act most effectively through voluntary organizations when the domestic and public domains were still connected; as urban growth continued, households became privatized and politics became formalized, eroding the in-between territory of neighborhood and kinship networks through which women had previously organized. Ryan, *Cradle of the Middle Class: The Family in Oneida County, New York, 1790–1865* (Cambridge: Cambridge University Press, 1981), 233–39.

3. Hamilton Child, comp., *Gazetteer and Business Directory . . . for 1872–3,* 121.

significance. The women did not speak at these meetings, nor did they vote to decide which side had carried the day, but their presence in the audience mattered nonetheless. Men discussed the question of female influence in front of their wives and daughters, sisters, aunts, and cousins. They spoke as husbands and fathers, brothers, nephews, and cousins, not as abstract "men"; in this setting, men's as well as women's identities were largely defined by their family connections. Furthermore, the gathering occurred in one of the most inclusive places in the locality. No wonder, then, that the question was "decided in the affirmative."

Farm Organizations

The farmers' groups established in the Nanticoke Valley before the advent of the Grange in 1874 confined their membership to men. Local agricultural societies were sponsored by the Broome County Agricultural Society and organized by the community's established office holders and commercial elite. They directed their regular educational programs toward men, for they presumed that adult male heads of families made the decisions about farm operations. Only when the local societies planned fairs did they involve women. In 1880, although all the officers of the Lamb's Corners Agricultural Society were men, two of the five members of the Fair's executive committee were women. Women superintended and judged six of the sixteen categories of exhibits that year. Men took charge of the livestock (including cattle and poultry) exhibits, displays of fruits and vegetables, ploughing demonstrations, and exhibits of farm and dairy implements. Women supervised exhibits of "butter, cheese, and culinary" items, domestic manufactures, painting, fancy work, ornamental needlework, and flowers. This division of responsibility bears little resemblance to the actual or even notional gender division of labor on Nanticoke Valley farms; although it acknowledges some of women's work, it ignores women's participation in dairying, poultry raising, fruit growing, and gardening, and it marginalizes women's responsibility for processing farm products by confounding it with purely domestic and even decorative pursuits. Women were represented on the executive committee not as integral participants in the farm economy but as practitioners of domestic arts and as organizers of sociability.[4]

4. These generalizations are based on the "Rules and Regulations for the Ninth Annual Fair of the Lamb's Corners Agricultural Society," September 22, 23, 1880, and

The farmers' clubs were somewhat more inclusive. Designed to increase popular interest in agricultural improvement by emphasizing practical rather than "book farming," the clubs met in district schoolhouses rather than in the villages and drew their leadership from ordinary farmers rather than from the community's elite. Although the lectures held by farmers' clubs during the winter on such topics as "Grass Lands," "Care of Stock," and "Making Farmers Attractive" were attended primarily by men, practical demonstrations were held "at the residences of the different members" so that "the families of the members" could participate in the inspection and discussion of farm operations.[5] The jubilees sponsored by the farmers' clubs were even more inclusive. Designed to appeal to all the residents of open-country neighborhoods, they considered a wide range of topics, from recent scientific discoveries to questions of moral philosophy and current political issues; invited speakers sometimes made the opening presentation, but local men usually carried on the discussion. The farmers' clubs recognized women both as working members of farm families and as persons with intellectual and political interests, but they still regarded men as the economic decision makers and political actors for their families.

The Patrons of Husbandry was the first farm organization to open its membership to women. The democratic and cooperative ideology of the Grange extended to matters of gender as well as economics, and the establishment of the Unity Grange in 1874 involved a radical transformation in local political culture.[6] Just as joining the national

the program for the "Nanticoke Valley Agricultural Society Thirteenth Annual Fair," Lamb's Corners, October 6, 7, 1886.

5. Child, *Gazetteer*, 121. The list of topics comes from the diary of William Marean.

6. A significant connection between the temperance and the farmers' movements in the early 1870s pushed farm organizations to accept women as equal members and, eventually, to support woman suffrage. The Independent Order of Good Templars, which expanded after the Civil War, accepted women as members and office holders. As early as 1869, a group of Good Templars in Oswego, New York, formed the Prohibition party, admitted women as delegates to its founding convention, and endorsed woman suffrage. By 1873–74, women Templars were involved with the Women's Christian Temperance Union as well. The "home protection" argument for prohibition, coupled with the conviction that men would never pass prohibition laws on their own, made woman suffrage seem consistent with the preservation of feminine domesticity. The presence of women temperance advocates and the general acceptance of the "home protection" argument were crucial in the Grange's commitment to gender equality. For information about the connections between temperance and suffrage, see Ruth B. A. Bordin, *Woman and Temperance: The Quest for Power and Liberty, 1873–1900* (Philadelphia: Temple University Press, 1981), 4–8, 123–31. Donald B. Marti documents the participation of women temperance activists in the Grange and their agitation for gender equality within the farm organization in "Sisters of the Grange: Rural

movement meant taking a stand against capitalist shippers, processors, and monopolists and espousing alternative forms of economic organization, so founding a local Grange required men to allow women to participate in, rather than merely observe, political debate. The inclusion of women was firmly established in the Grange before it spread to this region, so local men were following national policy in admitting women to membership. At the same time, there is no record of resistance to women's participation in local granges; men who adopted Grange principles did so wholeheartedly.

The ideology of gender relations which characterized the Patrons of Husbandry at the national level was firmly egalitarian and deeply rooted in the experiences of farm families. Participants in Grange ritual repeated this credo: "Woman was intended by our Creator to be the helpmeet, companion, and equal of man—the perfecting half added to his hemisphere—thus completing the fully-globed orb of our common humanity."[7] This image of gender relations contrasts clearly with the dominant image of gender differences in white urban middle-class culture and represents a direct critique of "separate spheres." The distinct realms pertaining to women and men are hemispheres, not spheres, and each is incomplete without the other; only when masculine and feminine are fused is "our common humanity" fulfilled. This is quite different from the notion that man is generically human and woman is the gendered other; the credo sees both men and women as gendered and emphasizes their unification rather than the differences between them. The credo had more than a metaphorical meaning in the Grange. Women and men were regarded as partners in production and the joint heads of farm families. In this perspective, women's distinctive responsibilities provided no basis for their exclusion from or subordination either within the organization itself or in the cooperative commonwealth the Grange sought to establish; rather, the inclusion of women was a matter both of justice and of necessity. The Grange recognized and celebrated the contributions of women to family farms and rural communities. Equally important, it relied on women to sustain their families' com-

---

Feminism in the Late Nineteenth Century," *Agricultural History* 58 (1984): 247–61. The direct connections between the local Good Templars' Lodge and the Grange cannot be traced except through individuals who belonged to both, but the lodge provided a local precedent for the equal membership of women, and the temperance papers members received furnished ample arguments for the extension of those principles to the political domain.

7. This early Grange credo is reprinted in Charles M. Gardner, *The Grange—Friend of the Farmer, 1867–1947* (Washington, D.C.: The National Grange, 1949), 191.

mitment to Grange principles and to organize the social activities that made Grange membership a way of life. As community organizers, women planned activities that nurtured cooperation among farm people.

The ideology of gender relations that informed Grange practice was deeply consonant with gender relations in local farm families and in informal social life, although it was sharply at variance with the traditional organization of politics. Women participated in Grange activities as family members, attending meetings with their husbands, fathers, and brothers. Four ritual offices were reserved for women; female members elected the Three Graces ("Ceres," "Pomona," and "Flora," or grain, fruit, and flowers) and a lady assistant steward, giving women a way of organizing collectively as Grange women. Women sometimes served as chaplain, lecturer, and secretary. All members were eligible for these offices and all voted in the election. The chaplain took responsibility for leading opening and closing prayers, the lecturer arranged for speakers or gave talks of an educational nature, and the secretary recorded the group's proceedings and conducted its correspondence with other granges. Women who served in these offices spoke in public and acted as the group's representatives in the wider community, as well as occupied positions of formal leadership within the local Grange.

From the beginning of the Grange movement in the Nanticoke Valley, women were active participants in the organizational work and assumed positions of responsibility. In the Unity Grange, founded at Mt. Ettrick in 1874, Lucy Howard Councilman and Ezra J. Councilman were among the first officers; this husband-wife team was elected assistant steward and lady assistant steward of the Broome County Pomona Grange when it was formed the next year.[8] Lucy Ann Riley may never have held Grange office but she accompanied George to meetings as well as to Grange-sponsored social events from the summer of 1874 on. George Riley recorded the initiation of a number of couples to Grange membership and the election of five women as officers of the Unity Grange in 1875. The same patterns prevailed in the Glen Aubrey Grange, founded in 1887, and the Maine Grange, founded in 1890.

Within Broome County as a whole, women comprised a significant proportion of Grange membership.[9] Most women joined with their

8. *Official Directory and History of Broome County Granges, Patrons of Husbandry* (Binghamton, N.Y.: Patrons of Husbandry, 1941), 11.

9. These generalizations are based on the histories of all the local Granges in the county included in the *Official Directory and History of Broome County Granges.*

husbands, although some men joined without their wives. Leadership, too, tended to run in families. Men held the highest offices and occupied the majority of positions not specifically assigned to women. The women who were chosen to fill the offices reserved for members of their sex, and who were occasionally elected to the offices of chaplain, lecturer, or secretary, were usually related to male officers. Their position, however, was based not on that of their husbands but rather on the way they conducted themselves in the discharge of their duties and on their dedicated service to the organization as a whole. The policies that gave women a distinct role in ritual and reserved specific offices for them increased women's participation in the formal side of local activities; instead of simply playing a supportive role, they assumed definite responsibilities. If women did not often go beyond the positions and activities that Grange structure established as exclusively their own, they were not confined to that place either. The Grange incorporated those aspects of local society and culture which stressed the mutuality of gender relations and the joint activities of husbands and wives, and it was marked by both the strengths and limitations of that approach. The result, although not perfect equality, was a principled commitment to equal rights and a greater degree of legitimate power than women attained in any other organization in the rural community.

Having established equal rights within the local granges, the New York State and National Grange organizations were gradually but determinedly pushed into advocacy of woman suffrage by their women members. As Donald B. Marti has pointed out, the Grange's later claim that it supported suffrage from the start will not bear examination.[10] Although the equal membership of women was established at the beginning of the Order of Patrons of Husbandry, founders had a variety of opinions about woman's place in the social order. Caroline Hall, the niece of Oliver Hudson Kelley, was active in the establishment of granges in Minnesota and served as lady assistant steward of the National Grange during the early years; she recruited women as members and was a persuasive advocate of women's equality. The Declaration of Purposes adopted at the 1874 national convention concluded with the statement that the Grange

10. Marti's "Sisters of the Grange" is the most recent analysis of the process though which Grange women successfully pushed the organization to commit itself to woman suffrage. For an earlier account, see Gardner, *The Grange*, 191–201. Oliver Hudson Kelley, *Origin and Progress of the Order of the Patrons of Husbandry in the United States: A History from 1866 to 1873* (Philadelphia: J. A. Wagenseller, 1875), includes a tribute to Caroline Hall's influence, as well as a caution that relatively few women assumed leadership positions in the organization.

sought "to inculcate a proper appreciation of the abilities and sphere of woman." Grange members had strikingly disparate views about how to define women's "abilities and sphere." Feminist Grange members such as Marie Stevens Howland, who advocated communal living, sex reform, and Fourierist socialism, put forward a radical vision of gender equality during the early 1870s. The Rev. Aaron B. Grosh, the first chaplain of the National Grange, took a more conservative position. He believed that "woman needs our Order far more than does the sterner, hardier sex," for farm women were confined to a dull round of domestic chores and enjoyed fewer opportunities for social intercourse than men. At the same time, "the Order needs her for man's improvement"; woman's presence would exert an elevating moral influence on the men.[11] Although the principles Grosh espoused supported gender integration within the Order, he did not extend these principles to the world outside the organization. Grosh believed that women should never act politically. Drawing a clear boundary between the family-based order and the public political domain, he likened women's participation within the protected circle of the order to their "voting for officers or for resolutions in a sewing circle," a church-sponsored women's organization. Some Grange men, at both the state and national levels, resisted the conclusion that their principles necessarily implied equal rights in the political arena.

Grange women, some of whom had a background in temperance agitation, pushed for an explicit commitment to woman suffrage. In 1875, the Ladies' Committee of the New York State Grange urged Grange men to "increase the opportunities of woman outside the Grange as well as in." This provoked considerable controversy over the question of suffrage in the state Grange newspaper *The Husbandman*. Canastota resident and temperance advocate Ella C. Goodell became the spokeswoman for the suffrage forces, arguing that "woman's sphere" centered in the home but embraced the world. Eliza C. Gifford, whose husband became the master of the New York State Grange, took up the banner in the early 1880s. In 1881 she persuaded the New York State Grange to declare that equal suffrage

11. A. B. Grosh, *Mentor in the Granges and Homes of Patrons of Husbandry* (New York: Clark and Maynard, 1875), 119–25. What this might mean in practice is suggested by Grange historian Charles M. Gardner, who discussed the reason why separate and unequal rituals for men and women were given up early in the Order's history: "At a certain point in the initiatory progress the women were halted while the men were put through the intricacies of the 'field work,' which was highly emblematic, but which was ultimately discontinued because of the tendency toward roughness in its exemplification." Gardner, *The Grange*, 196.

was an expression of "one of its fundamental principles." The National Grange took a similar position in 1885, but rescinded the resolution in 1886 when it ruled that suffrage was a state rather than national issue. The New York Grange continued to support women's equality, cooperating with the New York State Woman Suffrage Association and the Women's Christian Temperance Union's suffrage campaign throughout the 1890s. In 1893, New York's Gifford again persuaded the National Grange to declare itself in favor of woman suffrage.[12]

There is no evidence of how Nanticoke Valley Grange members felt about these questions during the late nineteenth century, although local women and men served as delegates to the state conventions at which the issue was debated and brought the news back to the local granges. By the early twentieth century, when the Grange movement underwent a significant revitalization, both male and female members of the Nanticoke Valley Grange were firm supporters of woman suffrage. Their commitment to equality and gender integration took other forms that were quite significant at the local level; for example, they initiated mixed seating at religious services and supported equal participation in church governance as well.[13]

The limitations on women's equal participation which the Grange failed to change or challenge pertained not so much to politics as to economics. Women were not directly involved in the economic activities organized by local granges. The consumers' cooperatives that were among their first undertakings were conducted entirely by men. Men also controlled the producers' cooperatives established in the Nanticoke Valley during the last decade of the nineteenth century. The cooperative creameries, although legally separate from the Grange, were founded by active Grange men and embodied its economic vision. Judson Riley's account of the affairs of the East Maine Creamery Association attests that it was an exclusively male institution. The transfer of butter making from farm to factory put it firmly within the realm of men's business activities and involved an extension of masculine control over the dairy process. The cooperative constitution of the East Maine creamery did not modify the gender-defined character of the enterprise. During the years that Judson Riley served as a director and treasurer of the East Maine Association, in fact, creamery business took him away from home and out of his

12. For some details of these controversies within the New York state organization, see Leonard Allen, *History of the New York State Grange* (Watertown, N.Y.: Hungerford-Holbrook, 1934).

13. Ralph M. Young, Diaries, 1913–45; Ralph M. Young (1894–1984) and Margaret Young Coles (1918–87), interviews by author, 5 & 11 July 1982.

wife's company more often than did any other community activity. Lillie Pope Riley attended one annual meeting of the Creamery Association with her husband, but Judson spent at least one evening a week and several days a month on creamery affairs. Business matters, whatever their political persuasion, remained a masculine preserve.

Women were active participants in the regular meetings of local Granges and in the special events these groups put on for other people in their community and for grangers from other communities. This was not a matter of women's serving refreshments after men talked about business or politics. Women presided over meetings, spoke before mixed audiences, and offered their views in open discussions. Descriptions of Grange activities in Broome County before the turn of the century suggest that grangers created a politicized and egalitarian version of traditional participatory and gender-mixed forms of rural culture. Their public activities resembled the "exhibitions" and "entertainments" with which rural residents were familiar, but the pieces people recited and the songs they sang had a political message; equally important, women were not confined to singing and playing the piano, but delivered orations as well. The *Official Directory and History of Broome County Granges* published in 1941 by the Patrons of Husbandry includes a set of rhymed verses that Martin Sherwood, the master of the Upper Lisle Grange, "wrote and sang at one of their meetings in the gay nineties."[14] Composed for the conclusion of a Grange festival in which two sides competed against one another in writing essays, speaking, singing, and storytelling, the verses describe the program in humorous detail and suggest the character of gender relations in local granges. Women and men customarily referred to one another as "Brother" and "Sister," rather than by the titles "Mr." and "Mrs."; the equality and ease presumed to characterize relationships among siblings were extended to the entire membership. The account does make some allusions to conventional conceptions of gender: "Brother Greene told us how Sweet butter we could make," and "Sister Greene she told us how Our house that we should keep." Although the speakers were male and female, in Master Sherwood's version the activities of butter making and housekeeping were shared rather than gendered. And for every conventional image there is an unconventional one: "Adams held the baby while His wife she sang a song," and "Sister Goetcheus treated us To female oratory." Some verses find humor in gender reversals. Consider these verses:

14. The Upper Lisle Grange was founded in 1886. The verses were "furnished by John Sherwood, son of the first master," and reprinted in the *Official Directory and History of the Broome County Granges*, 33–43.

> Brother Johnson climbed a tree
> And then came down again
> And Sister Day thought that was
> So just like a man.
>
> And if instead of Johnson there
> Had been a woman there
> She'd doubled up her little fist
> And she'd have killed the bear.

Although humor based on such reversals sometimes supports rather than undermines convention, this account suggests a friendly contest over gender questions. When Brother Sherwood retailed Sister Day's boast that she would have killed the bear from which Brother Johnson fled right after he said that "Brother Landers told us of The wings that ladies wear," he rendered problematic the notion that women are "ladies," much less angels. In Grange activities, women and men could interact with freedom and familiarity as well as mutual respect.

Churches

The Protestant churches were the largest and most numerous gender-mixed organizations in the Nanticoke Valley. Membership was open to individuals on the basis of their spiritual experiences and theological convictions, without regard to their sex, family status, or social position. In principle, every soul was of equal value and the inclusion of all people was the ultimate objective. In practice, of course, Nanticoke Valley residents did not participate in religious life as isolated individuals. Husbands and wives, parents and children attended religious services and church-sponsored social activities together; while they were not necessarily all church members, they usually belonged to the same congregation. The social relations of gender and generation, kinship and neighborhood, class and ethnicity shaped congregations' composition and modes of action.

Women and men occupied unequal positions within the Nanticoke Valley churches, just as they did within American Protestantism as a whole. Although women comprised the majority of all church members throughout the nineteenth century, experiencing conversion and affiliating with the churches in greater numbers than men, they did not serve as ministers or church officers in the major denominations.

The contradiction between an egalitarian theology and a male-dominated polity had been a central feature of Protestant religious life since the Reformation; women were attracted to the churches in part because their spiritual worth was recognized, yet they were not allowed to serve as official spiritual leaders or participate equally in church governance. Men monopolized positions of lay leadership as well as the ministry. As deacons or elders, men advised the minister and acted on the admission of new members and the enforcement of gospel discipline within the church. Some denominations had separate organizations to administer the church's temporal affairs; these were composed exclusively of men. As trustees of religious societies, men managed church property and financial matters. In both the secular and the spiritual realms, then, men dominated the church hierarchy even though women predominated among the membership. It was in congregational life, that variegated set of activities which constituted the social experience of institutional religion, where women made a central place for themselves. Largely because of women's efforts, men and women cooperated in congregational life. Church activities were more integrated than those of any other community-wide group besides the Grange, and they were unquestionably the most inclusive. Church-sponsored functions were often the only social activities in which Nanticoke Valley couples jointly participated beyond their kin groups and neighborhoods, and they played a crucial role in generating mutuality in the social lives of rural residents.

The membership of most valley churches was characterized by a predominance of women and by the presence of dense kinship ties.[15] On average, 62 percent of church members were female; women comprised 55 percent of those who joined during revivals and when buildings were constructed, and 70 percent of those who joined during less active periods. Some women were the only members of their families to belong. Still, they did not conduct their religious lives as disconnected individuals; instead, they drew other members of their families into the congregation. While women could not guarantee that their husbands would experience conversion, most could see to it that they faithfully attended on the means of grace. Similarly, while women could not ensure that their children would grow in grace as surely as they grew in stature, they could "train them up in the nur-

15. These generalizations are based on a detailed analysis of the membership records of the Maine Congregational and Methodist churches and the Union Center Congregational and Methodist churches. (The available Baptist Church records contain only aggregate membership statistics.) The Methodist classes generally included a somewhat larger proportion of men than the Congregationalist churches did.

ture and admonition of the Lord" and hope that they would enter the covenant as soon as they reached maturity. Popular religious literature told pious women that they could set a powerful example for their household; their "influence" might help bring all the members of their family to God.

The membership rolls of Nanticoke Valley churches demonstrate that many women succeeded in drawing the young people and even the adult men in their families into the circle of church membership. Most youths who were converted during seasons of revival were the children of church members; daughters joined in greater numbers, and at younger ages, than sons did.[16] Many young church members married within their own denomination. Some couples joined the church separately but simultaneously a year or two before they married, suggesting that conversion and courtship went together. Women who married outside their church but within the local community seldom changed their affiliation; instead, their husbands often joined their church, either soon after the wedding or when the children were baptized. Only women who moved into the Nanticoke Valley when they married local men customarily gave up their previous affiliation to join the church to which their husband's family belonged. Some pious women married men who did not belong to any church. Their husbands sometimes joined the church when their children were baptized or converted; in a few cases, the men professed their faith only in old age. One particularly striking example is found in the membership records of the Maine Congregational Church. Lucy Muzzey Bean joined by herself when she and her husband, Frederick, moved to Maine. Lucy's oldest daughter professed her faith at the age of fourteen, the same year her youngest daughter was baptized, and her second daughter was accepted into the church at the age of seventeen. Lucy's unmarried sister and her youngest daughter joined the church when they were in their early thirties. Lucy and Frederick's sons never joined the church, although several of their sons' daughters did. But the piety of the women finally reached one male member of the family, for Frederick Bean, Sr., professed his faith in 1880. According to the church records, the seventy-two-year-old "superannuated" blacksmith was "examined for membership at home and baptized (he has been in ill health for a long time)" just a month before he died. Some spouses and children of church members re-

16. These two tendencies were independent and mutually reinforcing. Young men whose mothers belonged to the church were much more likely to be converted than those whose mothers did not. The disparity was somewhat less among young women. However, nonmembers' daughters were still more likely to join the church than nonmembers' sons were.

mained outside the fold; the "genealogy of grace" was not infallible. But grace definitely ran in families, and it tended to follow the female line through both descent and marriage.[17] In spite of their predominantly female membership, then, the Nanticoke Valley churches were not women's organizations but associations of families within which women played a crucial mediating role. The kin-based pattern of church membership was at least in part the result of women's deliberate efforts to integrate the people closest to them into their religious organizations.

If women's piety had influence, it did not give them power. Women could speak in prayer meetings, which were held on winter weekday evenings for church members, and during special revival services for members and potential members alike. During the late nineteenth century, however, "covenant meetings" became less popular and revival services became more formalized, so women's voices were heard less often than before. Only in those Sunday schools which held separate classes for women and men did women assume the role of teachers and preachers; mixed Sunday-school classes for adults were almost always led by men. Although women and men both attended interdenominational Sunday-school conventions, these were educational gatherings. Men were selected as delegates to the regional conferences of their denominations where official decisions were made.

Nanticoke Valley residents were not entirely unacquainted with women missionaries and evangelists. For example, in 1895 and 1896 the Maine village churches engaged a husband-wife team to lead a series of winter revival meetings. Mr. Van Gorden did most of the preaching while Mrs. Van Gorden directed the choir, but she spoke at two Sunday-evening services as well. A few women spoke before local audiences by themselves. While the men who heard them remarked on their gender, they seemed to feel that these women's extraordinary spiritual gifts and unusual experiences gave them the right to speak in public. In 1893, for example, Judson Riley wrote: "We attended meeting at the M. E. church and listened to a girl who has

17. Other historians have found similar patterns of conversion and affiliation in the evangelical churches of New York and New England during the nineteenth century. Mary P. Ryan, "A Women's Awakening: Evangelical Religion and the Families of Utica, N.Y., 1800–1840," *American Quarterly* 20 (1978): 602–23, coined the phrase "genealogy of grace." Curtis D. Johnson, *Islands of Holiness: Rural Religion in Upstate New York, 1790–1860* (Ithaca: Cornell University Press, 1989), 53–67, found evidence of maternal influence on young people's conversions during "second stage" revivals in Cortland County, which is just north of Broome. See also Nancy F. Cott, "Young Women in the Second Great Awakening in New England," *Feminist Studies* 3 (1975): 15–29.

recently been converted and is now preaching and studying. She is only fifteen years old and is very smart" (8 October 1893). Vernon Davey went to the Presbyterian Church at East Maine in 1896 "to hear Miss Delia Fuller a returned missionary speak" (25 October 1896). Although a few women were making inroads into the ministerial profession, the majority of women church members did not enjoy greater opportunities for religious expression at the end of the nineteenth century than they did before.

The contrast between the established denominations and the radically evangelical Christian Church of Glen Aubrey illuminates the position of women within both types of religious organizations. The sexes were almost equally balanced in the membership of the Christian Church. There was a high proportion of married couples among its members, but the church also attracted men and women as individuals. While women did not predominate among church members, they had a more equal status among the Christians than they did in any of the other churches. The Christian Church was nonsectarian and nonhierarchical. Elders were elected by members; there were no settled ministers. A description of one of the "fellowship meetins" suggests their participatory character: "The meeting was opened by Singing, then reading of the Scripture by Elder Besemer, prayer by Brother Yeomans, followed by Sister Besemer and Brother Besemer. Then after prayer the Brothers and Sisters spoke of the love they had for the Master, all gave in thare testimony that Christ was presus to them" (1 August 1885). The titles "Brother" and "Sister" expressed the equality and kinship of all souls in Christ. Although men served as elders, trustees, and clerks in this society as they did in the other local churches, women were not excluded from positions of responsibility. Sometimes husbands and wives served together: J. W. and Samantha Adriance were conference delegates in 1881 and 1886. Women also participated in deliberations concerning the acceptance of new members and the discipline of wayward ones. When a prospective member recounted his or her spiritual experience, all church members listened and decided whether he or she was ready for admission to membership. When a sister was charged with an offense such as Sabbath-breaking or quarreling, a committee of women was appointed to question her and make a recommendation in her case.[18] Women in the Glen Aubrey Christian Church did not need to organize separately to attain equal participation in religious life. Because

18. In the established denominations, men interrogated and admonished women accused of similar offenses; however, these churches disciplined their members less often after the Civil War than they had before.

of the conjunction of radical evangelicalism and persistent localism in this group, women were granted a legitimate and integral place within the church.

In the established denominations, women's organizations were primarily responsible for the gender-integrated character of religious life. During the late nineteenth century, a variety of groups designed specifically for women were founded within the churches. Female benevolent associations and missionary societies, which had existed in other places a half-century earlier, took root in the Nanticoke Valley after the Civil War. Ladies' aid societies, which had developed more recently to increase women's financial contributions to the churches, spread to the local community during the last quarter of the nineteenth century. Through these organizations women could associate with one another to support particular causes and to expand the social and educational programs of their local churches. In some places, women's organizations constituted a "separate sphere" within the churches, a delimited realm of activity within which women could legitimately exercise initiative and build strong bonds of sisterhood.

What is most striking about the activities of women's organizations within the Nanticoke Valley churches is how often men participated. Men regularly attended the gatherings of the Methodist and Baptist sewing societies and of the Methodist Ladies' Benevolent Society. Women did hold some afternoon meetings without their husbands, but these were often followed by social affairs. Leroy Benton recorded: "After dinner I took Mary and Mother down to Mrs. Browns to the Sewing Society. I went down to the village . . . came back and took supper to the Browns" (16 August 1876). This pattern, in which women got together to sew in the afternoon and were joined by their husbands in the evening, was typical of informal socializing among neighbors; when it was adopted by the sewing societies the only difference was that women sewed for charity rather than themselves. The meetings of the Baptist and Methodist sewing societies which William Marean recorded resembled the rest of the couple's social activities in all but their name: William often accompanied his wife, and the meetings were usually held at the homes of relatives. George Riley, too, went with Lucy Ann to meetings of the Ladies' Benevolent Society. When the group met at their house, he remarked that they had "5 loads and 8 horses and 20 persons, had a good time in general, hope all was satisfide." Most of the guests were married couples (10 July 1874). The women's charitable societies, then, incorporated gender-mixed patterns of sociability and turned them to religious purposes.

Nanticoke Valley women did not use their organizations to construct a distinct domain within the churches. These organizations did
give women a legitimate means of collective action, and women certainly took advantage of them to compensate for their exclusion from
positions of formal power. However, they sought not a semiautono-
mous separate sphere but rather integration and equality in all aspects of religious life. In the perspective and practice of Nanticoke
Valley women, the enlargement of existing areas of commonality and
the creation of new forms of mutuality among women and men was
the most promising route toward the realization of the equality and
dignity which women were promised by Protestant theology.

Ladies' Aid

The ladies' aid societies sponsored most of the public social events
in the church calendar, and their monthly or twice-monthly socials
were planned to involve entire families. These groups represented the
formalization of women's role in the financial support and furnishing
of the churches.[19] The meetings were integrated right from the start.
On 14 February 1878, when the Maine Methodist Church Ladies' Improvement Society gathered at the Rileys', George identified the fifteen people who attended as "Mr. and Mrs. Councilman," "G. W.
Davey and wife," and so on. That same day, William Marean wrote
that "Deborah and I went up to G. W. Rileys with Uncle Matthew to
Aid Society."

The earliest organizational records that have been preserved are
those of the Ladies' Aid Society of the Congregational Church of
Union Center, founded in 1881 with a written constitution and formal bylaws. Its purpose was stated in broad terms: "The object of this
society shall be to contribute to the support of the gospel, the furnishing of the church and to all benevolent objects." Its membership
was defined equally broadly: "Any person may become a member of

19. The first county history noted that when the East Maine Presbyterian/Methodist
church was built in 1872, "it was furnished through the efforts of the ladies, who
raised seventy-five dollars for the purpose." H. P. Smith, ed., *A History of Broome County*
(1885), 504. These women did not incorporate, but they made a distinct and collective
contribution rather than submerging their individual donations under those of their
husbands. When the Maine Methodist Church was repaired and refurbished in 1877,
George Riley recorded that the Ladies' Improvement Society contributed the sum of
thirty-three dollars. This group did not disband once the repairs were paid for, but
constituted itself as the Ladies' Aid Society and became a permanent feature of church
life.

this society by signing the constitution and bylaws and paying into the treasurer the sum of twenty-five cents." Twenty-five people signed their names to the constitution and bylaws and paid their dues at the first annual meeting. Nineteen were women, all but one of whom were married; the six men who joined did so with their wives. Although the society was not for women only, it was definitely a women's organization. Women were elected to fill all of its offices and they conducted most of the business of the society by themselves, but the group worked in close coordination with the men who controlled the church's temporal affairs. The first official act of the society provided "that a committee of four gentlemen be chosen to confer with the trustees of Cong. Ch. relative to mooving the orchestra to the west end of the church, remove the beer barrel from the pulpit, varnish the church, and repair the church generally" (10 February 1881). Before long a committee of women was appointed to confer directly with the male trustees, but the two groups always cooperated on financial matters.

The official records of the Maine Methodist Ladies' Aid Society do not begin until 1890, twelve years after the group was formed. The constitution stated: "Any person of good moral character may become a member of this Society by signing this Constitution and paying ten cents per month. Gentlemen may become honorary members by the payment of ten cents per month but shall not have the privilege of voting." This provision kept control of the society firmly in women's hands; men could provide financial support, but they were relegated to the role of silent partners in the organization. By 1890, the Methodist women were confident of their ability to manage their own financial affairs; they met with the male trustees when necessary, but they made many decisions on their own.

The women who joined the ladies' aid societies were long-time church members. In the Union Center Congregational group, most of the officers and many of the members came from families that had joined the church when they moved to the community; these women had grown up in the church and professed their faith in their youth. Mothers, daughters, and sisters joined the organization together and held office simultaneously or successively. Most of these women's fathers and husbands were also prominent in the temporal and spiritual affairs of the church. The Ladies' Aid Society of the Union Center Methodist Church, founded in 1884, had forty members in 1897. All were female. Thirty-four were married; the six single women members were listed with their mothers. While most were church members, some were not. The majority of these women were

new to the community and joined the church after becoming involved in the society. A few women maintained a dual affiliation with
the Methodist and Congregationalist churches of Union Center; having grown up in one church and married into the other, they sought
to forge ties with their husband's kinswomen by joining the ladies' aid
society of his church even though they did not give up their original
affiliation.

If the ladies' aid societies of Union Center sometimes united
women from the locality across denominational lines, the Maine
Methodist Ladies' Aid Society linked women from different localities
who belonged to the denomination. The Maine society included
Methodist women from all the neighborhood classes and churches
that formed part of the Maine charge. Women from Allentown and
North Maine were as active as those who lived near the village. During the fifteen years covered by the minute books, seventy women
were named as holding office, serving on committees, or hosting
socials at their homes. While single women formed only a small fraction of the membership, five single women served as officers and two
occupied the presidency. Women who were active in the society
had especially close ties of kinship with one another. Daughters followed their mothers into office, while sisters who had married and
moved to different neighborhoods were reunited at meetings and on
the board.

Women were recruited into the ladies' aid societies through ties of
kinship and friendship. In turn, the societies sought to extend those
bonds of sympathy and mutual support to their entire membership
and, through them, to the congregation as a whole. The constitution
of the Union Center Methodist Ladies' Aid Society stated simply that
its primary purpose was "to promote Christian fellowship and love
among members of the Church and Society." The last article of the
bylaws of the Union Center Congregational Ladies' Aid Society, entitled "Fraternal Courtesy," spelled out part of what that meant: "As
this society is a christian association endeavoring to glorify God, It is
expected that the members will cultivate mutual affection for each
other that in concord and good fellowship we may cherish and preserve and further the prominent features of our society—viz. Friendship, Love and Truth."[20] At the same time that these organizations

20. Significantly, these documents did not use the language of "sisterhood" but
rather the language of "fellowship" and "fraternal courtesy" which was conventional in
the established churches. The use of terms that are masculine in gender to denote
what is universally human is one mark of male domination. But rural women did not

capitalized on the dense interconnections that made rural residents intimate with one another's lives, they also sought to control the destructive consequences gossip might have among their members.

The ladies' aid societies did not always succeed in avoiding conflict, especially where money was involved. "Fraternal courtesy" within the Union Center Congregational Ladies' Aid Society was severely strained during its second year. The dispute began with a difference of opinion over the suitability of an organ purchased for the church, but it culminated in the loss of half of the original membership. The dispute became so serious because it involved questions about the propriety of the treasurer's use of society funds and the role of socially prominent people in the church. Nanticoke Valley residents' sensitivity to class differences and their unwillingness to discuss them openly made the issue impossible to resolve. On the other hand, the Union Center society took care that economic differences among its members would not lead to either ostentatious displays of wealth or an undue burden on poor women in the provision of food for meetings. Its bylaws specified not only what each person attending a social had to pay but also exactly what the woman hosting the gathering should provide: "Every member who shall entertain the society and furnish supper shall be restricted to the following articles for the table—viz. bread or biscuit and butter, beef or cheese or pickles, two kinds of cake, one kind of sauce, and tea. And any member refusing to conform to above regulations shall pay a fine of fifty cents each." The society was concerned to prevent competition among members as to who could serve the better, or at least larger, supper; not only would such competition feed the vices of gluttony and envy, but it would also tend to exclude poor women from participation.

The Maine Methodist Ladies' Aid Society minutes interpreted "the harmonious and kind feeling that was exhibited" at their meetings as "an Omen of Peace and Prosperity" (22 May 1891). In practice, if not in principle, prosperity was just as important as peace. The constitution stated that the group united "to aid the general work of the

---

counter by adopting feminine terms for their own associations; rather, they claimed the conventional terms for themselves. While Nanticoke Valley women may not consciously have been asserting their right to an equal and undifferentiated place in the Christian community, they certainly refused to mark their own activities with the feminine gender. Their language emphasized the qualities of Christian character which all church members were supposed to share, not those presumed to distinguish women from men. Similarly, local women stressed not the separateness of their own organizations but rather the continuity between the ladies' aid society and the church as a whole. In this regard, their language certainly parallels their activities.

church, financially and otherwise." The Maine Methodist group's records provide a fairly complete and quite representative picture of the financial side of ladies' aid society operations. The regular gatherings for members and their families generally brought in between $5 and $15. When relatively little money was raised because attendance was low, the minutes stressed the fellowship of those who were present: "The Society of the M. E. Church was entertained at Mrs. Elias Pitchers Tuesday afternoon and evening Feb. 13th 1894. Were entertained by Miss Hattie and Eunice with speaking and reading. Not largely attended but a very enjoyable time. Receipts $4.05." Receipts from the regular socials totaled between $50 and $75 each year and amounted to about half of the society's annual income. Direct cash contributions were relatively unimportant; the society sought many small contributions and did not accept large donations from individuals. The special events the society organized for the congregation and community generally raised another $50 or $75 each year. Church festivals and suppers might yield $15 to $25, while the profits from selling ice cream and cake in the center of the village on Decoration Day ranged from $20 to as much as $50.

Over time, the contributions of the ladies' aid societies comprised an increasingly substantial portion of the total budget of local churches. The women of the Maine Methodist Ladies' Aid Society set ambitious goals for themselves. In 1895, they agreed "to endeavor to raise $250 to pay the parsonage debt" in full, which took them two years (11 April 1895). Then they turned to the support of the church itself, a function formerly left to the male-dominated Methodist Society. By the turn of the century, the Ladies' Aid Society was regularly paying substantial sums on the church mortgage and donating the balance of the treasury to the minister's salary. The women officially assumed responsibility for the church debt in 1903. Not only did they pay off the mortgage in two years, but they also paid for repairs to the church and the organ, purchased a pump for the parsonage, and increased their annual contribution to the minister's salary. The ladies' aid societies of the other churches assumed similar responsibilities. When the Union Center Methodists purchased a parsonage in 1898, the Ladies' Aid Society committed itself to furnish and maintain the building. The records of the Maine Congregational Society document the increasingly substantial financial contributions the Ladies' Aid Society made to that church's budget. Between 1893 and 1896, the Ladies' Aid raised $406 to repair and refurbish the church; in 1897, it raised $167 to refurnish the parsonage. These were the only expenditures made on the church properties during those years.

The men of the Congregational Society remained responsible only for raising the minister's salary.

The women of the Nanticoke Valley made a place for themselves in the financial as well as social affairs of their churches. This was a gradual and unobtrusive, but nonetheless significant, process. Financing the purchase, construction, and repair of church property and raising the pastor's salary had traditionally been the responsibility of male trustees and church officers. Although women had always contributed to the support of their churches, they had formerly done so as wives and their contributions had been subsumed by those of their husbands. The ladies' aid societies changed all that. Women made a distinct and collective contribution to church finances, and over time they voluntarily assumed responsibilities that had formally belonged to men alone. Organizing suppers, baking cakes and serving ice cream, and giving musical recitals all appeared to be quite womanly activities; so did buying furnishings for the parsonage. But for the women themselves, the ladies' aid provided experience in conducting meetings, planning and carrying out programs, and handling substantial sums of money. Within "ladies' auxiliaries," women appeared to be acting solely in the interest of the church as a whole rather than in their own interest. But religious women refused to be submerged within the male-dominated structure of the churches or to be confined to a "separate sphere." The social activities they sponsored included the men in their families and congregation, and the success of these gatherings enabled women to expand their role in church affairs. Just as joint participation in informal social events helped create mutuality between husbands and wives, so the gender-mixed activities conducted by the ladies' aid societies helped generate equality between women and men in the churches.

The history of the ladies' aid societies makes it clear that the integration of social life was a positive goal of Nanticoke Valley women. The urban ministers who originated the ladies' aid societies intended to provide women with a distinct, limited, and subordinate domain of activity within the church which supported the institution without threatening its male domination, but rural women turned it to different ends; they sought to expand their collective power within the church and to promote more gender-integrated modes of social action. These two aspects of women's strategies were inextricably related; women attempted to mitigate the inequalities of the gender system by enlarging the dimensions of joint activity in social institutions. Through their collective activities, too, women created occasions for a family-centered mode of sociability.

Women believed that in families, as in the church, sharing enhanced mutual respect; a common social life strengthened men's commitment to their wives and children and supported the position of women in marriage. Neither the isolated conjugal family nor male-dominated civil society offered women many resources. Women responded to their predicament by emphasizing the intermediate territory of kinship and neighborhood, informal contacts and local associations. This simultaneously offered women resources with which to work and the freedom to define their own ends. These were the most flexible of social relations; women could shape them in such a way as to bridge some of the divisions and counterbalance some of the asymmetries that arose out of gender relations in other aspects of life and labor. While the extent to which women could actually redress inequality and overcome gender divisions was limited, the meaning of their choices and the direction of their effort is nonetheless clear. The integration of social life was one form of the mutuality and reciprocity women sought to sustain and enhance in all aspects of their relationships with men. This was a common choice and a collective commitment. Women directed their solidarity with one another toward the achievement of greater sharing with men.

CHAPTER TWELVE

Conclusion: Mutuality as
an Empowerment Strategy

Rural women did not occupy a "separate sphere" during the late nineteenth century. Although women were not equal with men, they were not confined to a distinct domain of social life. Women were denied independent land-ownership, assigned to subordinate positions in their families, and excluded from equal participation in civil society. They relied on their mothers, sisters, and daughters for support in the common transitions and unexpected crises of family life. But women neither elaborated their shared experiences into a female-defined subculture nor turned to female networks as an alternative to their relationships with men. Rather, they strove to create mutuality in their marriages, reciprocity in their performance of labor, and integration in their modes of sociability. Individually and collectively, rural women responded to inequality by actively enlarging the dimensions of sharing in their relationships with men.

In rural communities, the elements of conjunction between women and men outweighed those of disjunction. Women, in the most salient aspects of their lives, were defined primarily in direct relation to men rather than in terms of their difference from men. This situation presented women with both a problem and an opportunity. The difficulty was that the possibilities for autonomy were highly circumscribed, and the resources to which women had independent access were strictly limited. Rural women had few means of support outside of the households in which they lived, and their interactions with men in their families and kin groups were both immediate and powerful. Women could, however, attempt to redefine the terms of those inter-

Pollard family. Nanticoke Valley Historical Society.

actions. They could meet men as much as possible on common ground rather than in situations that were shaped by gender difference; they could focus their energies on those aspects of life in which sharing provided some basis for equality rather than on those marked by hierarchical divisions. Thus rural women emphasized the familial, rather than feminine, dimensions of the crucial transitions in their lives. They voluntarily participated in the most highly valued and least gender-marked forms of productive labor. Equally important, women could draw on the resources of social networks beyond their immediate families. The joint patterns of sociability women sustained in their neighborhoods and community organizations helped overcome elements of gender separation within their households. This was a collective response to gender inequality; rural women were dedicated to the creation of a common culture of reciprocity and respect among women and men.

The strategies women adopted to nurture mutuality in cross-gender relationships were based on certain social-structural conditions that provided women with a base on which they could build and resources on which they could draw. First, kinship was the central mode of social organization in the rural community. Men and women were committed to family farms. While men inherited paternal land and women moved to their husbands' farms when they married, they both intended to pass the farm on to their sons. Although daughters were excluded from succession, mothers were essential to the inter-generational reproduction of farm families. Kinship also bound rural households together. Relatives shared resources between as well as within households and across as well as along generational and gen-der lines. Women were especially active in providing care for depen-dent kin. In turn, women were able to rely on their relatives not only as a recourse in case of death, desertion, or disaster but also as a resource within their marriages. The closeness of fathers, brothers, and cousins protected women from the arbitrary power of their hus-bands, while the support of mothers, sisters, cousins, and nieces pre-vented them from being overwhelmed by illness, exhaustion, or isolation. In rural neighborhoods and communities, kinship served as a model for friendship. The ubiquitous presence of kin ties across gender lines legitimated mixed modes of sociability, so unrelated women and men enjoyed some of the freedom from constraint which brothers and sisters and cousins enjoyed. Norms of mutual aid were extended from nearby kin to unrelated neighbors, so that long-term reciprocal caregiving, not short-term exchange or calculations of ad-vantage, defined neighborly interaction. Women were active agents in maintaining and extending the kinship system.

Second, the agricultural economy united men and women in the work of family farming. Farmers engaged in commodity production, but they organized their own labor process; neither the long arm of the market nor the dictates of suppliers and processors controlled the organization of production. Furthermore, just as farm families used the means of production they possessed or could mobilize from within their kin group, so they relied almost solely on the labor sup-plied by their families and kindred. This fact alone meant that the gender division of labor had to be somewhat flexible. While the con-ventional division of labor allocated distinct tasks to men and women, it also required close coordination as women completed labor pro-cesses men had begun. Joint responsibility for the dairy operation constituted a domain that women and men shared. The close proxim-ity between the barn and the house enabled women to engage in the work of the dairy while they were also minding children and tending fires. Although household and workplace were not separated on farms as they were in nineteenth-century cities, the specific character of farm operations did affect the degree of women's participation in income-producing work. The active involvement of women in the dairy process, coupled with the centrality of dairying to the agricultural economy of the region, ensured that at least this form of women's work was recognized and valued by men. Nanticoke Valley women believed that their integral role in the dairy operation provided a basis for mutual respect and joint decision making in farm households.

The integration of women and men in the farm family economy and in the kinship system supported and reinforced each other. Both involved joint rather than separate modes of activity; both helped to mitigate the hierarchical nature of property and authority relations between men and women. Women situated themselves strategically in both the kinship system and the agricultural economy, mobilizing the resources and taking advantage of the opportunities each offered for gender integration and equality. Although the rural economy and the dense, kin-based settlement pattern provided women with the foundations on which they could construct joint modes of work and social life, these structural factors did not guarantee that such mutuality would develop automatically. The degree to which husbands and wives, friends and neighbors enjoyed relationships of mutual concern and respect testifies to the achievements of Nanticoke Valley women. Women responded to their position in the gender system by acting to enlarge existing areas of commonality and create new modes of sharing between women and men. In struggling to improve their own lives, women enhanced the quality of life for men as well.

Women nurtured gender equality and integration under conditions of male dominance and over against the ideology of separate spheres. Although the ideology of separate spheres failed to correspond to the actual situations of many groups of women in the nineteenth century, it nonetheless became hegemonic in urban middle-class culture. Ideologies do not necessarily reflect social experience; rather they shape the ways people interpret their situations and interact with one another. The ideology of separate spheres concealed gender inequality at the same time it reinforced male dominance, making it quite effective in reducing gender conflict within those groups who adopted it. Nonetheless, ideologies must enable people to make some sense of their social experience and conduct orderly relationships with others in order to be accepted. Rural women, whose lives so directly contradicted the prescriptions of separate spheres, rejected the terms of the dominant ideology. They did not retain traditional modes of thought based on hierarchical relations between women and men either, even though inequality was still deeply embedded in women's and men's relationships to the land. Rather, they constructed an alternative vision of gender relations based on their experience of kinship and labor. To some degree this vision remained implicit in women's practice, but in crucial contexts women explicitly advanced this vision as an alternative to both male dominance and separate spheres. In attempting to secure community-wide acceptance of their model of gender relations, women were consciously and collectively countering the hegemony of ideologies of gender division and inequality.[1]

Just as women's strategies for sustaining and enhancing mutuality were based on the bonds of kinship and labor, so women sought to maintain a particular relationship between the kinship and economic systems. Women attempted to ensure that long-term norms of reciprocity, not short-term calculations of advantage, predominated in the interactions in which they were centrally involved. Women maintained an alternative both to the middle-class model of separate spheres and to the traditional model of patriarchal dominance, counterposing a model of human relations based on mutual aid. This was founded in their experience of kinship, but they extended it to both marriage and friendship. Men's kinship relations had already been permeated by the metaphors of the capitalist marketplace, not so much because men were more involved in the market than women were (although men's status as property-owning household heads was certainly significant in this regard), but because men adhered to an ideology of republican independence. The notion of republican independence which arose in civil society and the notion of the yeoman farmer which was its rural expression were profoundly gendered; their masculine character was inherent in their cultural meaning. Women, on the other hand, espoused a notion of interdependence based on continuing reciprocity among kin, which constituted an

---

1. This formulation of how subordinated groups challenge dominant ideologies follows the approach outlined by Sarah Eisenstein in *Give Us Bread but Give Us Roses: Working Women's Consciousness in the United States, 1890 to the First World War* (London: Routledge & Kegan Paul, 1983). Eisenstein, who did not live to complete this brilliant Marxist feminist work, sought to analyze the consciousness of working-class women holding paid jobs outside the household at a time when the dominant culture decreed that woman's place was in the home. She developed a theory of how subordinated groups construct "negotiated" versions of dominant ideologies to accommodate their experience or create alternatives to them on the basis of their practice. Eisenstein established the sources of resistance and alternative visions in women's social experience; in her view, a common consciousness and collective action are crucial to the formation of counter-hegemonic visions.

alternative both to the exclusive male representation of households and to the short-term, instrumental relations of the marketplace. What is most striking, finally, is that rural women collectively sought counter-hegemony, attempting to make their model of human relations normative in their community, rather than retreat to a separate subculture.

In the process, women not only ameliorated their own situation within rural society but also created a bulwark against the penetration of capitalist social relations. When farm people sought to resist the capitalist marketplace, they did not act to defend themselves as individuals independent of outside interests, as "yeoman" farmers, but rather organized themselves collectively as families of men and women to control their dealings with the market.[2] Farm organizations like the Grange were characterized by gender integration as well as cooperation among households; according to this radical rural ideology, equality and mutuality characterized both gender and class relations. Nanticoke Valley women, then, advocated a model of interdependence as an alternative to both male dominance and capitalist social relations.

Women beyond the Nanticoke Valley

How common were the conditions in the Nanticoke Valley, and how often did other groups of women adopt similar strategies to deal with their situation? Placing this small community in the larger context of rural America reveals that although rural society was much too varied for any one community to typify the whole, the Nanticoke Valley did share crucial structural characteristics with other regions in which family farming rather than plantation agriculture predominated.[3] Rural settlement patterns have generally been

2. For a discussion of the "yeoman" ideal and of the basis of the farmers' and Populist movements in "habits of mutuality" and informal cooperative associations among rural households, see Steven Hahn, *The Roots of Southern Populism: Yeoman Farmers and the Transformation of the Georgia Upcountry, 1850–1890* (New York: Oxford University Press, 1983), 50–85; Lawrence Goodwyn, *Democratic Promise: The Populist Movement in America* (New York: Oxford University Press, 1976).

3. The conditions of racial domination and economic exploitation under which African American slaves and freed people labored on southern plantations during the nineteenth century made their experience of labor very different from that of white property-owning farmers in the North and Midwest. However, the centrality of kinship to the African American community and the active participation of black women in productive as well as reproductive labor resemble the patterns found in the Nanticoke Valley. My conceptualization of kinship and gender relations has drawn on studies of African American communities, especially Edward Magdol, *A Right to the Land: Essays in the Freedmen's Community* (Westport, Conn.: Greenwood Press, 1977), which uses the

kin based. Kin groups have secured adjacent farms under various forms of land distribution, from the communal settlements of New England through the speculative market of the mid-Atlantic to the Homestead Act of the Midwest. Fathers have passed land on to some sons and secured nearby farms for others through a variety of strategies, while daughters have married inheriting sons and gone to live on their husbands' farms. Open-country neighborhoods based on kin clusters have been the predominant pattern of settlement since the eighteenth century, even in New England; most nucleated villages developed with the expansion of commerce in the nineteenth century.4 Rural communities passed through the process of settlement in various ways. As the available land was taken up and farms became too small to subdivide, farm families modified their inheritance strategies, sending some children to developing regions or placing them in nonagricultural occupations. The temporal conjunction between the culmination of settlement and the expansion of capitalist economic relations varied significantly between the eastern seaboard and the Mississippi River, but in a broad region of the North stretching from the Appalachian ridges to the edge of the Great Plains the culmination of settlement and absorption into the capitalist market occurred simultaneously.5 Kin groups remained fundamental to rural society as settlement matured. Indeed, rural depopulation was often accompanied by an increase in the density of kin ties among those who remained in rural communities.6 Kin worked together, routinely shar-

---

term "ethos of mutuality" to describe the extension of kin-based relations within the freed people's community, and Elizabeth Rauh Bethel, *Promiseland: A Century of Life in a Negro Community* (Philadelphia: Temple University Press, 1981). Similarly, although Hispanic residents of the rural Southwest had a distinctive historical experience of conquest, expropriation, and eventual absorption into the wage labor force, kinship and mutual aid were central to their culture. Sarah Deutsch, *No Separate Refuge: Culture, Class, and Gender on an Anglo-Hispanic Frontier in the American Southwest, 1880–1940* (Oxford: Oxford University Press, 1987), shows how involvement in the market intersected with the older system of autonomous communal villages; although men were initially drawn into wage labor to a greater degree than women were, both men and women sought to sustain a balance between the two which, they believed, served their individual and collective best interests.

4. Donald W. Meinig, *The Shaping of America: A Geographical Perspective on 500 Years of History*, vol. 1, *Atlantic America, 1492–1800* (New Haven: Yale University Press, 1986); John R. Stilgoe, *Common Landscape of America, 1580–1845* (New Haven: Yale University Press, 1982).

5. Kenneth A. Lockridge, "Land, Population, and the Evolution of New England Society, 1630–1790," *Past and Present* 39 (1968): 62–80; James A. Henretta and Gregory H. Nobles, *Evolution and Revolution: American Society, 1600–1820* (Lexington, Mass.: D.C. Heath, 1987).

6. Hal S. Barron, *Those Who Stayed Behind: Rural Society in Nineteenth-Century New England* (Cambridge: Cambridge University Press, 1984).

ing labor and machinery and assisting one another when ill health, bad weather, or low prices put family farms in jeopardy. Patterns of visiting, church membership, and participation in community organizations all followed the lines of kinship networks.

The other fundamental feature of Nanticoke Valley society, women's continued participation in income-producing farm labor alongside their husbands, was less universal.[7] Dominant cultural norms dictated that free white women should not work in the fields except when assisting their fathers and husbands at haying and harvest.[8] Some ethnic groups maintained their traditions of sharing outdoor labor; German women were especially likely to work in the fields with their men. Most native-born groups believed that field work was degrading for women. They regarded African American women as little better than animals because black women could chop and pick cotton as well as men, while they pitied immigrant women who worked in the fields as laboring drudges exploited by abusive husbands. In arable farming regions, then, women could not secure an honorable place in the agricultural economy by joining in the production of the primary cash crops.

Farms specializing in growing grain for national and international markets had a very clear gender division of labor which corresponded to the distinction between market-oriented and subsistence production; men engaged in commodity production, while women reproduced the farm family. On these arable farms, even though the household was not separate from the workplace and the family was not distinguished from the enterprise, gender divisions nonetheless approached the prevailing pattern in the urban lower middle class. Farm women often conducted small market-oriented operations, especially poultry flocks, and they usually controlled the proceeds from the sale of eggs and chickens. But such operations were generally peripheral to the farm—indeed, men referred to them colloquially as "sidelines"—and they were regarded as a source of petty cash or credit rather than as a substantial contribution to the farm income. Equally important, women's independent commodity production did

7. Carolyn Sachs, "Women's Work in the U.S.: Variations by Regions," *Agriculture and Human Values* 2 (1985): 31–39, summarizes regional variations and historical changes in the work of American farm women. For an overview and collection of documents on rural women's history which includes Native Americans, Hispanics, and African Americans as well as European Americans, see Joan M. Jensen, *With These Hands: Women Working on the Land* (Old Westbury, N.Y.: Feminist Press, 1981).

8. In 1840, the French traveler Alexis de Tocqueville pronounced this to be a fundamental difference between European peasant culture and American farm families. Alexis de Tocqueville, *Democracy in America*, trans. Henry Reeve and Francis Bowen (New York: Random House, 1945), 2: 223.

not provide a basis for shared labor and decision making between husbands and wives. Instead, it resembled the myriad of ways that lower-middle-class urban women found to bring in money—taking in boarders and lodgers or selling confectionaries and cooked food—which did not require them to leave the household or gain access to the capitalist marketplace. These income-earning activities were often hidden in the household and men did not count them as work.[9]

Dairy farming offered women the opportunity to participate fully in the primary income-producing labor of the farm. Since dairying had traditionally been women's responsibility, there was no question of women's ability to perform the work or of the propriety of their engaging in it. Indeed, women's cool hands and cleanly habits were sometimes described as advantageous to the production of high-quality butter, and the placement of the buttery between the barn and the kitchen enabled women to attend to the dairy process without neglecting their other domestic duties. Traditionally, butter and cheese were produced primarily for home consumption, although the surplus might be sold to other households. As cities grew and industrial villages proliferated during the late eighteenth and early nineteenth centuries, the market for dairy products expanded. Farm women responded by increasing the scale of their dairy operations and producing butter and cheese for sale in relatively distant markets.[10] By mid-century, farms began to specialize in dairying. As the scale of dairying increased, men became more involved in the labor process, not only providing fodder for the growing herds of cattle but also participating in milking and even butter and cheese making.

The gender division of labor in dairying diverged significantly between regions. In New England, women withdrew from or were pushed out of the dairy process as it became commercialized. By mid-century only hired girls went to the barn; it was regarded as unladylike for a woman to wade through the mud and manure of the farmyard, to tuck up her skirts while milking, to consort freely with the men in the barn, and to carry heavy milk pails back to the buttery. When the dairy operation became a substantial source of farm

9. Dorothy Schwieder, "Labor and Economic Roles of Iowa Farm Wives, 1840–80," in *Farmers, Bureaucrats, and Middlemen: Historical Perspectives on American Agriculture*, ed. Trudy Huskamp Peterson (Washington, D.C.: Howard University Press, 1980), 152–74, argues that the work of women on arable farms was essential for the establishment of enterprises as well as for the survival of the family, yet was not recognized as valuable by men.

10. The best account of the expansion of dairying is Joan M. Jensen, *Loosening the Bonds: Mid-Atlantic Farm Women, 1750–1850* (New Haven: Yale University Press, 1986), 79–113.

income in New England, then, it came under masculine control. Some historians believe that men asserted their control over dairying to retain a monopoly on commodity production and farm households' dealings with the market. Farm women had had independent relations with the market in New England during the late eighteenth century; many had sold their own butter and cheese. During the early nineteenth century, women in rural New England could engage in more lucrative forms of commodity production and paid labor outside agriculture. As the putting-out system of manufacturing penetrated the countryside, rural women wove cloth, sewed shoes, and braided palm-leaf hats, depending on their location. These forms of household industry did not ensure women an integral place in agriculture, but they did provide women with an independent source of income as well as contribute to the farm family economy. Women in New England, then, may have withdrawn from dairying because they had alternative ways of earning money.[11]

In New York and Pennsylvania, women did not retreat from the barn. While men participated in the increasingly arduous labor of milking many cows and processing large quantities of cream, women retained their place in butter and cheese making. The example of New England makes it clear that this represented a conscious and collective choice; women in the mid-Atlantic region did not cede the dairy operation to men as it became more central to the farm and more oriented toward the market. Although the causes for the divergent paths of New England and mid-Atlantic farm women are not entirely clear, the consequences are striking. In New England, the gender division of labor on dairy farms was as sharp and rigid as on arable farms, while in the mid-Atlantic region women and men shared both the responsibility for and the labor of dairying.

Many women in the upper Midwest worked in the barn and "helped" in the hayfields. The regional origins of midwestern settlers had some influence on the gender division of labor. Migrants who came from the mid-Atlantic and the southern uplands brought traditions of women's participation in dairying with them, while New Englanders treated milking as a masculine responsibility.[12] But it was the German and Scandinavian immigrants who settled in the upper Mid-

11. Thomas Dublin, "Women and Outwork in a Nineteenth-Century New England Town: Fitzwilliam, New Hampshire, 1830–1850," in *The Countryside in the Age of Capitalist Transformation*, ed. Steven Hahn and Jonathan Prude (Chapel Hill: University of North Carolina Press, 1985), 51–69.

12. John Mack Faragher's study of a midwestern farm community, *Sugar Creek: Life on the Illinois Prairie* (New Haven: Yale University Press, 1986), suggests that New Englanders had a clearer gender division of labor than migrants from the mid-Atlantic.

west and shifted to dairying after the collapse of the wheat boom who most closely resembled Nanticoke Valley families in their sharing of labor across gender lines.[13] In Norway, Sweden, and Denmark, women customarily took care of the cattle and made butter and cheese.[14] They continued to do so in America, first for family subsistence and then for commercial sale. As Scandinavian farmers expanded their dairy operations, men joined women in the barn but did not displace them.[15] The establishment of cooperative creameries for the manufacture of cheese and butter also increased men's participation in the processing of dairy products. Still, a substantial number of women continued to churn butter in the household.[16] Farm families in Wisconsin and Minnesota flexibly divided their labor within the context of joint responsibility for the dairy operation. Since they too settled in kin-based communities whose solidarity was reinforced by a common ethnic culture, they shared the same structural conditions as Nanticoke Valley farm families.[17]

In families from the southern uplands, women customarily did the milking and made dairy products; men regarded working with the milk cows as beneath them.

13. Eric E. Lampard, *The Rise of the Dairy Industry in Wisconsin* (Madison: State Historical Society of Wisconsin, 1963).

14. The best recent account of women's work on farms in Norway during the nineteenth century is found in Jon Gjerde, *From Peasants to Farmers: The Migration from Balestrand, Norway to the Upper Middlewest* (Cambridge: Cambridge University Press, 1985), 34–45, 193–201. Gjerde maintains that adaptation to American conditions involved a significant shift in the gender division of labor, as men not only performed the field work but took over the care of livestock; the gender division of labor came to coincide with the division between commodity production and domestic work. However, Gjerde did not continue his study through the conversion from mixed farming to large-scale dairying, nor did he examine records kept by women; rather, he relied on the recollections of Norwegian American men who grew up on midwestern farms. Bodil K. Hansen, "Rural Women in Late Nineteenth-Century Denmark," *Journal of Peasant Studies* 9 (1982): 225–40, discusses women's responsibility for the dairy process in Denmark.

15. Jane Marie Pederson has documented the continued participation of Norwegian women in milking and barn chores as well as haying during the late nineteenth and early twentieth centuries. Relying on diaries and other first-person accounts from both women and men, Pederson has demonstrated that (at least until the 1920s) women's work in the barn was regarded as normal rather than exceptional and that men recognized the value of women's contribution to the family income. Pederson, "After the Frontier: Family and Community in Rural Wisconsin, 1870–1970" (Ph.D. diss., Columbia University, 1985).

16. Farm families with smaller herds—including young couples just getting started, older couples who had reduced the scale of their operations, and families with little capital—were more likely to make butter at home.

17. A number of studies detail ethnic settlement patterns in the upper Midwest. For Germans, see Kathleen N. Conzen's "Historical Approaches to the Study of Rural Ethnic Communities," in *Ethnicity on the Great Plains*, ed. Frederick C. Luebke (Lincoln: University of Nebraska Press, 1980), 1–18, and "Peasant Pioneers: Generational Succession among German Farmers in Frontier Minnesota," in *The Countryside in the Age of*

The centrality of kinship to rural society and the centrality of
women to commodity production provided the women of the Nanticoke Valley with a basis for constructing an ideal and practice of integration and equality in gender relations to counter the ideology of
separate spheres and the reality of male dominance. To show that
rural women elsewhere adopted similar strategies would require similar scrutiny of daily life on family farms and in open-country neighborhoods, a task few historians have yet undertaken for the settled
communities of the upper Midwest.[18] Studies of rural communities
during the late nineteenth and early twentieth centuries document
the active participation of women in organizational life. Women
made a crucial contribution to the establishment of schools and
churches, building institutions on the framework generated by informal cooperation as well as within the structures of public life.[19]
Women joined men in the farmers' movements of the late nineteenth
century. The platforms and practices of rural reform organizations
suggest that those conditions sometimes gave rise to a distinctly rural
form of feminism.

Many historians have failed to recognize rural women's actions as
feminist because women did not organize separately from men or
proclaim that women's and men's interests were opposed, but rather
espoused a vision and practice of gender integration. Marti has documented the feminist perspective of women active in the Grange and
their persistent and eventually successful efforts to ensure that the
organization adopt a position in favor of woman suffrage.[20] Grange
women proclaimed that mutual respect provided the only stable
foundation for farm family solidarity and sought to assure equality

---

Capitalist Transformation, ed. Hahn and Prude, 259–92. For Swedes in the Dakotas and
Minnesota, see Robert C. Ostergren, *A Community Transplanted: The Trans-Atlantic Experiences of a Swedish Immigrant Settlement in the Upper Middlewest, 1835–1915* (Madison: University of Wisconsin Press, 1988). For Norwegians, see Gjerde, *From Peasants to Farmers,*
137–67. Sonya Salamon and her associates are doing comparative research on settlement and landholding patterns in German, Irish, and "Yankee" ethnic settlements in
Illinois: Salamon, "Ethnic Communities and the Structure of Agriculture," *Rural Sociology* 50 (1985): 323–40, and Salamon, "Ethnic Origin as an Explanation for Local Land
Ownership Patterns," *Research on Rural Sociology and Development* 1 (1984): 161–86.

18. Most research has focused on the process of settlement rather than on the patterns of family and social life after the maturation of rural communities.

19. Seena B. Kohl, "The Making of a Community: The Role of Women in an Agricultural Setting," in *Kin and Communities: Families in America,* ed. A. J. Lichtman and
J. R. Challinor (Washington, D.C.: Smithsonian Institution Press, 1979), 175–86, describes this process on the Canadian prairies.

20. Donald B. Marti, "Sisters of the Grange: Rural Feminism in the Late Nineteenth
Century," *Agricultural History* 58 (1984): 247–61.

between women and men in rural communities. The organizational structure of the Grange gave women a place of their own, but did not confine them to that place; rather, women used their distinct organizational role as a base for their integration into the larger group. Grange women's feminist radicalism was rooted in a vision of kinship extending throughout the community, nurturing mutual aid and cooperation rather than dividing people into buyers and sellers or into "independent" male heads of household and their "dependent" wives and children. The anticapitalist and feminist implications of this vision were inextricably connected. Rural women sought to maintain forms of social relations to which both the value of women's labor and the values of equality and reciprocity were fundamental.

There are substantial parallels between the Grange and the earlier forms of rural radicalism which gave birth to the women's rights movement. Recent studies of the roots of antebellum reform, especially Nancy Hewitt's analysis of women's activism in Rochester, New York, have established that the equal rights tradition from which self-conscious feminism emerged was distinct, socially and organizationally as well as philosophically, from the tradition of social reform in which women claimed the right to act as agents of benevolence. Participants in the equal rights movement were from rural, rather than urban, backgrounds and were still integrally involved in family enterprises.[21] Judith Wellman's research on the signers of the 1848 Declaration of Sentiments at Seneca Falls, New York, reveals that they were involved in dense and far-reaching kinship networks, resided in large and flexible households that often expanded to incorporate friends, and sustained cooperative relationships among women and men in work as well as in spiritual life and political action.[22] It was these women, whose rural roots nurtured reciprocity and integration in social relations, who first claimed equality with men in all areas of civil society.

This distinct tradition of rural feminism continued into the twentieth century, when rural women's groups such as the Women's Christian Temperance Union joined the woman suffrage movement and women participated actively in agricultural protest movements. Farm women claimed the right to participate as fully in family decision making as they did in farm labor, and eventually they asserted their

21. Nancy A. Hewitt, *Women's Activism and Social Change: Rochester, New York, 1822–1872* (Ithaca: Cornell University Press, 1984).
22. Judith Wellman, "Women and Radical Reform in Upstate New York: A Profile of Grassroots Female Abolitionists," in *Clio Was a Woman: Studies in the History of American Women,* ed. Mabel E. Deutrich and Virginia C. Purdy (Washington, D.C.: Howard University Press, 1980), 113–27.

right to have their name on the land as well. Farm women maintained this tradition of gender integration despite the best efforts of experts in agricultural and home economics to impose the ideology and practice of separate spheres on farm families so that they would function more efficiently within the capitalist marketplace and conform to the dominant urban culture.[23] Rural feminism has not always surfaced organizationally, but it has flourished at the grass-roots level as rural women have secured formal as well as informal power within local communities and exercised that power to sustain gender-integrated and cooperative modes of collective action.

23. Mary Neth, "Preserving the Family Farm: Farm Families and Communities in the Midwest, 1900–1940" (Ph.D. diss., University of Wisconsin, Madison, 1987), decribes the maintenance of customs of gender integration despite pressures from the agricultural establishment. Her paper "Farm Women, Gender-Based Work, and the New Agriculture, 1900–1940," presented at the Seventh Berkshire Conference on the History of Women, Wellesley College, June 1987, describes the customary participation of women in farmwork and barn chores and the efforts of agricultural reformers—some of whom were women—to institute more gender-divided labor practices in an attempt to improve rural women's lot. Neth, "Building the Base: Farm Women, the Rural Community, and Farm Organizations in the Midwest, 1900–1940," in *Women and Farming: Changing Roles, Changing Structures*, ed. Wava G. Haney and Jane B. Knowles (Boulder, Colo.: Westview Press, 1988), 339–55, provides an especially lucid account of the way customary gender-integrated modes of sociability underlay the forms of collective action adopted by rural people.

Selected Bibliography

Diaries, Family Papers, Interviews

Allen, Belden. *The Spencer Family.* Glen Aubrey, N.Y.: privately printed, 1900. Files of the Town Historian, Maine Town Hall.

Ames, Dorothy Lawton (1905–), and Leigh Ames (1903–). Interviews by author. 1981–83. Archives of the Nanticoke Valley Historical Society.

Atwater, Fanny Dayton (1866–?), and Mary Alice Dayton (1867–?). Interview by Robert J. Spencer. 1940. Files of the Town Historian, Maine Town Hall.

Benton family. Papers. 1836–1924. Collection of the Gates-Gunsalus family.

Benton, Helen Davis. Diary. 1874, 1877–78, 1888–89, 1891, 1893–94, 1897, 1914, 1928, 1931–37. Collection of the Gates-Gunsalus family.

Benton, John W., and Rosella Leadbetter Benton. Letters. 1862–65. Collection of the Gates-Gunsalus family.

Benton, Leroy M. Diary. 1876. Collection of the Gates-Gunsalus family.

Blanchard family. Letters. 1848–51. Archives of the Nanticoke Valley Historical Society.

Bowers, Clement Gray (1894–1973). Interview by Robert J. Spencer. 1941. Collection of Janet Bowers Bothwell.

——. Memoirs, including interviews with Lamont Montgomery Bowers and Frederick Taylor Gates. c. 1922–23. Collection of Janet Bowers Bothwell.

Bowers, Lamont Montgomery (1847–1941). Memoirs. c. 1922–23. Collection of Janet Bowers Bothwell.

Bronk, William, and Amelia Bronk. Letters. 1894–98. Collection of Leigh and Dorothy Ames.

Carley, Jennie [m. Graves]. Diary. 1864. Collection of Jennie L. Whittaker.

Women's writings are listed under their names at the time they wrote the document. If a woman later married, her married name is given in square brackets.

Carman, Myra Dudley (1885–1989). Interviews by author. 1983. Archives of the Nanticoke Valley Historical Society.

Curlhair, Nora. Diary. 1886–97, 1904–41, 1947–50. Archives of the Nanticoke Valley Historical Society.

Davey, Vernon. Diary. 1889–97. Archives of the Nanticoke Valley Historical Society.

Dence, Louisa Carley McIntyre. Diary. 1878. Archives of the Nanticoke Valley Historical Society.

Gates family. Papers. 1795–1885. Collection of the Gates-Gunsalus family.

Gates, Byron Chandler. Diary. 1869–73, 1876–78, 1882–1905, 1907–13. Collection of the Gates-Gunsalus family.

Gates, Frederick Taylor. *Chapters in My Life*. New York: Free Press/Macmillan, 1977. Manuscript, 1928. Collection of Janet Bowers Bothwell.

——. *Our American Ancestry*. Montclair, N.J.: J. J. Little and Ives, 1928.

Gates, Livingston Theodore, and Agnes Brockett Gates. Diary. 1876. Collection of the Gates-Gunsalus family.

Gates, Russell Buck. Diary. 1881, 1882, 1884, 1892–94. Collection of the Gates-Gunsalus family.

Gates, Velma Leadbetter. Diary. 1893, 1913–16, 1931, 1935. Collection of the Gates-Gunsalus family.

Gray, Lyman Burrell. Letters. 1862–63. Collection of Janet Bowers Bothwell.

Gunsalus, Louise Gates (1894–1982), and Paul Gunsalus. Interviews by author. 1981–83. Archives of the Nanticoke Valley Historical Society.

——. Interview by Janet Bowers Bothwell and Ian Mylchreest. 1982. Archives of the Nanticoke Valley Historical Society.

Gunsalus, Paul, and Louise Gunsalus. *A Record of the Descendants of Thomas and Anna Rowley Leadbetter*. Maine, N.Y.: privately printed, 1980.

Hogg family. Papers. c. 1868–1924. Collection of Anita Jackson [m. Dunbar].

Howard, Grace [m. Paisley]. Diary. 1888. Collection of Anita Jackson [m. Dunbar].

Jackson family. Papers. c. 1900–1984. Collection of Anita Jackson [m. Dunbar].

Jackson, Anita [m. Dunbar] (1902–   ). Interviews by author. 1984. Archives of the Nanticoke Valley Historical Society.

Johnson, Amy L. Papers. 1892–93. Collection of Evelyn Bailey LaDue.

Johnson, Belle North (1887–?). "East Maine History." Interview by Robert J. Spencer. 1957. Files of the Town Historian, Maine Town Hall.

Johnson, Mrs. Harry [Belle North] (1887–?). "Recollections of Brockett Hollow." Manuscript, undated; written for or transcribed by Robert J. Spencer. c. 1957. Files of the Town Historian, Maine Town Hall.

Ketchum, Lala [m. Marean]. Letters, Diary, and Poems. 1861–65. Files of the Town Historian, Maine Town Hall.

McIntyre, Chauncey. Diary. 1856–62. Archives of the Nanticoke Valley Historical Society.

McIntyre, Chauncey F. Diary. 1875, 1878, 1883–87. Archives of the Nanticoke Valley Historical Society.

Marean family. Papers. 1846, 1870–1947. Collection of Leigh and Dorothy Ames.

Marean, William A. Diary. 1878–79. Collection of Leigh and Dorothy Ames.

Merrill, Semira Omans. Letters. 1862. Collection of Jane Daniels Youngs.

Mooers, Lucy Jane. Letters. 1846–47. Collection of Jane Daniels Youngs and Deborah Youngs.

Newton, Elizabeth M. Riley. Memoirs. 1898. Files of the Town Historian, Maine Town Hall.

Osterhaut, Jane Paisley (1834–1924). Memoirs. c. 1900. Collection of Anita Jackson [m. Dunbar].

——. Papers. c. 1868–1924. Collection of Anita Jackson [m. Dunbar].

Paisley, Nellie. Diary. 1891. Collection of the Smith family.

Riley, George W. Diary. 1865–89. Archives of the Nanticoke Valley Historical Society.

Riley, Judson. Diary. 1876–97. Archives of the Nanticoke Valley Historical Society.

Rozelle, Eldon M. (1883–1960), and Louella Richards Rozelle (1883–1957). Papers. c. 1937–54. Archives of the Nanticoke Valley Historical Society.

Rozelle, Richard J. (1911–). "The Generations." c. 1982. Archives of the Nanticoke Valley Historical Society.

——. Interviews by author. 1982. Archives of the Nanticoke Valley Historical Society.

Smith, Ina [m. Marean]. Diary. 1899. Collection of Leigh and Dorothy Ames.

Stevens, Halsey, comp. *Philip Councilman (1760–1834) of Nanticoke, Broome County, New York, and His Descendants.* California: privately printed, 1937. Files of the Town Historian, Maine Town Hall.

Vandemark, Lucretia Ketchum. Diary. 1893. Collection of Barbara Yarrington.

Warner, Martha [m. Marean]. Diary. 1872. Collection of Leigh and Dorothy Ames.

Wheaton, Timothy S. McGowan (pseud.). Diary. 1868–72, 1881, 1882, 1885, 1887–1916, 1918, 1921–22. Collection of Dorothy Ames.

Young, George W. "Buying a Farm on Small Capital." *American Agriculturist* 118 (14 August 1926).

Young, Ralph M. (1894–1984). Diary. 1913–45. Collection of the Young family.

Young, Ralph M. (1894–1984), and Margaret Young Coles (1918–1987). Interviews by author. 1982. Archives of the Nanticoke Valley Historical Society.

Local Church Records and Histories

Baptist Church

First Baptist Church and Society, Maine, N.Y. Minute Book, 1835–1960. First Baptist Church and Society, Maine, N.Y., and files of the Town Historian, Maine Town Hall.

"Historical Notes Regarding the First Baptist Church and Society, Maine, New York." Manuscript, 1960. Based on the Church and Society's Minutes, the Anniversary Minutes of the Broome and Tioga Baptist Association, and

H. P. Smith, ed., *A History of Broome County* (Syracuse, N.Y.: D. Mason, 1855). First Baptist Church and Society, Maine, N.Y., and files of the Town Historian, Maine Town Hall.

Christian Church

Glen Aubrey Christian Church. Records, 1854–87. Files of the Broome County Historian's Office, Broome County Public Library.

Congregational Churches

First Congregational Church of Maine and the First Congregational Church Society. Records and Minute Books, 1819–1916. Includes records of the East Maine Presbyterian Church. Congregational Church, Maine, N.Y. Transcription by Robert J. Spencer in the collection of Janet Bowers Bothwell.

Lainhart, Grace. "A History of the Maine Congregational Church." Manuscript, 1957. Congregational Church, Maine, N.Y., and files of the Town Historian, Maine Town Hall.

Union Center Congregational Church and Society. Records, 1841–1941. Congregational Church, Union Center, N.Y., and files of the Town Historian, Maine Town Hall.

——. Ladies' Aid Society. Records, 1881–1917. Congregational Church, Union Center, N.Y., and files of the Town Historian, Maine Town Hall.

Methodist Churches

Garrett, Mildred [m. Hawver]. "A History of the Maine Methodist Church." 1973. Methodist Church, Maine, N.Y., and files of the Town Historian, Maine Town Hall.

"Historical Records of the Lamb's Corners Church," 1873–79. Included in Mildred Garrett [m. Hawver], "A History of the Maine Methodist Church," 1973. Files of the Town Historian, Maine Town Hall.

Maine Methodist Church. Records, 1851–1900. Methodist Church, Maine, N.Y.

——. Ladies' Aid Society. Minutes, 1890–1906. Methodist Church, Maine, N.Y.

Maine Methodist Circuit. Records, 1860–99. Methodist Church, Maine, N.Y.

Union Center Methodist Church. Records, 1825–1962. Union Center Methodist Church, and files of the Town Historian, Maine Town Hall.

——. Ladies' Aid Society. Records, 1883–1911. Union Center Methodist Church, and files of the Town Historian, Maine Town Hall.

Woodward, Shirley L., and Leslie Oliver, comps. "Union Center United Methodist Church: Sesquicentennial, 1825–1975." 1975. Includes selections from A. J. Chafee's *History of the Wyoming Conference*. Files of the Town Historian, Maine Town Hall.

Local Histories, Censuses, Maps, Documents

Asher and Adams' New Topographical Atlas and Gazetteer of New York. New York: Asher and Adams, 1871.

Babbitt, James C. "The Maine Community Band: A Brief History, 1873–1973." In *A Short History of Maine*, comp. Shirley L. Woodward. Maine, N.Y.: Town of Maine, 1973, 38–41.

Beers, S. N., and D. G. Beers and Assistants. *New Topographical Atlas of Broome County, New York, from Actual Surveys*. Philadelphia: Stone and Stewart, 1866.

Bothwell, Lawrence. *Broome County Heritage: An Illustrated History*. Woodland Hills, Calif.: Windsor Publications, 1983.

Boyd, Andrew, comp. *Boyd's Binghamton City and Susquehanna Railroad Directory*. Binghamton, N.Y.: H. E. Pratt, Bookseller, 1871.

Child, Hamilton, comp. *Gazetteer and Business Directory of Broome and Tioga Counties, N.Y. for 1872–3*. Syracuse, N.Y.: published by Child and printed at the Journal office, 1872.

——. *Map of Tioga and Broome Counties, New York, to accompany Child's Gazetteer and Directory*. Albany, N.Y.: Weed, Parsons, 1872.

Corbin, John P. *Practical Hints on Dairying, or, Manual for Butter Makers*. Whitney's Point, N.Y.: n.p., 1871.

Edwards, Uriah. "Journal of my travels to the West. . . ." 20 September 1828. Manuscript, New York State Library.

Everts, Ensign, and Everts. *Combination Atlas Map of Broome County, New York, Compiled, Drawn and Published from Personal Examinations and Surveys by Everts, Ensign and Everts*. Philadelphia: Everts, Ensign and Everts, 1876.

Garrett, Helen Knapp, comp. and ed. "Early Scotch Settlers of West Chenango." *Whitney Point Reporter*, 1901–2.

Gifford, Franklin, and Emile Wenig. "Map of Broome County, From Actual Surveys by Franklin Gifford and Emile Wenig." Philadelphia: A. O. Gallup, 1855.

"Historical Sketches of Maine." *Whitney Point Reporter*, 9, 23, 30 July 1914; 6, 23, 27 August 1914.

"Historical Sketches of Union Center." *Whitney Point Reporter*, 10, 17 December 1914.

Ingalls, Earl H. "History of Maine: Town of Maine, Broome County, New York." Manuscript, c. 1943. Files of the County Historian, Broome County Public Library.

——. *A 125 Year History of Maine Lodge, No. 399, Free and Accepted Masons, 1856–1981*, ed. Lawrence R. Rice. Maine, N.Y.: Masonic Lodge, 1981.

Lamb's Corners Agricultural Society. "Rules and Regulations for the Ninth Annual Fair of the Lamb's Corners Agricultural Society at Lamb's Corners,

New York, Wednesday and Thursday, September 22nd and 23rd, 1880." Archives of the Broome County Historical Society.

The Lamb's Corners Eagle. 1 (18 July 1874). Lamb's Corners, N.Y.: Jos. A. Brooks, 1874. Files of the Town Historian, Maine Town Hall.

Lawyer, William S., ed. *Binghamton: Its Settlement, Growth, and Development and the Factors in Its History Together with a History of the Villages and Towns of the County.* N.p.: Century Memorial Publishing Company, 1900.

McGuire, Ross. "Lumbermen, Farmers and Artisans: The Rural Economy of the Nineteenth Century." In *Working Lives: Broome County, New York, 1800–1930.* Binghamton, N.Y.: Roberson Center for the Arts and Sciences, 1982, 1–39.

The Maine News, 1 (10 June 1876). Maine, N.Y.: W. L. Brooks, pub. and ed., 1876. Files of the Town Historian, Maine Town Hall.

"Maine of To-Day." *Whitney Point Reporter,* 29 May 1903.

Mylchreest, Ian. "Men at Work: Labor in the Nanticoke Valley." Manuscript, 1983. Archives of the Nanticoke Valley Historical Society.

Nanticoke Valley Agricultural Society. "Nanticoke Valley Agricultural Society Thirteenth Annual Fair, Lamb's Corners, New York, Wednesday and Thursday, October 6th and 7th, 1886." Archives of the Broome County Historical Society.

New York State *Census.* Agriculture, Manuscript Schedules, Towns of Maine and Nanticoke. 1855, 1865, 1875.

——. Agriculture, Printed Reports, Broome County. 1855, 1865, 1875.

——. Population, Manuscript Schedules, Towns of Maine and Nanticoke. 1855, 1865, 1875, 1892, 1925.

——. Population, Printed Reports, Broome County. 1855, 1865, 1875, 1892.

New York State Department of Agriculture. "List of Butter and Cheese Factories in the State, together with the Amount of Product . . . and a Summary of each County arranged by Towns." *Annual Report of the Commissioner of Agriculture.* Albany, N.Y.: State Printer, 1892–1898.

Official Directory and History of Broome County Granges, Patrons of Husbandry. Binghamton, N.Y.: Patrons of Husbandry, 1941.

Osterud, Nancy Grey. "Land, Identity and Agency in the Oral Autobiographies of Farm Women." In *Women and Farming: Changing Roles, Changing Structures,* ed. Wava G. Haney and Jane B. Knowles. Boulder, Colo.: Westview Press, 1988, 73–87.

——. "Mechanics, Operatives and Laborers: Factories in the Valley, 1870–1930." In *Working Lives: Broome County, New York, 1800–1930.* Binghamton, N.Y.: Roberson Center for the Arts and Sciences, 1982, 41–101.

——. " 'She Helped Me Hay It as Good as a Man': Relations among Women and Men in an Agricultural Community." In *"To Toil The Livelong Day": America's Women at Work, 1780–1980,* ed. Carol Groneman and Mary Beth Norton. Ithaca: Cornell University Press, 1987, 87–97.

——. "Strategies of Mutuality: Relations among Women and Men in an Agricultural Community." Ph.D. diss., Brown University, 1984.

——. "The Valuation of Women's Work: Gender and the Market in a Dairy

Farming Community during the Late Nineteenth Century." *Frontiers* 10 (1988): 18–24.

Plat Book of Broome County, New York, compiled from County Records and Actual Surveys. Des Moines, Iowa: Northwest Publishing, 1908.

Seward, William Foote, ed. *Binghamton and Broome County, New York: A History.* New York and Chicago: Lewis Historical Publishing Co., 1924.

Smith, H. P., ed. *A History of Broome County.* Syracuse, N.Y.: D. Mason, 1885.

Spencer, Robert J. "Glen Aubrey: A Brief History of the Village of Glen Aubrey, Town of Nanticoke, County of Broome, on the 125th Anniversary of the First Town Meeting, 1832–1957." *Bulletin of the Broome County Historical Society* 6 (1958): 3–13. Manuscript version, c. 1957, in the files of the Broome County Historian, Broome County Public Library.

———. "I See by the Paper." Manuscript, 1957. Files of the Town Historian, Maine Town Hall.

———, and Clement G. Bowers. "Notes on the History of the Town of Maine." Manuscript, c. 1941–57. Files of the Town Historian, Maine Town Hall, and the collection of Janet Bowers Bothwell.

Swan, Eleanor Brown. *Story of the Valleys: Town of Nanticoke.* Nanticoke, N.Y.: Town of Nanticoke, 1981.

Tucker, Harriet E. "Maine Village in Rhyme—1874." Manuscript. Files of the Town Historian, Maine Town Hall.

United States Census. Agriculture, Manuscript Schedules, Towns of Maine and Nanticoke. 1850, 1880.

———. Agriculture, Printed Reports, Broome County. 1850, 1860, 1870, 1880, 1890, 1900, 1910, 1920, 1930, 1940.

———. Industry, Manuscript Schedules, Towns of Maine and Nanticoke. 1850, 1860, 1870, 1880.

———. Population, Manuscript Schedules, Towns of Maine and Nanticoke. 1850, 1860, 1870, 1880, 1900, 1910.

———. Population, Printed Reports, Broome County. 1850, 1860, 1870, 1880, 1890, 1900, 1910, 1920, 1930, 1940.

United States Geological Survey. *Topographical Map, Apalachin and Binghamton Quadrangles.* Edition of May 1904, published 1908, reprinted September 1909.

Wilkinson, J. B. *The Annals of Binghamton, and of the County connected with it, from the earliest settlement.* Binghamton, N.Y.: n.p., 1840; reprinted Binghamton, N.Y.: Broome County Historical Society, 1967.

Williams, J. E., comp. *Williams' Binghamton City and Broome County Directory for 1881.* Binghamton, N.Y.: J. E. Williams, 1881.

Woodward, Shirley L., comp. *A Short History of Maine, New York.* Maine, N.Y.: Town of Maine, 1973.

———, comp. Vertical file, population of the Town of Maine, compiled from manuscript census schedules, church records, cemetery records, newspaper obituaries, and genealogies. Archives of the Nanticoke Valley Historical Society, Maine, N.Y.

Index

Note: [m. ——] = married name.

Library of Congress Cataloging-in-Publication Data

Osterud, Nancy Grey, 1948–
    Bonds of community : the lives of farm women in nineteenth-century
New York / Nancy Grey Osterud.
        p.   cm.
    Includes bibliographical references and index.
    ISBN 0-8014-2510-7 (alk. paper)
    ISBN 0-8014-9798-1 (pbk: alk. paper)
        1. Rural women—New York (State)—History—19th century.   2. New
York (State)—Rural conditions.   I. Title.
    HQ1438.N57O88   1991
    305.4—dc20   90-41814